# 360 Degree Virtual World

## A 360 Degree Life of a Human in a Virtual World

Ekambar Kodali

ATLANTIC
PUBLISHERS & DISTRIBUTORS (P) LTD

Published by

**ATLANTIC**

**PUBLISHERS & DISTRIBUTORS (P) LTD**

7/22, Ansari Road, Darya Ganj, New Delhi-110002
Phones : +91-11-40775252, 40775214, 23273880, 23275880
Fax : +91-11-23285873
Web : www.atlanticbooks.com
E-mail : orders@atlanticbooks.com

**Branch Office: Chennai**
Phones : +91-44-48531784, 28291383
E-mail : chennai@atlanticbooks.com



Printed & bound in India by Atlantic Print Services

# PREFACE

I am writing this book after almost seven long years of debate within myself on several different issues. The debate that I had was, whether it is possible to give an experience of real time to the reader by this book. I doubt it, but I want to write it to face the challenge. Whatever I am trying to do here is supposed to be carried out by several persons. I am trying to present things in brief.

The Americans and the British have established virtual systems successfully across the world by projecting some of the 'jokers' as 'experts' and have been fooling the world for their benefit and profiting at the loss of others. They are building their wealth on others' poverty. In order to prove this, several different prevailing understandings need to be proved wrong. For this purpose, I need to give some details of those systems. Is it possible? Let us see.

Here, I will give you a simple example: I hope you have seen the *Dracula*. In such movies there will usually be a candidate who adores Dracula, sympathizes with him, and also tries to serve him. Similarly, here in our society, America and Britain have created such disciples for their ideologies through education system and other systems. They work for the benefit of America and Britain. You will understand how that has been happening for several decades on this earth successfully.

What is this book all about? Is this a book of life, a book of economy, a book of politics, a book of management, or what? You read and decide what it is. My objective of writing this book is to make the reader understand the black holes, not the black holes of universe, but of this human world.

One thing is sure that reading this book will add some triggers to your thoughts that change your thinking pattern. That is the objective of this book.

I am sure that this would become the base for several other thoughts in many different persons, but I wonder whether, if anybody else has written this kind of document on practical incidents in the last 200 years at macro to micro level, or would write it in future. If anyone writes it in future, I am sure they will take this document as a basis for their work.

All I have done in writing this book is putting down my understanding of this world. You may already have a knowledge base, and some of what I have written may be understood by you differently. Please put together your knowledge and my ideas and derive the right meaning. This is the other intent of this book.

The book may sound like I am writing my autobiography, but I am not. I am trying to give you details along with a timeline as they have been along with the information that I have received. Of course, I am writing this book for my self-satisfaction as well, i.e. I am living a life with complete understanding of this world, better than others.

The book is all about understanding. Some will call it a perspective. However, in my opinion perspective is the lateral stage of understanding. Understanding is the lateral stage of interpretation. Interpretation is the lateral stage of earlier knowledge base. The final result inside the humans, which is perspective, would have different hues before it becomes a conclusion that results as deliverable action from a human being, based on his or her needs. I hope I have explained well about the chain.

As I said earlier, this book is all about my understanding of different things around me, which are common to all of us. However, my understanding of the same would be different from others. I have been finding this difference for quite some time. The reaction from me has also been different from that of others. I sometimes have been reacting with the core reason, which is found irrelevant by others. A fact is always a fact.

Perspective does not change the fact. To identify the fact is the ultimate goal of this book.

In today's complex world, which is sliced and diced into several sections under the name of subjects and specializations, putting together such subjects and specializations to give a meaning is a challenging task. However, what I am trying to expose is, in the successful establishment of concepts, virtual concepts. Some of the meaningless concepts, which are not valid at all, are also promoted as 'correct' ones and are established as scientifically correct ones. Some unscrupulous fellows are promoted as experts and are being used to profit from others and suppress them.

Notice here that this projection of the 'expert' is on virtual things. In India, virtual things are always 'correct' when they are accepted by powerful and strong people and 'wrong' when they are not accepted by the powerful and strong.

However, the actually 'correct' never changes. Here, my effort is to bring out the actual correct, though I am not considered as an expert. Now it is up to the reader to decide at the end of the book, if I am an expert or not. But be cognizant of the fact that on virtual things, nobody can be considered as an expert.

The total time taken for me in achieving this maturity of writing a book on the subject is 14 years. I initially felt it as a financial issue, then felt that it may be an economic issue; after some time felt it as a political issue, then, when I started focusing on the management aspect, I felt that it is a management issue, but at the end I figured out that it is a ruling issue. I have named this as 'economic terrorism'.

Initially, I used to find errors in several different real-time situations but not accurate reasons. Later, my continuous and consistent effort in understanding such errors led me to find the accurate reasons. Reasons lead me to the right cause. Investigation of causes leads me to know how those causes are being created. I felt then that they were human errors. But at the end what I found was, that it is a highly intellectual technique of this world which our ancestors called *maya,* or skill, or expertise, or miracle, and what not!

In simple words, I can tell one thing, a destructive weapon made by metals or chemicals or any other such material or instruments is not required to destroy any nation or society and turn it to ashes. Just a small concept is enough to do the job that is as large as or even bigger than an asteroid hitting the earth. By concepts, thought patterns can be corrupted to the extent that it does the maximum damage without being noticeable or traceable. For example, cigarette smoking was promoted as an activity good for relaxing, and we all know how big nonsense it is, but it is successfully adopted by the society and innumerable people are destroying their lives with it.

I attended a soft skill program where a psychologist asked each of us to write what he or she thought about himself/herself. Then he asked each of us to write about others in the program, anonymously. The final result was an astonishing one for me. Similarly, reading this book will have an astonishing effect on you.

The information provided in this book is not complete, but the book is self-contained. The first chapter has very important details and it works as a platform for the reader to understand the rest of the book. There will be questions in the book. Those questions are for the reader to think on the subject and the pertinent issues, and find answers.

Issues which I have been mentioning in this book are pure systems. Systems program our behaviour and personality. You may recall the Lord Krishna's words in *Bhagavad Gita*: "We humans are just actors, living life on the directions of forces created by God". System in which we live is "GOD".

Individual names which I have mentioned in the book are all made to behave by the systems and there is nothing personal against anyone. My focus is to change the future India and the world, and in this respect, the book is a systems analysis book that helps to correct ourselves.

You have chosen reading this book means, you have started resolving the global problems or disorders, global warming, pollution, poverty and corruption.

**Ekambar Kodali**

# CONTENTS

# 1 3D ↔ 2D

We all know that as creatures of this world, we live in a world of 3 dimension. When we look at each other in our daily life, our eye catches the image, the brain processes the image and we experience the feel of 3 dimension. Of course, there are several additional characteristics such as ambience attached to that 3 dimension image.

We use words to illustrate the 3 dimension world. Authors use words to illustrate the 3 dimension objects. Artists draw pictures to illustrate the 3 dimension objects.

Sometimes using pictures is easier than using words to illustrate 3 dimension objects and associated circumstantial ambience.

However, here is one significant point to be noticed. Both artists and authors use paper and pencil, objects from 3D world to create 2 dimension objects on a paper using pencil.

Now the 3 dimension has become a 2 dimension.

Any human who goes through the details in 2 dimension has to use the brain power to create a 3 dimension image in real time.

Now this skill of 2D to 3D transformation by human is the very challenging one, where each individual will have his/her own capability of forming the 3D image from 2D details.

For example, look at the following picture (Fig. 1).

A person who has never seen either one of the objects in 3D world will form his/her own 3D image in his imagination.

**Figure 1:** Is this a ball or cone or cycle wheel or what?

This difference in imagination capability of human plays a major role in the human world while judging intelligent capabilities of individual human and also synchronizing the thoughts of two or more individuals.

Now the world where we are living is also the same. This difference in understanding makes a lot of difference in our success.

For example, until the point we had Google Earth in computer world, every individual on earth was relying on 2 dimensional maps or 3 dimension Globe Toy to create an image of the earth in brain.

The Google Earth and the capability of zooming in and out has given a new perspective to the same.

Earlier this zooming in and out used to be invisible and used to be done by the brain of the human in his/her own imaginary world to create an understanding of the details in 2 dimension world.

The information gathered from 2 dimension world in bits and pieces are being put together in the brain of the human to form an imaginary object in the thoughts of the human.

Now this is usually referred as joining the dots.

The zooming in and out is usually what we do it using our brain imaginary power and refer it to as the scope of the vision or small picture to big picture, wider vision, close look or broader look, etc.

Another most important point surfaces here is "Angle of Vision."

If the above circle is a ball in 3D then the lines if representing the lines on the ball, the above picture is representing viewing the ball from one specific angle. The 2D image will vary by angle even by smallest fraction of change in vision.

So this angle of vision also makes a lot of difference. If a ball has half red colour and half black colour, then representing it on paper requires more pictures. This is similar to 24 frames animation.

Another important aspect here is Human and his/her understanding.

Human brain processing is as similar as computer processor. A computer processor gets programmed by a human and based on the inputs received, the computer will deliver the responses based on the logic written.

We as human being are nothing but intelligent natural computing machines. Unlike computer, human gets programmed by the information received by him/her from his/her surroundings where he/she lives.

We take input and understand and then react based on our need. We again wait for results of our reactions and again calculate and calibrate, and process and react again. So it is a continuous process.

We must analyse the above said with respect to our society that has been changing and giving input to us and impacting us and our behaviour.

So this entire book and its interpretation is based on your imaginary power and right angle of understanding.

Hope you are all aware of virus effect on computers. Similarly, Indians and their brains are virus effected. Now this book I am envisioning as Anti-Virus. However, this is only a small micro anti-virus targeting to clean or kill some key Trojan virus.

At the end, My Imaginary Object and Your Imaginary Object should match each other exactly. At the same time, they should be exactly, same. If I say 0, then you should see 0, if –1 at my left side then you also should be able to see –1 at your left side of 0, and similarly for +1 at opposite side of 0.

The first and final one is remember that we are trying to form a 3D object from 2D details that I am writing in this book.

**What is said is not important, what is understood is important.**

India has economic document which usually they refer it as "Astrology document". It is Panchangam.

There one can find, four characteristics of economy.

Income (Aadhayam) – Expenditure (Vyayam) which is nothing but Income – Expenditure or Credit – Debit – Quantity based.

Success/Respect (Raaja Poojyam) – Failure/Insult (Avamanam) which is nothing but Success Vs. Failure – Quality based.

Even in Management analysis, there will always be exactly the same two types, Quantity and Quality of forecasting before the start and analysis after the end.

Everything that I mentioned here in this book are all from real time.

# 2 INTRODUCTION

I started an effort of making people, especially people in ruling chairs, understand what is economy and economic analysis in 1999 with an aim of explaining economy in real terms for the numbers being projected as indicators. This may sound strange but it is true which this book will prove you. India, and especially third world, has problems in a very unconventional manner that people of those nations can not understand easily.

I chose the name INDIANOMICS to my "unconventional" effort. This name is to tell the world that these economic details are in the Indian Dimension. You may find this name in CNBC TV channel but I named my effort earlier than that program in CNBC TV18.

Through this book, I am trying to give you the experience of Economy based on currency world as similar as the experience that Google Earth gives you. Of course, this is book and not Software.

Where do I start is always a matter? How do I explain is another challenge that I always have?

I will start from the point when I started getting different thoughts in my mind, those are different from others. Also I will write it as I am explaining my experience by being in the situation. However, there is one significant point to remember here, as an author I am writing my experience. In my experience I am at the Center of my experience, in 3D world, I am at the Center means, I am at the Center of a Ball where 360 means I will be receiving information from all angles around me. This includes starting from childhood.

I am receiving information to my peripherals like Eyes, Ears and other information sensitive devices and my brain processes all of them and then "an understanding" which is the process in my brain that results into a perspective in me. Remember that I already have a knowledge base from my childhood till the point of my experience in time.

Also remember that some of my Knowledge base is my perspective, and may sound to readers that it is insufficient and false understanding.

The reader may conclude it as one Dimension of Understanding of the entire issue. Here, I would like to give you one of my experience.

After I returned to India from USA, I contacted several Political Parties.

One of that was Loksatta Party hailed from Hyderabad and headed by Jayaprakash Narayan, a former IAS officer; the party that was having the identity as started by intellectual and have all intellectuals. I vaguely remember the name of a person, I think it ends with Varma, as I remember, he was general secretary of the party who was experienced in participating in the employee unions. He was retired government employee.

I went to them with a belief that I would get good support from them because I had been sending several emails to their respective party emails with my analytical details. After they heard all that I said, they simply ruled it out as "your dimension that you are finding it as right one is for you". I was shocked.

Their version of conclusion was, a "baba" trying to sell his ideology that he believes as "correct", a political party tries to project their thinking as their ideology and promotes it, and similarly, I have been hanging to an understanding that I have been finding meanings in them and have been carrying to each door to sell my ideology or understandings. I was shocked and ended the meeting as I have not come to them with some ideology but facts which I would like to pass them to people as information so that people would start understanding the facts. They rejected it.

Similarly, I went to meet all media companies with confidence that I would get some support from them, because I had been sending different perspectives of the contemporary issues to their respective Editor's email. Some of them were published in papers as letters to editors.

One of the senior journalists suggested that "these are very big subjects and do not fire the gun from your shoulder, but fire it from somebody else's shoulder who might be powerful so that you don't get into troubles from unwanted means, especially from government itself". He warned me about intelligent forces of government tracking me and my activities. Not sure, if they were as nobody had ever contacted me.

One of Communist Party President also said the same to me as they are large issues which he could not handle.

The Senior Journalist did not realize that I had been doing these activities since five years by then, this was in 2004.

One thing what I understood was, there is a need to carry my effort through different means that is not conventional to spread the knowledge.

One more thing is, I have to work with the same systems whose bugs I have been targeting to fix.

I believe I have created the platform as prerequisite with whatever I have written till now to read and understand this book. Let us get into the subject.

I will start with my introduction.

You know my name as an Author. I am an engineering graduate and a Computer Software Systems Analyst and MBA in Technology Management.

My profession is Understanding the Real Time requirements/Problems of the Business Users and Develop a Software that helps them in simplifying their business activities and increase their business efficiency. In this endeavour, there will be errors, and I need to do Root Cause Analysis to figure out the Cause that is causing the Error and rectify it. The starting point and triggering point for a Root cause analysis would be the "results" those are not as expected.

Now my job responsibility is again related to developing a 2 Dimension in a 3 Dimension device for a 3 Dimension Human world Object, which is Business User.

My thought pattern in my brain always switches its imaginary process at every given point of time during my job performance.

In Computer world, User and Software Engineer always face opposite to each other. Software Engineer should be able to visualize and document what user requires. The same will be later presented through Computer Interface.

My Understanding was one of my knowledge base.

At one point of time I got this crazy idea of using these job skills of mine on real time world. Of course, this did not start all of a sudden in my life.

I lived in India for 28 years before I moved to USA. I worked in India for four years before I moved to USA. I not only worked as Software Engineer but also used to do business along with my father. It was a Trading Business. Hence, I also had some business knowledge and experience.

I started my career in 1993. It was the starting time of economic reforms era in India. Lot of new industries were coming up. Especially, most of them were 100% Export Oriented Units (EOUs) due to government policies. Bulk Drug Manufacturing Units, Aqua farms and many more Export Oriented Units.

One important thing that I highlight here is, as I have been living in Hyderabad, I used to have a scooter to travel around the city. Earlier days, I used to travel, return home and was able to have my clothes in good condition to wear again on the same day or next day. But later, I used to find carbon dust on clothes. Of course, everybody might have noticed the kind of pollution spread across Hyderabad or other places across the nation.

I will give one funny fact about Indian dumbness here that is related to Scooter. Petrol per Litre used to be around ₹25 and Lubrication oil used to be ₹54 per litre. Scooter requires Lubricant oil at 2% Petrol Quantity. This additional quantity used to give Additional mileage. However, people used to find this as additional benefit at low cost without calculating the actual costs.

This is to inform you about the same change in the environment and pollution under the name of Development after 1990.

Here I would like to add one fact that I found earlier to 1990, until India became a place for supplier of bulk drug industry as a hub, the first world nation's environment was in horrible conditions till the extent that fish were not growing in any natural water reservoirs. Water was polluted till that extent was the situation in those nations.

This is one more important point to remember by readers about destruction or deterioration started happening under the name of Economic Reforms. Remember here that 100% EOUs were having 100% tax rebates.

Hundred per cent EOUs came into existence because of lack of Forex. This is one large and most important fact to recall now and remember. What is that Forex? US$ or UK Pound. Recall here the situation of Mortgaging the Gold by then Prime Minister Chandrasekhar, with UK for Forex in order to import fuel and fertilizer.

I always wanted to start a small scale manufacturing unit. I never wanted to do a job. During then, the kind of jobs available were mostly in Sales/Marketing. I was more interested in establishing a dealership of a large company or small manufacturing unit so that I can be settled easily.

Everybody was suggesting to go for a trading business because manufacturing was not good at all.

However, my efforts did not stop. During then, I found several large multinationals purchasing Indian sick companies and reviving them. I knew a company that purchased a sick company in plastic net manufacturing and turned it into a successful business by establishing a good marketing network around the nation easily. Of course, I was not wealthy to do all that but I was looking at manufacturing ancillary components sort of units. However, out of interest I used to study the information about such activities of large companies.

I looked at HDPE Sack manufacturing/Cement Sheets manufacturing etc. small scale units. There were several sick units across the State. I also worked on establishing a Cold Storage as well. When I started looking at Cold Storage, there were only 7 or 8 cold storage units in India. I chose cold storage industry, looking at the kind of transformation happening during then in Indian market and demand for storage of Food products. I could not get good help.

I also tried to establish a Scooter Dealership but could not, due to several other reasons. However, all such failures gave me knowledge of how to look at industry and how to look at a project etc. Also, came to know about what kind of policies were available in India for Industry development.

During 70s and 80s, government at different levels created several different industrial promotional programmes and also poultry and dairy industry. Several graduates or others had started several industries—poultry and dairy. This was to develop entrepreneurship, generate employment and leadership in technology as well.

Majority of the industries were gone sick due to several reasons, such as dynamics of the market, rapid change in technology, and many more.

When I was collecting the information on project reports, I always used to find the out-dated information and the current projects used to cost almost 10 times the price mentioned in the project reports. Also the Small scale sector that was supposed to be at around ₹1 lakh has become minimum of ₹10 lakh + Working Capital.

This means, investment requirement raised. Also several industrial machines were outdated.

Several Aqua farming industries came up and busted later due to several reasons. In simple, several 100s of 100% EOU with 100% tax rebates came up for forex earning requirement.

During late 60s several public sector units were started. Why government of India started PSUs was for two different purposes. One purpose was to develop science and technology capabilities of the nation and the other to meet the large investment capital required for large industries.

Several PSUs used to suffer a lot with Employee Trade Unions and their strikes. Why? Several reasons. But some or other benefits to them in some or other way as labour issue or right to have it, etc., were there.

One major thing needs to be understood is, work sincerely so that your present contribution would build platform for future generations: wealth was completely destroyed and the purpose of PSUs was defeated completely. PSUs, those have monopoly option and have no Competition, only survived and cherished, for example, OIL PSUs, Defence PSUs, BHEL sort of companies.

Look at this from Country point of View. I am not saying this newly. I am trying to have you keep this as one point of Failure of the nation which would help you get the 3D 360 degree view later.

The objective of development of Technology was busted. Means adopted to it were in different dimensions. They are: Rise in cost of living, Employee Union problems, etc.

After 1990 itself, software industry started picking up in India.

When I was working in India, since I was a Software Engineer, I with an experience of three years was drawing a salary equivalent to five times of any average Indian monthly income that too a person with experience of 20 years. That was three times of my father's salary at retirement.

Before I moved to USA, I was in Chennai outskirts where the company after I joined, raised the salaries by 100% to all workforce. First change that I saw due to such rapid raise in Salaries was the auto-rickshaw prices in that locality. All Software engineers used to, one way to say that, throwing money for engaging autos. Peak hours, general public used to suffer like anything due to this.

This is Important to read and understand. I was in a bus stop waiting for a shared auto, where shared auto prices were also doubled and noticed an Aged Person, with Syringe into his vein on his hand with plaster around it, and hardly able to stand with the help of a stick and with a small kid beside him trying to engage an auto to take him to hospital, that was visible from the place we were, but far to walk for him with some medical problems. He could not engage because of a sudden rise in auto fares and also excess income being earned due to shared autos used by Software Engineers whose salaries were abnormal to that region.

The Aged person out of frustration commented about the change in situation and the spurt in auto rickshaw charges due to raise in software engineer salaries.

What one needs to understand here is the Quantity of Money to Software Engineers made available in the form of salary.

The starting range was ₹9,000 per month and highest range was ₹2,00,000 per month when the local income levels were at less than ₹9,000.

This change in a software company was a major hit to the local house rents, auto rickshaw charges, food price in some hotels.

I felt bad about the old man while living in India but I was only able to pity to his situation but not able to recognize the reasons. Even the above reasons were not to my notice while I was in the situation in my life.

I was proud to draw the fat salary; my parents were proud for getting such large salary. One thing the reader should remember here is the Quantity of Money in Numbers.

This was my third job in three years. When I went to get Visa for USA, the counter visa officer asked me a question about why did I change the job frequently, and why am I going to USA? I was pretty straight to him in my answer as "For more Money". I found people praying while standing in queue for VISA. Here I should say this that I never aspired to go anywhere outside Hyderabad and now my fate led me to go for USA visa. I was not in any mood to pray also.

I always aspired to settle in small business on my own without any bossism by anybody. Why I am saying this, when you are failing continuously you will definitely start looking for reasons for such failures. This has been happening to me always due to failure in my ambitions.

Let me give you one simple example about the "Success" of "Failures". Theory of Probability was created by two mathematicians who were losers in Gambling. The influence of that subject is so humungous at unbelievable levels.

From India, I first went to Atlanta where my company headquarters were there. I lived there for three months before I took an assignment from my company side in Cleveland.

Till I moved to Cleveland, I did not have any idea about the chillness of winter and snow. I had never seen snow in my life. Temperatures below 0 degree Celsius were not in my experience of 28 years. Temperatures at 11°C in Hyderabad were most chilled ones for me till that point. In Cleveland, I first experienced different life. Then I remembered the Indian movies where heroine and hero dance in below 0°C temperature places with laugh and pleasantness. I remembered the way how I used to understand while watching movie and what the reality was.

Not only environment but also the work culture, living conditions, living style, shopping style and what not. One more major change that I noticed was deserted localities and roads. Probably, a person may see 1 or 2 persons in a day on an average unless visited a supermarket.

When I reached USA, first thing that I was asked to do was to go to Social Security registration office to register the social security number. Read more details about this Social Security System in Unique ID Chapter.

I was with my friend for a couple of months before I moved to my own apartment in the same complex. I was not having any friends or acquaints or relatives in USA. Only my company and company officials were known persons, so if I need to talk to anybody with affection then only option with me was calling India. I used to get minimum of US$900 per month telephone bill.

I used to travel 13 miles every day to work by city bus. Early morning at 5:55 AM, I need to get into bus which used to take about 2 hours to reach the downtown Cleveland where my client's office used to be. At evening 5:55 PM again I used to get into the bus to reach back the house in another 2 hours.

In local city bus, I and my friend used to be only two Indians majority of the time. I used to hear lot of conversations between commuters in the bus. I used to pay attention in order to pick up quick understanding of American accent and slangs and also to improve my American accent and slang. This city bus travel really provided an opportunity to get into the inner side of the society of USA.

There was conversation between two mothers, at their age of around 45s with daughters at teenage.

They were talking about the challenges being faced by them as mothers. Also some incidents from their neighbourhood teenage girls and their corresponding mother's troubles. I was completely shocked by the conversation.

Such conversation, I never expected I would ever hear in USA. There were resemblances between India and USA. Mothers were concerned about their daughters. They were also afraid of the sexual relations by their teenage daughters and the age and the disturbance or loss of concentration on their future career and negative consequences due to false emotional faults usually committed by teenagers at that age. All those were resembling to the same in India among Indian families. Not only about teenage daughters but also about teenage sons.

Till that point, I as everybody from India were in the impression that USA does not have family structure. They have free sex. Their teenagers are encouraged to have sex as they feel like. They propose and have sex as similar as food when feel hungry. These were the impressions. Also the Hollywood movies created an impression that people there wear very less clothes. Especially, as young male Indian I was also having interesting thoughts towards American females in USA.

All of those wrong understandings in my mind were completely shattered. I understood that there are good family values in USA but they have a very clear and crisp social values than several stupid values that Indians have in their society. In fact such values in India are merely due to several apprehensions in Indian society. I don't mean that India does not have social values but there are differences. There are merits and demerits in both USA and India.

Life was going on.

The next incident that changed me and my internal cognition process again occurred. This time it was in the form of telephone bill. I got a huge telephone bill from AT&T telephone company. My calling plan was wrongly mentioned and calculation was 50% higher than my negotiated price. I did not have any proof of the negotiated price. Everything was recorded and accepted over phone. I was completely upset and worried about the large bill of US$1300. I was more worried about losing US$400, equivalent to ₹20,000 and was remembering the kind of complications one had to go through with Indian government Telephone department in order to get rid of the discrepancies in the telephone bill in India and how one has to go through all legal hassles and consumer courts. I was really worried for ₹20,000. I was hopeless about correcting that. One more point here is I did not even have the name of the person to whom I spoke and did my negotiation. We all know that in India when such problems occur, Indians usually try to locate the person/s who are all involved in the incidents. When I mentioned, my friends said to call up AT&T and talk about it. They assured me of getting corrected right away over phone call. But I was sceptic. I called on AT&T and got cleared the bill discrepancy right over telephone. I was relieved from all my tensions. This was another impact on my psychology and confidence of dealing things in USA.

One more very important thing that I have always been noticing about living in USA is about the cost of living. If we go to Supermarkets, we can find huge choice of products to buy from. However, many of them are imported to USA.

One more interesting thing is about the facility available to buyers. Different super markets have different policies; however there is one common thing between them. It is about "Return Policy". Any customer can buy and use it and return it if not satisfied. In other words, if you need it or not, like it or not, used it or not, but you can return in 15 days to 3 months duration if you have receipt in hand.

I was initially surprised. Initially when I was having the same level of thoughts as anybody else, I always admired it. Later maturity of understanding led me to the point of reasons for it.

Even bananas in USA are imported. Same with tomatoes. Unless the product is machine harvested, rest everything is imported for USA from surrounding nations or from around the world. Since the US$ rates against other nation's currencies have always been appreciating, the prices of food products used to be lowering.

To know the reason for capability of absorbing the costs of "Refund Policy", we need to recall the kind of purchase policies and refund policies that the giant retail stores have from their suppliers. Majority of those suppliers are from Third world nations like India.

Here I must give you some information about the kind of losses and hardships that Indian exporters used to face on the name of Quality Assurance exercise at the shores of the USA after they land their products at USA shores. The weakness with exporters was the bulk market and bulk payments and appreciating US$ that used to give them unexpected profits in terms of their native currency.

*Reader should remember this to create the understanding of 360 degrees.*

Life was going and I was happy in receiving more and more money at low expenditure. Large amount of savings. I once read a serial written by an editor in Telugu weekly "Andhra Bhoomi" about his travel experiences in USA. I remembered him of mentioning about milk that is used to mix in coffee decoction was called as Creamer. He also mentioned one should ask for Creamer instead of milk to mix for making coffee but the fact was different. Milk was also available. The purpose of making Creamer availability was different which is not contextual. I am mentioning this—hear to show that how impressions get created within people those have never seen it.

In my childhood, my grandmother's relative was moved to USA as doctor and I remember of overhearing a conversation that USA is such a rich place where even servant maids use cars.

The next impact on me was when I travelled from Cleveland to Pittsburgh with my friend in his car. First time long distance travel. During that trip I started observing the engineering miracles. Roads, Bridges, Traffic Signs, Traffic Engineering, Road Safety Engineering, Bridge Architectures, Road Side Help facilities, Traffic Policing System and many more where Technical, Managerial and Organization skills are well reflecting everywhere in every aspect of whatever we are able to see with our eyes around us.

Highly Organized, Well engineered, Fool Proof and No wastage.

I recollected our engineering college principal Professor Droothrot's "inspirable" story during the farewell day.

An engineer, a lawyer and a doctor had reached the Prairie Gates where the person at the gate asked each one to give details about at least one act of their life time that can be considered as a "credit" to get into heaven. We know that Doctor is a default gainer in such incidents. Lawyer is the second one who claimed that he fought for acquitting an innocent. Engineer is the one who can't claim at least one hence, resulted him to be sent into hell.

After some time, both doctor and lawyer were enjoying the comforts of heaven, they thought of visiting their engineering friend in hell. What they found when they reached hell was astonishing to them. Hell has more heavenly facilities than heaven itself. This is what an engineer is capable of.

Here I advise reader, please don't relate the conventional present Certificate Course of our education as a reference of identifying an engineer.

USA is an example of what a human is capable of. A Hell is transformed to Heaven. Also how heaven on earth, land of Gods of history, India has become hell on earth. Not India alone but several other nations due to this "Economic Terrorism."

I used to wonder what could have made USA or Europe successful or better than India!

USA also used to have horrible conditions during initial days of automobile booming and urban formation. However, what I understand was, Mother Nature made them to develop discipline in them. Since temperatures always stay in cold around ZERO or below ZERO levels, any traffic jam will be a hell for them to live in those cold temperatures outside. Mother Nature will kill them.

Whereas in India, such indiscipline acts do not show any lethal impact from Mother Nature which is the reason for a natural behaviour characteristics in Indians as "Ok....let it go."

My savings were good, I was able to send money to India. My father was able to purchase a house. We were able to repay all our debts. We were happy. I was happy receiving more money. Whenever Rupee falls in Forex Market I used to be happier than earlier as every other person like me then in USA.

At the same time, I was finding more and expenditure rising during those days in India. More and more industries were going sick in India. I used to hear people talking about loss in all sectors and rising input costs and cost of living.

My wife joined me and I bought a car and we were living well with all joy of life. The next major incident that triggered some thoughts in me occurred after some time when I was waiting in hospital visitor gallery for my wife who was pregnant and was having check-up by her gynaecologist.

A person, aged around 80 or above, white fellow, came near me and was trying to sit about two seats away from me, and said "bakshish dev". I did not notice that expression as I was not expecting it. He repeated again. I was surprised first and then looked at him as I was having a doubt if he was begging me by sitting beside me. His attire was good and was not reflecting any beggar symptoms. I asked him how he knew about that phrase. He explained about his Second World War days, staying at Kolkata and how he used to find beggars on road. He ended stating that "Doesn't India have lot of beggars"? It sounded very offending and insulting to me. I responded stating that "Doesn't USA have Beggars?"

However this did not leave any impression on me until I started facing different situation at home, in India and in USA.

I met my engineering friend in India when I returned to India to visit my parents after one and half years. He was unemployed and he was desperately looking for job but could not get any. He was upset and he was cursing his unlucky fate and was very upset that left a huge impression in my mind and on my heart. He was a wealthy fellow.

This brought back the earlier White fellow's remarks on beggars in India. A seed of question got created in my mind why there is difference between USA and India.

One more incident that impacted me was my friend's brother who was a military major and moved out of India in search of better life for kids. I told him the same words, "you are motivational to us and your moving out of India is very big jolt to people like us."

This was mostly accumulated further and further as and when I started seeing more and more problems.

One of the most influential one was the suicide by farmer and a girl child of farmer writing email to, if I remember right, to CM of AP, and PM of India. I wrote an email then to Chandrababu Naidu (the then Chief Minister of Andhra Pradesh), stating that the letter was a "Souvenir" to ruling chairs of India.

I was able to see USA Senate though not as a citizen of USA but could not see Parliament of India though I am citizen of India.

I returned to USA and my life was as usual. Nothing much happened for another two years in my life. Same routine life. Counting money and savings and investing in India or in USA. Returning to India after good savings was only aim.

There was one incident that happened as a small discussion around genuineness of Gandhi and his selfishness during freedom struggle. I argued stating that if a person spared a time of his life for somebody that is enough to consider him as good man, one simple question is why should that man spend his time of life for somebody else?

I happened to stay in Bismarck in USA where the population is low that entire State of North Dakota. Population was only 600,000 in an area of 250,000 sq. miles. This is like a state of the size of Andhra Pradesh which has only a population of any district headquarters in that state. See how feeble population is, in such a barren land. However strange that you can find "fence" around land, those were owned by people there as well. I used to have a lot of time after work. No places to go around hence always used to stay at home and used to either watch TV or go through Internet.

I used to watch lot of old Hollywood movies and lot of History Channel Programs almost the rest of the day when I don't have any other self-training software programs. Here I should mention about my self-learning software skill. As a software developer, I have to keep on learning always new software packages in order to keep up myself to the market demand. I by now had learnt about 5 to 6 different packages. This new learning is because "I have been getting reset to one always due to change in the market". I was frustrated but no choice. Every time I have to update my resume to the suitability of the market demand with new skills. Remember here that I am a skilled labour.

*"Labour market" has been a very old market on this earth that can be found evidences of its existence 1000 years ago also.* Indians do not have idea about this market after British left India and until H1 was initiated by USA for skilled labour.

Now here watching those TV programs has created a change in my interests as well. Those old Movies and History programs, keeping aside the story line, they reflect more about the contemporary social conditions of the story and its time in the history. It gives you feel of living those days and understanding the kind of then society, culture and social, political and economic conditions then. History Channel used to transmit several programs, those would be in different dimensions such as technology history, political history, science history, economic history, finance history, etc. and many more.

This was when I started understanding the concept of Dating in USA for male and female natural mating process, what kind of circumstances had led to the development of such concept in the society of USA. Here I am putting down my interpretations based on the information I received from the context that I watched through different history programs. As a reader, you may have different information that might have resulted into different interpretation. Hence, please read this book from my dimension.

My interpretation with respect to dating concept is as follows. The entire European Immigrant life in USA and their society establishment in USA has some roots from their source land society, Europe. The long duration of globetrotting by Europeans Society for centuries together, such as British, French, Dutch, Portuguese, Spanish people migrating to other part of the world for trading to Europe from other parts of the world, those long years of globetrotting by the young European population on the globe led to a situation of creating this Dating Concept. Because the chances or scope for following certain social/traditional values and circumstances for their natural instincts were meagre and almost nil. They had to find a mating partner available within reach and proceed.

The settlers in USA from Europe were living in a vast land doing agriculture or other activities staying away far from each other relatives and without any clue as to who are their neighbours which led to situations where young persons of those settlers had to adopt techniques of finding opposite for sex. The social gatherings were more at church gatherings, in case there is church or some sort of religious gatherings. Since, in such immigrant life, where parents cannot follow any social rules to create a wedding system with others as similar as Indian society, parents have to let the young choose their own counterpart for natural urges and to continue with their life in future. Also since their life is immigrant life and the economy was new, most of the changes in their social life was as similar as animal world. Young has to find their own means of survival with their own will and wish. This is not similar to India where the framework of society, family and several more are rooted since centuries. This difference is one of major points that have been impacting freedom of thoughts in the minds of USA citizens. The same has been exactly opposite in India where one cannot have freedom of thoughts as he/she finds it reasonable.

I have seen and heard Indian immigrant parents with teenage kids expressing the concerns about dating in USA and who were trying to impose their Indian Social system in USA which was considered as "rude crude method" by people who are habituated to live there in a different society and having different understandings. Here they are as human as natural computing machines got programmed by the circumstances they lived.

I was also an immigrant and was imagining the situations that would lead into such sexual relations as dating that is not native to India. I could make out the reasons. In such small population available in USA, there is no choice for parent's options but individuals have to make their own choice.

I met a family which was migrated to USA long back and has been running a laundry shop. The man looks for "dependent" Indian women who would work for him at low cost in his laundry business. He belongs to a caste that never even thinks of getting into laundry business in India. This incident without saying told me that an individual adopts a profession that is available to him for survival purpose and no inhibitions would come in his way.

There was an Indian American movie on the same. An Indian "Origin" family, who had no clue about how India would be, migrated to USA from Nigeria, when there were extraditions by that government, whose girl child, at teenage, got used to watching the black society, studied and understood about black society, gets attracted to the black young man and always finds it not an issue, whereas parents were more worried about the good old traditions of Indian society and values and they pressurise her to marry an Indian origin person. Also the father who returns to Nigeria remembers his childhood days and cries a lot of leaving his birth place and staying away from his ancestors place to somewhere in USA which he feels as not his place. He could not own the new society where he has been living. His daughter kid was able to own the USA society where and all those Nigerian immigrants as her ancestral nation and society and was not finding any issue in dating a Nigerian native.

However in India, dating is considered with different understandings which we all know. Of course, knowing each other is also required but that culture is not there in India socially, and so much open talk is also not allowed in India.

Everybody talks about Valentine Day but what I wonder is, how many of them really consider hearing a open proposal for going out to a dinner. Indian social psychology is different from American.

This led me to explore why Indians were moved to Africa. I found that British/Europeans were migrating families to Africa where there is good tropical land available. I compared my skilled IT labour life with those old skilled agriculture labour life. No difference. Because, Indians have very good agriculture skills, especially in tropical crops such as sugarcane and many other agriculture products. They had good skills of cultivation and "supervisory" skills. Also they are good workers with discipline. I will talk about different skills later. Indians always live with fear of sin and sincerity. They behave as good as possible equal to intelligent computing machines, if programmed carefully with information, expected results can be achieved as expected.

During the same time, I happened to watch a Hollywood movie of 60s reflecting a "real time" story of then economic conditions of society of farmer with cow herd. In this movie an old man has been surviving with son and nephew. Old man dies of stress from his economic failures, resulted due to foot and mouth disease of his cattle. Government orders to kill all cows of herd and bury them. The disease was widespread in state and almost all the cow herds were put through the same process on government orders. Nephew who was very practical man is almost double the age of old man's son. Old man's son was more attached to his father's nephew but the nephew though was attached to the old man's son but being more practical, wants to leave old man's son to his fate and decides to move on with his life as he doesn't own any as successor from the old man. Story was heart touching. Leaving the story aside, since this was a movie based on real incident in America, the reality stored in my memory. One important fact is, there was no help from government to farmers as recovery from losses in terms of Finance. This explains, even farmers in USA also have problems. Even today it is true.

I started comparing the farmer life in USA and that of the same in India. I did not find much difference between both the places. In USA, 100s of acres will be cultivated by farmer using machines. Also as their crop pattern is, they cultivate only those crops which can be done by machines in bulk way. If at all, man power is required, they have to depend on foreign sources only. Too much production by farmers but less consumption due to low population. Due to this excess availability of everything, farmers do not get enough margin to their produce. However their input costs are lowered due to imports. The situation in India has been exactly opposite. There is huge demand for food due to population. But farmer, food production sector, has been suffering with large input costs and purchase power has been dropping in the society.

This reminded me of my childhood in India. In the next chapter I would like to take you to my earlier life.

# 3 HISTORY

*I was born in 1970, today what I understand is that the time of my birth and my life along with my contemporaries has been passing through a timeline of Indian society that is really very important change in the life of the Indian society. The same can be generalized to world. It was transformation and shift from its fundamentals or pillars to different fluid state.*

One important thing to be understood is, a society gets a character in a course of time, those characteristics take longer time to change also. Hence the difference between present characteristics to the same of 100 years ago could be very little.

As anybody, I used to go to my mother side grandfather's house for every holidays. My mother's father was an upper middle class farmer of his time with lot of agriculture activities along with lot of cattles. He used to have four pairs of bulls, almost 15 cows, and around 15 buffalos with one lead male servant with three supporting male servants. I will use the word "workers" instead of "Servants" to make it more meaningful in economic terms. I have seen the life of a farmer family very closely.

Several movies are made in Telugu to reflect the changes in farmer families due to economic and social changes that have taken place after independence of India.

Those were the days when quantity of land, quantity of children (sons), quantity of rice bags, quantity of cattle etc. and many more were considered as symbols of wealth.

One important observation relevant to my book is, once I went to my grandfather's place when harvesting was in progress. There were two kinds of workers. One job workers would be engaged during the harvesting season on job work basis only for harvesting purpose. The second set of workers are regular workers who work at home on regular basis throughout the year. Regular workers apart from those work in the house that usually would be cloth washer, barber, cobbler/leather processor, blacksmith and others those usually work for the needs of the farmer.

There are third kind of workers. They are domestic animals and cattle. There used to be interdependency between all creatures with affection and respect.

*Farming in India can be considered as one of the largest industrious activities as similar as Industrial Production house. Farmer used to be the head of his production house of Food Production.*

What is important that I want to say here is, every one of those regular workers used to get paid by paddy and not by money. I witnessed this transaction method when I was in my teenage of 13 years. Now do not get surprise about my memory power.

*This means barter system is there after 1970 as well in villages of India.*

Here I need to give some more information about my experiences of my life that was an input information to me and my cognition process in my brain.

My father was working for a fertilizer company. Coincidently its name was East India Distilleries Parry India Ltd.

Why I am saying this name is, it happened to be one of the old Corporates of British that was started around 230 years ago as a trading company by a British businessmen Parry Thomson and the business had transformed itself into a big corporate house when India gained independence.

I used to get feel of East India Company of British whenever I used to see all that related to that company.

The reason for mentioning this here is to let you know about the influence that it made on me as Corporate along with freedom fight stories in school books and outside.

I happened to live in different places due to his job transfers. I lived in 15 different places and cultures within India in my 28 year life. Every place has its own culture though they are not very far from each other.

Our resident location mostly used to be the district Head Quarters which is bit elegant than the villages. We used to have all modern facilities such as telephone facility, vehicle facility etc. which were provided by company for their business purpose.

I sometimes used to travel along with him to fertilizer markets, usually ranging from small villages without commutation facility to large towns. This has given me the opportunity to understand the fundamental sector of India and its trade. Also since the company in which my father used to work was a large corporate house of India, and since he was at middle management for long duration, I got the opportunity of looking at the Corporate Life Style in my house also. This helped me understanding the Corporates operating processes and procedures from the conversations of my father along with his colleagues or friends.

One of the major influences on me was their "campaigning programs" and the means they adopt to influence the thoughts of the consumer. There used to be a movie on van for the company promotion activities such as Movie Advertisements. I also saw that movie once. They also used to "adopt" land in villages to apply the chemical fertilizers in order to show the improvement which attracts the farmer to use it.

These are not uncommon. I am trying to tell you that how such programs have been influencing the behaviour of person from childhood itself.

One more interesting thing was, since agriculture was largest economic activity of India and fertilizer was the most desired commodity for farmers and the season of fertilizer is time bound and also the products have always been scarce in the market, however fertilizer products have large demands from society, this was completely being enjoyed by Company employees, it is one of the very highly valued property in the market and society. They used to enjoy a lot of value and respect from society due to their job.

This life style helped me experience different life styles which may be usually available to very limited persons and also corporate management culture.

During my fertilizer trading business, I saw the way how farmers used to get exploited by fertilizer dealers. One pesticide, by their colour will be sold at different prices but the fact was none of them had stipulated percentage of pesticide chemical. One farmer came to a shop asking for a remedy of leaf becoming yellow. The reason was due to soil but the farmer was made to buy a product of ₹300 worth liquid to spray on it which just works for a week due to its ingredients, but does not give any benefit to the farmer. I felt very bad about this when my father explained me what exactly happened. Farmers don't have any guidance. Scientists are not at all at their reach. Specializations are not anywhere near them. Take the case of my father who happened to be a agricultural graduate and working to sell fertilizer and pesticides and looking at profits on wrong sales. He was one among many in that sector.

I was not a reformer, and in fact I was also making money from his consumption but that left me with some understanding about the situation in the sector.

Though government has lot of infrastructure and programs but none of them were helping farmers in any manner. Everybody was looking to make money from farmers. One thing is evident that everybody was more interested in making more money.

Here, I should mention one more thing. In India, due to constant rise in cost of living, people started adopting all different kinds of practices to raise their income in terms of "money". There is one important matter related to conversion of farming land to non-farming purpose, especially coastal paddy lands to fisheries.

Earlier I said about my fertilizer business. I used to find large Grape farms around Hyderabad. Grape farming requires a large amount of investment for pesticides and fertilizers. However, the time available to harvest and cash yield would be very less. In addition, I used to find problems of pest and exploitation by pesticide traders and many more. I happened to interact, in fact, using them for my business purpose so called, advisors/consultants, etc. for grape farmers. Their words were like axioms for some farmers.

Also the same situation used to be there in tomato farming also with corn farming and in all different sector.

Input costs were raising and sale prices were not meeting their investments. Farmers were running into losses.

During my trading business, I used to pay bribes in sales tax office of government of Andhra Pradesh. Everybody used to put innocent face but at the end the work used to be done only when there was some payment made as bribe. Even today it is the same.

The complaint from society for such bribery behaviour was "low income to government employees", which was not true.

Here I should mention that in USA, I inquired about the kind of salaries that government employees get paid, which was not good at all, not even as good as India. However they used to be sincere towards their duty. Why? Why this motivation in USA and why that morale so high in USA? Why the same has been opposite in India? Initial days, there used to be a lot of sincerity in India and commitment by all Indian as patriot and service towards India and society, but that morale and, motivation is not there, why? What was it that made Indians loose the focus of their role responsibilities?

I do not have any answers. But remember these questions are important.

This trading business helped me understand the supply chain, warehousing, dealer network types, tax structures of government etc. Though I was observing the same activities since my childhood due to my fathers job, I got real hands on only when I started the business. Cost accounting, profit derivation, trade techniques, accounting, meaning of ledger, journal, debit, credit, invoice, cash receipt, interest rates, banking procedures, banking instruments, DDs, cheques and processes and many more were there that I learnt in this business unit.

# 4 SHARE MARKET–I

One more reason was that we lost a lot of money in Share Market due to which I had to move into a Software job. This was something I should detail here.

I graduated in 1993 when there were huge transformations in the Indian Economic Policies. P.V. Narasimha Rao as PM of India with Manmohan Singh as Finance Minister of India had initiated several "reforms" to correct the economy which was bankrupted. Here please remember the important words, *reforms* and *bankrupt* which I will mention again later in this book.

All know that Indian economy was not having enough "Forex" to meet its needs through imports. Indian Economy was "closed" economy and was in need of reforms to open up the economy. It was told by every expert through newspapers.

During that time only the stock market got the attention of the nation. Investment in stock market was given large promotion. Everybody started talking about share market, stocks, investments, etc. I do not want to detail about Harshad Mehta and other stock market scandals as they do not add value to my book in any manner. However, I would mention about one incident. The Indian Stock market crash was followed by Pakistan stock market crash. It was such a big crash; if I remember right, the market was crashed to 20% of its peak in just two days. It was attributed towards some change in economic conditions, industry outlook and the participants were foreign fund organization. I got the question as why would the indicators change such rapid pace that too in just difference of one or two calendar days.

Initially stock markets used to be at Mumbai, Chennai and Delhi only. Also those stock markets used to be as consortium centres of stock brokers. The stock market boom led to creation of Hyderabad stock exchange, Vijayawada stock exchange and many more stock exchanges around the nation. Later these small stock markets were closed. Large stock markets were converted into a commercial company with share capital and part of the share capital was sold for foreign stock exchange.

Here, one should pay attention as to why that stock market was converted into a commercial company? Why was it sold to foreign company? What was the benefit for India? Stock market is a company that always makes money and never loses any money at all, then why was it, instead of owned by government of India completely, made as a company and sold to foreign stock exchange? Who decided this? What information was given to the parliament or to any other ruling chair about this large decision that impacts the nation? If reader does some work here, there will be several bitter answers which would be mindboggling.

*Remember this as reader of this book. These are important questions.*

Everywhere there was fever of shares investment and making quick money. My father's steno when he was in office before retirement, he was very active in stock trading, introduced us to this stock market. When we looked around, several others were there in those activities. I have seen people "participating" heavily in stock market, either as IPO issuers, stock brokers, investors or advisors. Everywhere they were there. We also got excited and started investing in the market buying stocks on advices on our own reviews and knowledge from papers. The fall of stock market sucked up my father's retirement money of ₹4 Lakh that was a 26 year old savings. Even today we have share certificates which are not useful for anything.

Why am I saying, not for sympathy or to tell about my economic status, but about the way how stock market can be costlier for you. Imagine our family situation and my father's psychological tension. I wrote more about how stock markets are used for "virtual war" on nations by USA.

The stock market participation for almost about 1½ year gave me some understanding about Stock market investments and how to interpret the stock moves and reports and Government policies, etc., not gained expertise, but gained knowledge and familiarity with stock market jargons, parameters, and many more.

But since we had the trading firm that I started, my father who was having king size respect in that trade, became a trader to make living again on trading business. I opted to go for a job and luckily got the job in a software company.

My software career was started.

Software boom was everywhere. New companies started coming into market. I got quick jumps and reached a point where I started drawing large salary, and I got married and "luckily" got US visa as well and moved to USA.

# 5 1:1

While living in USA, I started focusing on what are the major differences between life in India and USA. One thing what I found about the major difference as anybody else able to notice, were the roads, uninterrupted electricity supply, telecommunications, cheap food, cheap fuel, cheap real estate, etc.

I used to observe one major characteristic of Indians in India. Mostly their thoughts, aspirations and requirements have always been hitting each other. I used to wonder how could they bring on to a streamlined thought patterns. I used to compare between India and USA analyse. What I felt was, roads are one of the common utilities where all people have common understanding in order to move around freely without hitting each other and without interrupting others. In India usually, there will be interruptions very frequently due to poor traffic system. Also lack of traffic engineering system on roads, several commuters step over on others route. This is an example how Indian's thoughts do not align well with others. I felt that this is one of the major reasons why USA has been very well organized and successfully able to keep its citizens well-coordinated with each other for successful social life in USA.

The most important thing that I found in USA was, one needs to be creative to grab his/her opportunity. I always used to have only one thought in mind, settle in a job in a small town in USA for life and do not looking back to India again. I did not intend to move back to India again.

I was in the conclusion that India was over crowded due to population and whoever has got the opportunity to get out of

India should always stay out and should never return to India again.

After I moved to Bismarck, there was one more incident that occurred in my life. It was my friend and colleague who was actively involved in Share Market investment in USA. All my friends used to invest there. But I used to stay away from it with fear of losing money again. I always used to discourage my friend, used make him cautious about dangers in stock market, how analysts speak and how stock market bursts. We used to car pool and have long discussions around the stock market analysis reports.

Living in Bismarck and watching several history programs and old Hollywood movies, the living conditions of Bismarck always used to raise one question. What for the reason human moved to this part of the earth? Why did not they choose to move away from here to more tropical areas? Bismarck always have temperatures below zero for 10 months of the year. One interesting thing that I observed was the nature behaviour, especially trees transforming their leaves from green to ripe state and then dropping them in just less than two or three days. Also when temperatures are good at the start of spring, leaves grow fast and become very green. The behaviour of trees in tropical areas, like India, and in other parts of USA is different. In some parts, trees take longer time to shelve their leaves. Nature is really a miracle. This change attracted me about how every creature on earth establishes its life style based on the circumstantial demands and obeys the Mother Nature.

Here I should mention one thing about agriculture in those areas. USA usually has below zero temperatures for most of the year. They usually go for two crops within five months. Farmers prefer to have below zero temperatures, this lowers the impact of pest problem. India has for long days of tropical atmosphere. Due to its temperatures, pest problem is more. All creatures need to survive.

Here I would like to add one incident related to the kind of science and technology developed in first world nations. Australia had a Rat Epidemic. There were so many rats that people were not able to find land to place foot to walk. Australian scientists developed wheat crop seed in such a way that if that is eaten by any creature then it will be dead. A food crop is converted into a killer crop. Understand the height of technology development in those nations.

However, India is able to produce all that to feed all its population (four times of population of USA but having only 1/3 of land size of USA) within its production and also able to export. Isn't this efficiency of expertise of India?

Bismarck and Fargo are very small towns. The change in Bismarck town in one year and also change in Minneapolis and Fargo areas gave me an idea about how economy gets build up in an area and then append that to state level and then append that to the nation level. However, this was only a starting.

The debates with my friend, who always used to say that all the analysts are highly qualified and their anticipations are scientific conclusions. He made good profit and the same details and my wife's interest made me focus on stock market again. I started focusing on several different analytical reports and other market and government policies and many more.

I have been living in USA since last three years and have been earning good income and the fall of Rupee has been making me rich and rich in India as well. I wanted to build my assets in India.

While I was leaving India to USA three years ago, I said to my friends that my aim is to buy about 50 acres of land in India and return to India. After that I changed my mind for settling in USA.

This was an evidence of "not my greed or ambition" but "the change in need of money" to meet the new economic conditions in India and around the world after I return to India. Also pay attention towards my changing preferences and priorities. Earning money is now changed to settling down in USA.

My first options of buying a flat for parents was completed. Also I had constructed second house for my parents. I invested into fixed assets.

A big endeavour that was not possible for a person who worked for 30 years in job and having middle class financial and social status, I was able to do in five years of career because of US$ value against Indian Rupees.

Remember here that I am having lot of quantity of money and I am moving that to India. The raising in quantity of money is raising as the rupee falls against US$.

I was looking at the options of investing in India. The situation in India was the same as explained earlier, agriculture was not doing well at all. Farmers were getting indebted faster than earlier. I have been taking back my decisions on buying agriculture land every time due to loss in agriculture. Investments were more, and yields were less and so support price for yields that was leading farmers getting indebted. Also I could see that manpower cost was raising along with more demands from workers and less delivery of services from workers. At every opportunity I was finding negative returns instead of positive returns. Even real estate prices were raising but rents were not to that level. Real estate prices were raised from ₹900 per Sq. Ft. to ₹3000 per Sq. Ft.

I was not able to find best place to invest, hence I invested in a cooperative bank settling for a 15% assured dividend every year on my capital which was almost 5% more than usual interest rates. This sounded to me reasonable. However this investment into bank made me to look at the options of understanding dividend and interest rates and their meanings, etc.

I wrote about the investment opportunities in India in Chapter 38 "Investments Opportunities".

One more History Channel program that changed my understanding was about the construction of Panama Canal. In this program, I first saw the details about the steam engine based earth dozers, diggers and dumpers and many more large equipment. This was an eye opener to me. As an Indian, I always had this understanding that the above said heavy earth equipment was new technology developments and did not have a clue that they were there in USA in 1800s itself. One more program that attracted me from History Channel was construction of Hoover Dam in worst economic depression of USA; where they used the refrigeration or heating technology for curing of cement pillars while constructing Hoover Dam. Such programs always used to create amazed feeling inside me and my technical interests. I am being an engineering graduate was not having idea of how a technology would be used in real time. In such huge depression of economy, how did the government raise money to construct the Hoover Dam?

What I understand from several different information that I had been through, as the government being the supreme it can plan its economy in whichever manner it wants and can create/print money to suit its economic activities. Here government has anticipated certain economic growth due to initiation of this new dam, pre-construction during construction and post-construction, that would create a debt in its economic accounting calculations and print/create that money as debt will later repay it by the collection of taxes generated from the new economy. See here, no debt from outside. Remember here that I will mention this again later when I talk about Indian Economy and its Planning.

In India we only know about the invention of electricity, telephone, flight and some of those inventions reached India, and are being utilised there.

This reminds me of another interesting technical equipment. I stood in front of this just to enjoy the technology invention. It was mechanical, the Flight Schedule display board in Frankfurt that I saw when I first travelled from India to USA. This triggered some sense about how the simple techniques in technology will be used for large purposes. The Frankfurt Airport Flight display unit was not electronic one but mechanical + electrical one with metal pieces that runs on using the principles of Metal, Magnets and Matrix. The mechanical display of letters resembles the segment display as show in the picture below. The movement of metal plates in the segments makes noise of Trrrr...Trrrr...I still remember of standing in front of it for half hour admiring it. It was similar to the following.

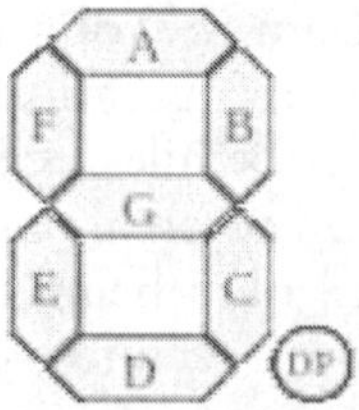


The History Channel programs gave me lot of information about how to use the learnt subject or techniques or technologies and how one can be creative or innovative.

I came to know about how people in USA get rich on new inventions those are not complex like proving $e = mc^2$ like Einstein.

A person invented the colour coding to identify the left leg shoe and right leg shoe. Invention of Yellow Pages, etc. are some of them.

One more interesting aspect that I found was, I have always seen that Indians are in the belief of the automation started only after invention of electronics. I was shocked to look at the kind of automation happened with pure mechanical engineering and timing cam techniques. Pay attention here on, no electricity or electronics or computers are involved in any of those old automations.

Also the use of electric motor for different purposes was very amusing to me.

What we need to understand here is the Technology Development and surrounding protections in the form of Patent Rights. Patent rights is something not well known and is in practice in India at all even today but this protection and royalty to knowledge and innovation has been there in western world since 1570. Here as an average Indian, one should start learning the value of documenting a Right.

It means there was value for a document in 1600s itself where in India, providing value to a document as representative of legitimacy is not there until British came into India and introduced the system of Registration system for land ownership or any other registrations.

Imagine the kind of gap in the knowledge and understanding between two different regions. There is a reason for this.

In India, there used to be feudal system where the small holdings were not having value. Whoever has power and strength would rule the place and as long as the interests of feudal powers are not challenged, everything in the society would be even.

I also learnt how people used to migrate to USA on Gold Rush. The History Channel programs and my moving to Bismarck, a place that is very less populated, changed my thinking pattern. In India change is not noticeable, due to large population. If at all any change occurs in India then that would be due to some external stimulation factor from foreign source.

I got the knowledge of how economy gets initiated due to movement of people and how economy gets established.

There is one important aspect here to mention, the rapid changes in the USA economy due the addition of foreign population to USA society through H1B Visas was very evident. The impact from simple food buying till buying cars which later converted into real estate after almost five years. There was huge real estate boom because many of the H1B holders had started gaining the permanent residency and buying houses in order to save tax.

Here one thing that I should add about saving tax. In USA, number of kids will impact the tax being paid. In USA, there will be 3 kinds of taxes on every tax payer. One is transaction tax that we pay while buying anything. Second is State Income Tax. The Transaction Tax + State income tax together usually stays at around 10 to 12%. Third is Federal Income Tax which would be around 20% and above.

I also happened to watch a lot of programs on stock market history in USA. Stock markets in Europe, USA in 1700s itself where Indians were only familiar of them in 1990s and after that, almost 200 years later. Of course, there used to be exchanges but percentage of people knew about them were very little.

I watched History programs the way how Ford started his Ford Company and what is its history and how the labour conditions used to be, etc. Such programs gave me information about how it used to be in those old days.

By now, many know the cause for labour revolution and labour laws evolution and Labour Day on May 1 in India and September 5 in USA. They celebrate the day when labour revolution was successful, we celebrate the day when the revolution was started. This is similar to left hand driving and right hand driving.

Also I watched programs about how the "currency" systems used to be. In earlier days, every bank in USA used to issue its own Currency Bills. There used to be different currencies in USA alone until Federal Government of USA adopted the Single Currency system in USA. This knowledge helped in understanding the multiple currency systems and fundamentally how to interpret the currency system.

This kind of information is not available to Indians at all which is the most important reason why Indians have been very poor in understanding things.

The normal living in Bismarck usually would be different from other part of USA itself. North Dakota is a backward state in USA. Bismarck being far from other places has some complications.

I purchased rice of 2 Pounds for US$7 in Bismarck. I was completely shocked. Tomatoes cost around US$8 per Pound during winter. During winter some times, highway connectivity also gets disconnected from rest of the world.

In supermarkets there, whatever chicken available usually would be defreezed frozen chicken.

Fruits or vegetables or any other food items have to be from far away places to Bismarck. Defreezed chicken used to be contaminated one. They used to stick "Fresh" on the defreezed chicken. The lack of proper food availability made me to inquire about how the local natives manage their food.

What I figured out was, local natives buy the whole cow in the nearby farm and keep it frozen in large freezers and consume it as long as they can.

There used to be a company, Swan, that used to deliver supplies to home. I tried that as well where we don't get right fresh food. I was completely frustrated. This explains that USA is not as perfect and comfortable as you think of.

Why the heck am I living here in this part of the world? Of course, for money, I know that. But, the same used to follow by another question, can't I earn the same amount by being in India?

Here I should mention one more important point. I used to get large income whereas my productivity was very simple and riskless. Just develop computer software code for the given functional specs and do unit testing. That is all.

I always used to watch tropical getaway opportunities. I also used to find getaway deals to Las Vegas from Bismarck during winter. Free accommodation and free food for 2 days 3 nights at US$220. Usually the same would be around US$500 to 1000.

Now who and how they are going to get compensated to get so much low price that is 25% of regular price.

After two or three months, I decided to drive down to Minneapolis to fetch groceries from there. I did this for three times during a year.

During that period my parents visited me. While seeing them off to India, I got the same question, why am I here for in this wide barren land? What am I getting? Nine months frozen place. No enjoyment. Why the hell people have been living here for? What is it that is making this place economically rich when compared with that in India or those other tropical locations on earth where there will be people and activities throughout the year?

As far as, it is relevant to me and for my family was money. More Money. The same answer which I said to the Visa Processing Officer in American Consulate when the first time I went for Visa.

# 6 USA MARKET—FOREIGN

During my life with my friend who invested in stocks, I happened to observe very closely several different economic indicators, Industrial Indicators, and many more.

One important thing that I understood was the world market has a hierarchical relation that influences the local economies as well.

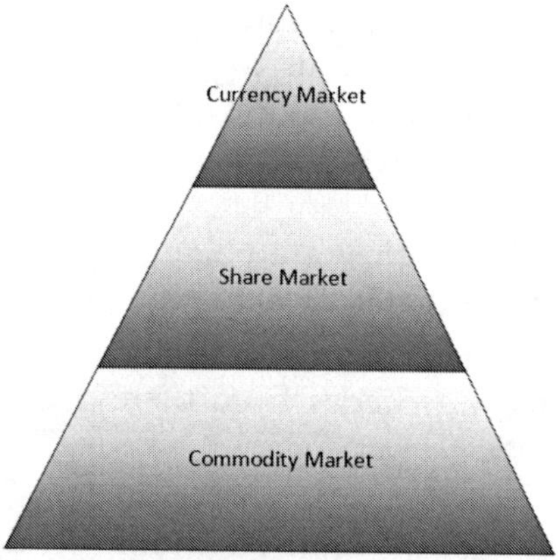


Top in the hierarchy is the Money Market where currencies trade each other. Second level is the stock markets and the third are Commodity Exchanges where natural resources will be traded.

Especially used to focus and understand the US Fed Chairman Alan Greenspan's statements on economy, I used to try to understand his statements as they used to be very vague and not understandable easily because the dimension and angle of his version is not able to be understood that easily.

The heated debates with my friend used to be very argumentative and I used to be always not able to prove my points about the genuineness of analyst's information. I used to watch CNBC always.

The day came when I also opened the stock market account after a lot of debates and pressure from wife. I was not interested to open because of the loss of money in India. I opened the account with the amount received as income tax return from IRS. I added some more money and invested in the stock market. It was not long enough that the day came when stock market was crashed.

Due to the investment in the stock market and online self-service account with "TD WaterHouse", we used to ticker of stocks and used to sell or buy by ourselves. With this, I got the opportunity to know the terms such as Stop Loss, Sell at Market, etc. and several other Stock market jargons. I was able to understand penny stocks, OTC, etc. and several different points in stock market.

Due to my participation in stock market I understood what is venture capitalism, how mutual funds gains benefits even before the companies get listed in stock market, how research companies get venture funds from mutual fund companies and many more.

Fund Management Companies would invest in new science and technology based R&D companies and by the time the products are created and come to the point of commercialization, the actual investments by Fund Management companies would become equivalent to peanuts and the new products bring value to their investment at the rate and levels of unbelievable amounts and the net worth based on the new business will be so huge, and market capital value would rise to that levels, that the venture will become successful in the near future which cannot be beaten up by anybody as long as the competitor is not ready to beat the invention of this company.

Here in India, mutual funds are equal to money pools operate in gambling house of share market.

The investment in stock market and the activeness and interest did not last for long due to crash in stock market. That was dot com burst. Many friends lost multiples of US$ 100,000s which was a big surprise to me about their financial loss's worth.

I lost about US$8000 which was not big amount but was significant in my view. The total loss of mine in stock market was rose to Indian ₹800,000 (in Indian market + USA Market).

This experience helped me understanding many more about stock market, finance, technologies and techniques, and many more.

In USA, all stock broking companies provide live tickers and live online share order execution facility with an assurance of execution in about a second or two seconds. Also about stock market trading jargons like stop-loss order, market order etc. Also during my stock market investments in India, I got opportunity to discuss with stock brokers and learn about the operations of stock market.

One important thing that I should highlight is about the fall of NASDAQ, only market orders were getting executed. I tried to sell my shares at lower price difference of around US$1 when compared with the last listed prices, my orders were not getting executed. Only if I put to market order then the shares were sold. They used to get sold at lower than my expected price; usually it would be 10% below the price of last traded price.

One of the most important things was the raise of stock market due to retail investor like me and its impact on the Stock market and Sensex. As a retail investor I don't care at what price I buy because my investment is always targeted at imaginary ambitious profit of double or triple of multiple of invested amount. Since the kind of facilities made available to retail investor by online stock trading companies are equal to a stock broker facilities, it was easy to understand how stock market operations could be.

Here I must mention about one of the historical incidences. During my earlier invest in stocks experience in India, there was an incidence that attracted my attention which even today I remember. *Pakistan stock market was crashed to the levels of 20% of its peak in just two days.* I was wondering why did it happen and why it happened and why should it happen. But the major reasons published in newspapers were withdrawal of funds by global investing firms.

See here again, *in USA, stock markets fell in 2 or 3 days duration to evaporate the profits from all accounts.* See here, numbers get piled up and numbers get evaporated. Stocks raise for several months and weeks but will fall all of a sudden abruptly. Why? Was it manipulated? Will there be government hands behind it? Especially USA government.

During the peak days of USA stock market, all the 401K retirement accounts of USA used to have bulged US$s and several of the years of investment went to the valuation of millions, and people were looking to go for early retirement. These are not my personal findings. These are reports of several different forums including Media.

Spending was rising in USA due to large amounts in accounts and less expenditure. If I visit super market, majority of the products used to be imported but still the prices used to go down. I used to wonder why and how?

However, the stock market and stock prices are like Water level in a water tank with water inlet and water outlet. It rises, there may be spikes of liquid due to disturbance of pouring in water but it rises evenly and falls evenly. When water is more pouring in than more venting out, levels rise and there will be disturbance on water surface. However, the final stage will be how much liquid is in the water tank. There will be evaporation of water as well due to heat in stock market as well in the form of wrong choice investments.

Also one should pay attention towards another major change in the stock market since 1990 is, during then, when stock markets were not integrated and globalized, there used to have value for P/E ratio and other figures like balance sheets and performance of Company. After the integration of Stock Markets globally, stock markets became a global legal gambling houses.

Here one must understand the kind of money flew into India that raised the Indian Sensex from 6000 to 25000.

In fact there was a time when Sensex was considered as symbol/indicator of the economic growth of the nation by several around the nation those are being considered as "Experts". This is the kind of knowledge that Market analysts spread across the nation through media. They have very limited knowledge on the numbers in Stock Market and try to use that limited knowledge as universal knowledge.

Since huge money flows into the market, every company, remember here; same industry and same tangible capacities, value have gone up.

The simple fact is Sensex has now become a symbol or an indicator of "Index of Foolishness of Indians."

A healthy Sensex is that which never rises in number though new economy is added to it.

Alan Greenspan himself used to give warning statements of overspending leading to rise in imports and rise in inflation. Such information was adding drops to the knowledge that I have about economy.

The study of different news articles and different details required for an investor involved in stock market investments and trading made me focus on Indian Economic Policies as well. This is the one which brought in lot of changes in my understanding on economy and especially related to that of India.

During the same time, some more changes I noticed around world. Indonesian currency was falling and fell to Rupiah 1500 against US$ (if I remember right) and the nation was going to a major debacle and people were fighting to fetch grocery before prices inflate further.

Also one more thing was Euro Creation in European Union. The reasons given were to establish a common ground in order to compete with the world. Euro creation gave me clue about the real significant of value of a currency.

What is to be understood here is, numbers are rising and numbers are lowering like water level. Similarly in the entire stock market, numbers rise and numbers fall and maintain an average of all positive and negative variations and the behaviour is again like water levels in a water tank.

However, there will always be only two participants who make money from this. It is the Stock Broker and Stock Market.

When Indian Stock markets were sold to foreign stock markets, an opportunity of no loss but always profit opportunity was given to foreign investor in India. How did that happen? How Indian Finance Ministry could allow it to happen? Are they not able to understand the angle which I am looking at?

These are large questions to delve through.

*During then what I found was mindboggling fact, Indian Government and all its entities involved in economical and financial policies were following suit of USA economic policies.* I found this behaviour of Indian Government and related entities very strange and surprise to me.

The first fundamental question that drew my attention was, there has never been any similarity between Indian Economy and USA Economy, the same policies cannot be adopted by Indian in any manner, but why and how India has been adopting all the policies of USA as they are and applying them to Indian economy? India has 3 times population of USA and USA has 5 times size of India. How on the earth the same policies blindly can be adopted by India with complete contrast characteristics against USA?

Now so far I have given you the information about my life time experiences those impacted my thought patterns in a linear manner as I remember them. The question about synchronized behaviour led me to look at more information about the same.

I tried to start a Chit-Fund Company in USA. This effort helped me understand how tough it is to start a business on Currency in USA which is different from India. One more information that I found during the same time was, American/British entities always keep a tab on the orders of making a currency printing machines by the manufacturer as well.

Earlier to this Chit-fund company, when E-Book concept was not there, I asked my company president to start an e-book online library. He was M.Tech (IIT) person but he was more interested towards body shopping only for quick business and he was not convinced for this concept.

*Now the knowledge that I acquired through different means started creating different thoughts those were opposite to the earlier thoughts.*

During the same period or earlier to that there was a loan disbursement by USA to Pakistan and at the same time some fighter jets and ammunition. The amount was around 300 million and 600 million worth military equipment.

Probably you won't believe, I wrote email to Musharaf as well warning about the kind of game being played by global forces. Then email was a major advanced mode of communication, hence he may have seen my email, it is my guess.

I also said that there is only one activity that will reduce tension in the region and start building a focus on economic development of the region on earth. It was trade relations between both the regions. As much more trade is established and a dependency is created between regions that much more harmony will be developed between regions. Of course, there were other issues surfaced in media.

He visited India, I don't mean I made him to do that, this is ridiculous.

I would say one thing, this part of world leaders or third world nation leaders have been facing large virtual walls created by media as equal to tsunami always. They will be subverted by such large tsunami of impressions created in the society which they have been leading through media by global forces.

How global forces create such situations, I have written later in this book.

Here regarding Share Market development, I should mention one very important thing.

There used to be a company called Andersen Consulting in USA. Later it became Accenture.

Andersen Consulting was caught in the malpractices of share trading and was convicted in court as well for those crimes. Price Waterhouse Coopers was also another company on the same grounds then facing charges.

I do not recall today but what happened was, both the companies were merged, dissolved and a new company was formed in USA as Accenture.

It was like, on a drama stage, drop of a curtain and change the background scene, raise curtain again.

I was completely shocked.

# 7 PROBLEM RESOLUTIONS

I closed my share account with TD waterhouse and stopped all Share Market activities. However, I have not stopped following the business news.

Here one thing I should mention is that, the Chief Minister of Andhra Pradesh was Nara Chandrababu Naidu, who was IT enthusiast, had initiated a cell for corresponding with him through email. I was not interested to buy a computer in my initial first year in USA during when I bought a product which can be interfaced with TV as Monitor and hook it up with normal Telephone jack and start browsing Internet using wireless keyboard and mouse. It was useful only for Internet browsing. I did not use it much but I had sent emails to Chandrababu Naidu and even got personal replies from him.

I was just enthusiast of sharing some ideas those may be useful to the state of Andhra Pradesh where NCBN, being CM, could implement the suggestions easily.

I told you earlier about my life because of my father's job and my initial business has given me a lot of insights of social conditions of villages in India. My new creative thinking developed from my cognition process after all the inputs and living USA started triggering solutions to the problem of society of India. I wrote several emails to NCBN on different issues. Not many but may be around 20 max in the three years.

Later after one year, I purchased a computer and started using it for different purposes which include the stock market trading.

I started addressing several different issues of our society while comparing the same with USA and different solutions suitable to them. He was doing "Janmabhoomi" program and he was interested in receiving new ideas.

There might be around 50 different suggestions belonging to several different sectors that I wrote to Chandrababu Naidu and to Finance Minister of India. Please refer appendix for more details about my suggestions. There are more than what I mentioned here.

I moved from Bismarck to Washington DC in USA. My life was as today is, no different from yesterday. Just trying to find some different experiences in life as living in USA was more monotonous and regular without change. How to kill the time after job was a major challenge? So watch as many TV programs or movies as possible.

I went to a Thailand restaurant where I found a person's picture. I inquired about whether, if they also have the similar "Baba" culture. I learnt that it is their King's photo which they do the prayers as God. I remembered history book knowledge from school days that in some part of the world or most of the world where old day feudal systems were there and the corresponding behaviour in society was about considering the King as the representative of God.

I went to Los Vegas where I saw the temple for Brahma which was a surprise to me as a person from India where the belief that Brahma God will not have a temple. Also I learnt that Indonesia, Taiwan, Cambodia, Burma (Myanmar), Malaysia and many more south-east nations have culture of Hinduism.

I went to several gambling houses in several different states in USA. In some states, gambling houses were not allowed on land. In such states, gambling business would be on large boats/ships. The final outcome what I learnt is, an opportunity of employment is closely related with needs. Needs can be divided as basic needs and weaknesses.

*The bottom line for good economy is a successful transaction between two parties for mutual benefit as understood, agreed and satisfied.*

Here I must mention one information that I came across. The largest wealthy business on this earth historically is "Sex" trade. One of the history documentaries that I saw was related to USA Gold Trail where "Sex" trade was a big trade along with liquor. Also one of the history studies revealed the same along the trail of Silk Route. Also the same was revealed in history studies that is the same and true during "Krishna Devarya" Kingdom in India.

This is not selling girls etc. This is nothing but having sex with a woman while paying something in return; may be gold or property, etc. or currency as well.

In USA there are legally run nude bars where women dance for money. It was an earning opportunity for women and entertainment for men. Don't misunderstand me. To get more details, please read the Unique ID Chapter.

Such incidents told me a fact that "opportunity of earning" is the result of "satisfying someone else's requirement willingly". In single word, "Needs". Needs could be necessities or weaknesses.

From the information that I have been receiving from my surroundings, I started understanding that there are several differences in understandings of people in India and outside world. Whatever considered as "not exists" or "not right" are not the same at other parts of the world.

*My close follow up of news articles around synchronized behaviour of Indian Economists led to catch my attention to one of the policies of RBI. It was devaluation of Rupee.* I was surprised about the statement. Until then I was happy to see the realization of my money from US$ to Indian Rupee. This news article surprised me. Why did they choose to devaluate?

Reasons given in newspapers were, Indian export market would become competitive on the globe. India can do more exports due to price advantage and also be able to earn more forex. OK. That sounds reasonable.

*The behaviour of RBI and other market analysts was appearing to me like a Symphony Orchestra supporting one other's activities.*

This was the time when I got interest to know why so much importance and stress on more exports. What is it that India imports and why India needs to be competitive in international market?

This made me focus on Indian Import needs data. That gave me information about the major requirements of India. Those are getting satisfied majorly by import from foreign nations.

One is Petroleum and the second is Fertilizer. Eighty per cent of Indian needs related to Fuel and Fertilizer are being satisfied by imports by India for which it requires US$.

Here I should mention one more historical information that I had in my mind.

The involvement in the stock market investment activities during 1993, gave me some information about liberalization policies, 100% export oriented units, 100% tax rebates to those units, etc. I also used to see information about complications in exporting to USA and quality rejections and loss of money by Indian exporters at US ports due to several different reasons.

During the same time there was some news articles around fuel price rise in India, deregulation of Fuel Price and giving freedom to Indian oil PSU marketing companies on retail price definition etc.

Since my father was in Fertilizer trade and since I also had initial experience in the same trade, I knew that there were subsidies to Fertilizer. There were demands on removing subsidies on fertilizers and fuel.

Already there is huge pressure on farmers due to continuously rising input costs, on the earth how can anybody give such advises to government of India or in media, was a most amazing question to me then.

There were news articles and comments around by several different so called economists or market analysts for removing all subsidies on fuel and fertilizer.

Such news articles drew my attention towards comparing the prices between India and USA. In fact it was not so formal.

I was filling my gasoline in my car in USA and found the price in US$ for gallons and just casually wondered how much would that be in litres.

Then I found shocking revelations in my calculations. USA market has 40% lesser price than that of in India. USA has different fuel prices at different locations. I used to pay around US$2 per gallon. About 100 miles away from the city, the same Gasoline costs, only around US$1.

I found this far lower price from my colleague who stay away by 50 miles from the city and comes every day by Virginia Railway to work.

I started looking for more and more information around this to figure out the reasons for such a large difference between USA and India. There is an important historical information that I remember should be recalled here.

The demands for deregulation of Petroleum Products Pricing and freedom to change the existing regulated regime of pricing by government to hand over decision power has been there for quite some time. When first time, government deregulated the price, one incident caught my attention.

That was, if I remember right, the petrol price was at around ₹28 or so. The price of the petrol was kept at ₹20 per litre for a day and immediately reset back to ₹28 per litre, reasons given were subsidy compensation I remembered this incident when I started comparing the prices between India and USA. I got interesting facts.

There are Subsidies on Petroleum bi-products. In order to compensate one product's subsidy loss, another product was kept at high price. Hence Petrol and Diesel prices were kept at high in order to compensate the losses of subsidies. That sounds logical to me. But that doesn't justify the large prices that is almost 5 times the raw material cost.

I started expanding spectrum of my analysis to larger products. I started noticing the day to day drop in prices in USA. I used to wonder how on the earth such large production is possible that can support the reduction of the prices of all products every week from earlier week prices. Most of the products available in USA supermarkets are imported ones.

This continuous thought process started bringing together the elongated dots and I am able to notice the lines between those elongated dots to form a different understanding about what is happening on earth.

# 8 CURRENCY VALUE FOOLING

First understand about the currency value in real time life of ours. What is it that we need to live on this earth? Primary one!

Oxygen. Say for example, if Oxygen is reducing in the air, then what?

That is what this Currency value to our lives in the economies built on currency.

New understanding based on the elongated dots and lines between them and picture, that I am able to see started giving me the second side of the coin.

US$ is being widely accepted by all nations for their Export Business. All businesses around the world are adopting US$ as their currency for their export business. Due to this, the appreciation in the US$ value against other currencies is leading to the following result.

Product is becoming cheaper in US$ terms so that USA consumers can buy them at lower price than earlier. However, the exporters are getting more money in their native currency when US$ is realized to their native currency.

However, there was one significant thing to be understood here, currencies were not freely allowed to trade each other, several nations, including India did not have that. RBI was deciding the price of the Rupee against other global currencies. This you can make out from the Intentional Devaluation of Rupee exercise for 10 years and more.

The following explains better. Here you need to use your math skills.

Indian is seller and American Buyer.

**Step 1:**

Indian has manufactured his product "P" at a cost of ₹35 and is expecting a price of ₹50 with a margin of ₹15.

*Scenario 1*

Say Product "P" Quantity "1" is sold at ₹50 and exported to USA at the same price.

Say US$ to Indian Rupee Currency Exchange rate is US$1 = INR 50.

Indian gets US$1 for his sale. At ₹50 for US$1, Indian has got his expected money.

*Scenario 2*

Say, US$ is appreciated against Indian Rupee, say by 10% which makes US$1 = INR 55.

Because of this movement in currency market, now the Indian has got ₹55 instead of ₹50.

Now, the fall of Rupee against US$ is resulted as 10% more profit for Indian.

*Scenario 3*

Product "P" Quantity "1" requires to sell at ₹50 and export to USA at the same price to make his ₹15 margin.

Say US$ to Indian Rupee Currency Exchange rate is US$1 = INR 50.

American asked for more Competitive Price than the Scenario 1 which is quantity 1 for US$1.

Competitive price could be in two ways, pay LESS US$ for the SAME quantity or SAME Amount of US$ for MORE quantity.

Now if US$ is appreciated against Indian Rupee, say by 10% which makes US$1 = INR 55.

Because of this movement in currency market, now the Indian can sell his product by offering a 10% discount. So LESS US$ for SAME quantity. Now Indian gets US$0.90 instead of US$1.

Now, the fall of rupee against US$ is resulted into SAME expected PROFIT, SAME expected SALE price for Indian when US$0.90 is realized into INR at ₹55 per US$1.

Indian made same ₹50 and Margin of ₹15.

American got the product at US$0.90.

The above said three scenarios are very important that the reader should read again and again to understand the depth of it.

Indian has sold his product for less in US$.

Indian has sold his product for same price in Indian Rupees.

Indian has made same expected margin.

Indian made profit in terms of money. American also made profit by 10%.

However, what is hidden here, *Indian has given away more resources for the less money.*

Now this is where the 360 degree plays a vital role to understand.

Indians have been losing more resources for lesser forex income. Is this only applicable to Indians? No. Not only to India but every nation across the world who have been believing and practicing the same currency value based on economic policies and exporting to USA have been losing the same way.

Here one more point needs to be focused on in order to understand more details. It is related to the characteristics of USA and its Economy. USA population does not increase as much as India usually. The USA population has been consistent since last several decades. It has always been around 30 crores. The consumption has always been stable. In order to maintain its population, USA allows immigrants. This population growth creates new consumption in the economy. During the last half of the 1990 decade and early half of new millennium decade, immigrant inflow through H1B created large new economy in USA.

The economy was in the form of new vehicle purchase, food, clothes, consumer durables, houses, telephone traffic and many more.

Here I will give one more information. When I reached USA, the situation in USA used to be: if an apartment is rented for 6 months, one month rent will be free, if the same is for 1 year, then two months rent will be discounted from the rent.

Similarly, banks used to give gifts for opening an account and also used to give US$10 as first deposit in the account. This kind of business strategies by companies tells that there is not enough consumption in the economy—either product consumption or service consumption.

This means, there are resource under utilization in USA and companies are trying to survive. How are they surviving? When USA economy was reviewed from macro level, one thing is evident the year over year reduction in prices of resources such as Gasoline. USA also imports 80% of its crude requirement but their import costs never changes due to constant price of US$ that is pegged with OPEC Nation's currencies. This was not hurting the fundamental expenditure in their economy which is quite opposite to that of India.

USA also imports several other resources from around the world. All those resources get very cheap due to US$ appreciation every year over other currencies such as Indian Rupee. This lowering prices at macro level provided more reduction in input costs to USA which became an advantage to USA.

When it comes to India, the loss of rupee value not only results in exporting more resources at devaluated price and getting us the same or lesser forex income. The loss of Forex Income is making us loose the power of importing fertilizers and fuel required for the nation. Not only this. The devaluation Rupee against US$ was making the Fuel and Fertilizer more and more expensive.

I wrote earlier about India's 80% dependency on imports of Fuel and Fertilizer. Focus here very carefully on both commodities: *Fuel is without which nothing can be done on this earth and Fertilizer that is core for Food Production inside India.* It means, Indian nation is completely dependent on IMPORTS. And that dependency was increasing every day.

If crude barrel is US$10 and US$1 = ₹50 then our import cost for a barrel of Crude is ₹500. The fall of Rupee against US$ from ₹50 to ₹55, increasing the import of Crude per barrel by 10% more. This raise of 10% at raw material would be resulting into multiples. I said earlier that Petroleum corporations were selling Petrol sort of Products at 5 times the price of raw material which was making the 10% increase in import price into 5 times multiplied as 50%. This raise in Fuel price and raise in Fertilizer prices are resulting as more expenditure on the entire nation.

*The above said bluffing game based on currency values was clear to me and hope the same for readers now.* If not, then read it again and again. Because this is the Secret of the current World.

If understanding this is hard for you, then just imagine yourself, after I figured out this major flaw or conspiracy in this, I was clueless about what to do with what I found and how to make everybody aware of this major blunder being committed by RBI.

However, I need to let somebody know about this in some or other way.

What is the blunder? *The blunder is RBI's "intentional" devaluation of Rupee.* RBI was devaluating Rupee stating that Indian Export market could be competitive only when it is devalued further against US$ and similarly with other top currencies.

The biggest challenge in front of me is, *I am not qualified in any manner*, at least 1% to talk about it.

The next biggest challenge is I am trying to claim that something was wrong. That SOMETHING was being done by MOST QUALIFIED and TOP EXPERT fellows.

I contemplated in myself for several days before I decided to do something about this finding of mine. I concluded it as, even experts may sometimes go wrong due to unknown reasons, why not we send email to just create awareness! May be my information could be equivalent to a small stone required to move a large stone. If useful, will take it, if not will throw it away. Who cares!! I am neither going to talk to anybody nor discuss with anybody about it as people may find me meaningless fellow. I dared to act on it. Since I will not speak to anybody about this, I will write and keep quite.

I looked around for options. I remembered my emails communication with Chandrababu Naidu, who was Chief Minister of Andhra Pradesh state in India. I wrote to him explaining in detail about my finding. Also I wrote to Finance Minister of India explaining the consequences.

That was the time when Rupee was devaluated from ₹42 to ₹46 by RBI. I concluded my email to CM of AP as please ask the RBI folks to justify their stand and get the facts if the devaluation really benefits in India.

I received the acknowledgement for email from Chandrababu Naidu. I also sent email to the Finance Minister of India. I did not receive any acknowledgement from the Finance Minister of India.

The acknowledgement received from Chandrababu Naidu, CM of AP and corresponding news articles on RBI actions and rolling back of rupee declaration gave me some confidence on my actions. I started delving through the information that I have.

This has created an interest in me about economy. I started developing interest in finding more and more information about all that related to economy.

I am by profession a systems analyst who always be in between real world and computer world. My job is to either create new systems or fix existing systems. In this effort, I always work on Root cause Analysis in order to figure out the right "Cause" that created wrong result which is ERROR. While doing so I have to think through several different options. Sometimes, the cause could be somewhere outside the computer system also.

For example, I was called for a problem in a system. The problem has been there for two years. All world renowned techniques were used to find out the cause for the problem. I was asked to look at it. What I figured out was, everything was perfect but the cause was in the cleaning up of garbage before deployment of new software programs. It was failing due to that. Nobody expected that it could lead to such a large impact on the machine.

Now I started using my technical skills on economy. This brought me to the level that I can see water and milk separately. What I mean by it is, water is the Currency based economy and milk is real time economy.

# 9 FUEL SECTOR

The next step that was incomplete on my part was the large fuel prices. What made them to be at that high price? I collected information about the same.

There were mind chilling/boggling facts around fuel pricing. Oil companies were minting money like hell from Indian society who were enjoying 300% net profits. I was shocked. Also the same with Indian government Large amount of taxes are being levied on fuel in order to make large tax income to government.

I started writing this time to the Petroleum and Natural Gas Minister of India. There were so many twists that every time I find one flaw, there will be some or other supporting reason that would be released by the Petroleum and Natural Gas Minister.

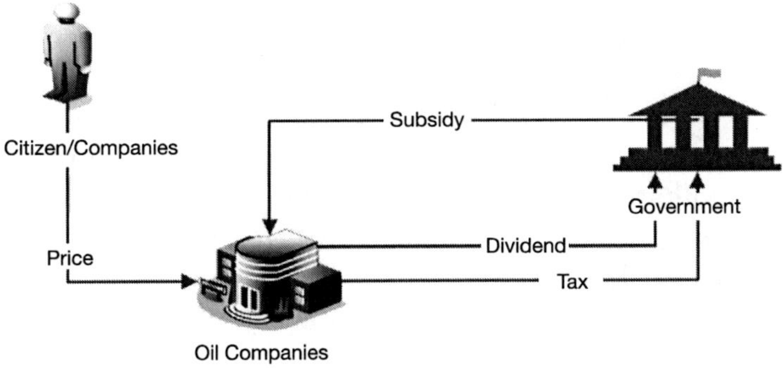


Does it make sense to have back and forth between Oil Companies and Government? But the oil companies have taken this back and forth advantage and started making double profits under the name of subsidy.

My findings were:

1. Large tax rates on petroleum products under the name of subsidy.
2. Actual Subsidy was small but the tax was being collected showing subsidy as reason was multiples of Subsidy amount.
3. Since subsidy amount was small but large taxes and large profits are on fuel being siphoned by oil companies from public which makes subsidy as not exists at all.
4. Oil sector was having multiple levels and multiple companies from exploration till retail business. At each level, individual companies are making their own industrial profits which was one more reason for large fuel prices in India.
5. Oil companies occupy 99% of Indian market and Government policies were biased to benefit the oil companies.
6. India used to import crude based on the price in either London Commodity Exchange or in New York Commodity Exchange price.
7. Crude which was explored and produced by ONGC was also being priced at the same levels of either London or New York Exchange in US$.
8. Monopolize the Indian Fuel market by three OIL PSUs with the help of government policies.

I used to send all my findings to PNG Minister of India, Mani Shankar Iyer and to Media as well. Strange that I figured out was there used to be actions by government not to correct the wrong but to cover the wrong and continue with the same error with new over cover.

What at the end resulted into is, PNG Minister was ousted for trying to correct the wrongs in the system, here I am not mentioning them as errors as they are not errors but very well calibrated wrongs properly placed to squeeze the nation's economy for government benefit.

Who is Government? Politicians who owns the PNG dealerships or contracts who have been enjoying the safe income avenues, oil sector employees, bureaucrats and government employees.

Government used to give statements about how government can manage its expenditure without oil sector income. This statement explains what kind of people are in the top chairs of India. They want to run government on oil income.

Government used to get huge tax amount on petrol prices. Oil companies used to make large profits. Government used to pay huge money as reimbursement towards subsidy to oil companies. At the end of the entire drama, again government used to get profit dividend from oil companies.

Oil companies used to have large reserves in their kitties, lot of idle money.

How this kind of large fuel price will impact the economy? Every one of us knows that without fuel nothing can be done in nation. When fuel is kept at such large price obviously it reflects as large expenditure on both industrial sector and other sectors as well due to large transport cost.

Repeated continuous emails to PNG Minister and to Finance Minister of India somehow created some movement in the administration but all the acts were only to cover the wrong and not to correct them.

Even today, Private Sector participation in fuel sector is completely destroyed due to Government policies. One such policy is, Government. PNG Ministry allocates licensing to retail outlets of Private industries also. Assess yourself how hard it is for a company that invested 1000s of crores in their refineries always go to Government to get licenses for every retail outlet and how that is going to impact the performance of the company.

Due to such corrupted system in the top bureaucrats and political circles, the situation has led to the point that private refineries stopped entering the retail business and limited their refining activities to contract basis service and make profits on them.

This kind of policies have created a situation in India that only public sector oil companies would monopolise the fuel business in India. In such situation there was another situation which started developing in the nation. That surprised me.

This was about Globalization of Indian Public Sector oil companies. Companies those are on large piles of cash reserves and 100% monopoly business with more than 51% Government stake, were trying to globalize in order to take up foreign oil exploration fields. For such efforts, Global Conglomerates' support was required. Anybody who is able to acquire major stake in the oil companies can rule the nation.

Here I should recall one of the major incidents happened during the NTPC public issue. NTPC that holds the entire Grid ownership in India, went to Public Issue during when a Foreign investor offered US$2 billion to get majority stake holding in the NTPC. Such investment would be so much worth one that probably referring it by comparing with a gold mine or even gems mine would also be an insult to the opportunity because this opportunity is several times larger valuable than any one of them. Indian Government may have to listen and behave as per NTPC owner. NTPC owner can dictate terms to the nation.

Somehow the Oil PSU globalization was stopped partially and care was taken that only companies those do not lead to threat situation to the nation would be globalized. I think it was ONGC that was globalized to compete in foreign land for oil field explorations. But Indian PSU Oil Companies could never be successful in any oil field acquisition through bidding anywhere outside India. Private globally wealthy Indian origin Corporate Giants also could not do any benefit or advantage to India and its oil sector.

At one point there was a discussion started developing about disinvestment of Indian Public Sector units. I was surprised about this. Also there was huge discussion in media about the over burden of subsidies on Indian Government.

*One thing what I noticed was, whenever there is some dent found I informed to the ministry and to media, new proposals were popping up. Also such new proposals were always very well calibrated and carefully structured ones. I used to really get shocked looking at the new proposals being floated through media.*

Here I should mention one thing about my effort. As I said earlier, I was writing emails to Chief Minister of AP and Finance Minister of India and PNG Minister, I started CC them to news media editorial emails. But as repeatedly stated I was not able to get the acknowledgements from any dignitaries. However, I used to find corresponding news and government announcements on the same topic only after I brought it up to the attention of the dignitaries.

When this was the situation in the Oil Sector, on finance side several changes were being developed.

Whenever the issue on oil prices is at boiling point, strangely political parties, media analysts and several others used to point fingers at private companies.

This was a surprise to me why on the earth everybody has been targeting Private Businessmen and projecting them as Criminals and Exploiters of the nation. I do not know the reason even today but one thing is sure that there is some misunderstanding or some other objectives are there with those targeting Private Companies.

If it is the same with any Multinational, situation would be different again. No comments from any direction will be there. Why?

One more major fact behind is, PSU Employee Unions are very strong in India and their role could be there behind this which is surfacing and visible through political parties commentators to keep their life easy and safe at the cost of the nation.

What is the final result, the 10,000s of crores of investment into oil refineries by Indian Citizen Investors through stock market in a public traded company are ended up as companies for contract jobs for foreign businesses and not for Indian Economy. Indians are not benefiting from it.

One thing what I understood was the employee union leaders though well-educated they do not have the vision beyond horizons and are also insecured of their own future and failed in showing progressive paths to employee unions.

This insecuredness has become a rigid reason that is hurting the economic growth of India. Somewhere this rigidity must be destroyed. How?

What is causing this insecuredness? Answer that I found for this question is "Financial" Stress and "Continuously" rising cost of living.

While I was writing different details on the fuel sector, I started noticing different twisted statements, remember here that *all my emails were CCed to media and MPs as well, and actions from Government.*

Initially government started saying that it is income for maintenance of government. It means government employees and bureaucrats and MPs get salaries from such Income. So they are not interested to reduce their income to fix the economy.

They started saying that Subsidy burden on government is huge. For this I will give some details. When Crude is processed, approximately 44% of petrol, 26% of Diesel, about 6% of LPG and 1% of kerosene will be yielded with other products of 23% around. Kerosene and LPG are being subsidized for which Petrol is being sold at premium and Diesel is being sold at actual/more than actual, and LPG and Kerosene at subsidy. Here actual means, with proper or more industrial margin to meet all expenses and profits; and Premium means, very high prices.

Following table is an example of Crude breakdown.

| | | | | |
|---|---|---|---|---|
| **Crude Price in US$** | **114** | | | |
| **Currency Conversion INR per US$** | 38 | | **Gallons to Liter** | **3.78541178** |
| **Crude Price per barrel in INR** | 4332 | | | |
| **Product** | | **Gallons per barrel** | **in Liters per barrel** | |
| | gasoline | 19.50000 | 73.81552971 | |
| distillate fuel oil (includes both home heating oil and diesel fuel) | | 9.20000 | 34.82578838 | |
| | kerosene-type jet fuel | 4.10000 | 15.5201883 | |
| residual fuel oil (Heavy oils used as fuels in industry, marine) | | 2.30000 | 8.706447094 | |
| | | | | |
| | liquefied refinery gasses | 1.90000 | 7.192282382 | |
| | still gas | 1.90000 | 7.192282382 | |
| | coke | 1.80000 | 6.813741204 | |
| | asphalt and road oil | 1.30000 | 4.921035314 | |
| | petrochemical feed stocks | 1.20000 | 4.542494136 | |
| | lubricants | 0.50000 | 1.89270589 | |
| | kerosene | 0.20000 | 0.757082356 | |
| | other | 0.30000 | 1.135623534 | |
| **Total Yield** | | 44.20000 | 167.3152007 | |
| | **Sale Price per Liter in INR** | **Price per Liter of Refined Fuel** | **Average Gains/Loss on Fuel in INR** | **% of Tax on Base Price** |
| **Retail Price of Petrol in India** | 70 | 25.89125186 | 44.10875 | 63.01249735 |
| **Retail Price of Diesel in India** | 44 | 25.89125186 | 18.10875 | 41.15624578 |
| **Retail Price of Kerosene in India** | 11 | 25.89125186 | -14.89125 | -135.3750169 |
| **Auto LPG in Liter Price** | 31.34 | 25.89125186 | 5.44875 | |
| **Domestic LPG per KG 1.6 lit = 1 kg** | | 41.42000297 | | |
| | 41.66666667 | 25.89125186 | | |
| **Gross Margin per Liter** | **15.77541** | | | |
| **Price where we are supposed to have our Fuel Price if Rupee is at 38 against US$** | **34.4202899** | | | |

Figures are based on 1995 average yields for U.S. refineries. One barrel contains 42 gallons of crude oil. The total volume of products made is 2.2 gallons greater than the original 42 gallons of crude oil. This represents "processing gain."

Because of such large prices, vehicles owners have started adopting fuel to pollute the air quality of India. For example, using Kerosene in vehicles.

Again I wrote a suggestion to CM of AP advising him of removing Kerosene from public availability and use it for Production of Electricity, and only provide LPG for domestic purpose. This was when the LPG was started providing to all families.

One more important fact is, every product usually would be transported using Diesel. Diesel being the fuel for Bulk Transport activities, if prices of Diesel are reduced that will reduce the transport cost of all products across the nation.

One more important impact from Petroleum Sector was, negative burden on Rupee value when Fuel Companies are buying forex for the Crude import. Government could make arrangements in such a way that Fuel Companies need not buy Forex money usually US$ from forex market and instead Government gives them the forex money from reserve at the price that it finds suitable, but the Government has been different.

Why?

This is because all the so called Economists, Financial experts of Government have been under the grim grip of some financial concepts which are properly established by Global Forces, not known by then to me as well. Everybody is afraid of his career and afraid of Global Forces, such as World Bank and IMF who support them in their career.

There is one more fuel that we use and are dependent on in our daily life. It is Electricity.

This doesn't require external resources to produce. However, the electricity sector is funded by foreign loans. Our electricity consumption will provide profit to foreign nations.

Here, the nation's welfare is compromised by individual prosperity which clearly reflects the division in the society of India.

This is as similar as Broken Milk. We as human having thoughts when consider as particles milk, that milk is now broken.

Also there is one more important thing, entire nation has higher taxes on fuel by about 25% than that in National Capital Region where Government employees live. Why?

Let us also look at the international situation in this regard. The intelligent Americans, go in a form to the Oil rich nations to implement their technology as investment. They go in another form as Financial System advisors. Also they go in another form as buyers. Again they go in the form of investment seekers with opportunity of investment back in America. Now what is left with oil rich nation is big zero. Oil gone, money gone. Since no knowledge and expertise, no advantage but dependency and loss.

# 10 INTEREST RATE

*When the Rupee's intentional devaluation was stopped*, until then RBI used to give Public statements on the next weak level of Rupee against US$ to improve the competitive position of India in Global market. Such statements were stopped.

However market analysts were still uttering through media statements. Especially business news papers were writing left and right on valuations and barking like hell.

I was wondering why!

Don't they know the meaning of Intentional devaluation in real terms?

We all know that we work to earn money. We work for "Time duration" to earn that money. It means, *by the time you earn your next Rupee, your expenditure is gone beyond your income. You are made to run behind meeting your expenditure.*

This is similar to dog race where dogs will be made to run behind a bait in the ring that dog can never reach.

We are made to fail before we reach our target by means of rising expenditure in terms of Money Figures.

Insufficiency is being created in the form of failures in terms of money. This insufficiency has been creating insecurity. That insecurity is making us cunning. That cunningness we are considering as symbol of intelligence.

*Since we did not have a clue about the core issue that has been causing us losers, we have been always sentimental in India. We call it sentiment but it is a psychological disorder that is developed due to fear of unknown reasons for our failures.*

I did not stop framing the facts together that I have been collecting and stored in my mind from the knowledge that I have been gaining from several different past and present developments in India. I was in USA and was able to go through the policies of Government of India one by one and corresponding data through internet. I recall the earlier said, policy announcements, especially in finance sector by RBI, I started analysing the related real time impacts.

I started focusing about all those impacting the rupee value. I started finding many different mind boggling details such as World Bank Loans to Public Sector. Another important fact that I found was, RBI and its board of directors, one of the top 100% EOU chairman would be as one of the directors in RBI. Such 100% EOUs get benefited by loss of Rupee value. He was none other than Narayana Murthy of Infosys.

RBI used to announce policy and immediately there will be market analysts who would start appraising it and also some industrialists. I used to get the first doubt how the heck this policy would be good for India. I could see the symptoms of coordination between different entities and the news developments in media, government and several other platforms. I used to get surprised about such coordination.

For example, reduce bank interest rates to divert the investments from fixed deposits to stock market. I used to wonder, why would a person invest in stock market for just a drop of 1% interest rate. The stock market investor's characteristics would be different from bank deposit investor.

I started focusing on the interest rates, the component of Interest rate and its significance. First I started, what are all the ways and means by which a cash holder would get return as interest to him/her.

(Here one disclaimer, I might use the terms he/him/his and may not use she/her. Please consider to use both genders wherever I used such phrases. Also this book seems to be a crude way of writing and composition, in fact I would like to keep it as it is to maintain my psychological state and its reflection to reader.)

I also started focusing on the RBI's earlier policies. I was surprised from two angles, RBI has always been using the same kind of announcements for years together. I could find the evidence of finding more options by top RBI persons which was reflecting the fact that RBI top guys have very limited knowledge on economy with currency. Even today, RBI during its credit policy announcement, says that alteration of interest rate by a fraction of percent will correct all the problems. That was really funny to me. To make you understand better, I will explain you from fundamentals.

What is an interest rate? What is its significance in the Finance World? What is its significance in the economy based on currency?

Till this point I was also not very well clear about the difference between ECONOMY and FINANCE. I only knew that the currency values are impacting the income of India from exports and India and Indian has been losing its/his income.

We must remember that some of Indians are getting benefited from such fall in Rupee. They are Export Oriented units who earn in foreign currency and gain from fall of Rupee.

My system analysis skills started playing their role in my mind and started creating picture of Finance and its impact on the real life of human society.

The answers to the questions on Interest rates are:

- Banks pay interest to the money they take as deposits
- Banks charge interest to the money they lend
- Financers charges interest on the money they lend
- Borrower pays interest to the money they borrow.

At the end, money receiver would have to pay some "Charge" to the source for having that money from the money source which is interest rate. Interest rate can be considered as demurrage of money for being with a person who does not own it.

Ok. So far so good. Now at the same time I got different perspective, this was developed from my maturity of thinking, I stopped looking at the Finance and started looking at numbers only. Just pure Numbers.

I started experimenting on numbers. The interest rate could be income to Source but the same is expenditure for borrower. The need for money for "an entity" is being satisfied by making the numbers available to that entity at an expenditure.

Rise in interest rate increases the income to Source and increases expenditure to borrower. In between, there will be brokers like NBFCs or Banks who append their operation costs/margin and lend money.

In one way, between individuals, the raise in income/expenditure is a kind raise in numbers, say for example, 10% of ₹100 is ₹10. If 10% is raised to 15% then that additional ₹5 is more income and at the same more expenditure in that circle of people.

Since this raise in income/expenditure due to change in the interest rates is creating new quantity of numbers, forget about Rupees or Dollars or other Currency to reflect Finance, but look at it as Numbers, the new 5 from the above example due to raise in interest rate, is additional "inflow" numbers that Source gets to spend and additional "outflow" numbers to receiver.

At the end, Receiver will not be able to notice the impact of the overall activities in that circle as he has burden due to MORE OUTFLOW but Source will impact due to MORE INFLOW. Source will try to spend more.

Also the same now increased the Numbers in the circle. Here the transaction is purely in numbers only and no real time activity is required to raise the numbers.

Say there are only 10 persons in the circle. Now these 10 persons have together has "1"s of total equal to 100 in between them 100. Now the raise interest rate will raise the Quantity of numbers automatically by % considered as interest rate. If we consider 10%, means the actual quantity of 100 will a utomatically become 110.

This number quantity is called Liquidity. Now the liquidity is considered as "Quantity" of "Currency" made available to the persons in the circle.

The quantity could be either created by raise or fall of interest rates but also raised from creating new numbers. All 10 in the circle may want to increase the number from 100 to 200 on their mutual agreement.

The conditions on which such raise in numbers will be allowed is a different story all together.

Now hope you have understood the terms "Liquidity" and "interest rate". Everybody who is familiar with finance policies announcement or economic policy announcement would be familiar with term "Inflation."

"Inflation" is a double edged sword. It requires special detailing which I will do it separately later.

Interest rate acts as accelerator or decelerator to raise the quantity of money or to reduce the quantity of money.

Here one other angle of interest rate is, the more quantity of money made available to the public through the rise in INTEREST rate will result into EXPENDITURE. This new numbers/money those get appended to the existing expenditure will result into more EXPENDITURE when look at the macro level of the circle.

My research on different avenues or options available to fetch interest rate to depositors revealed startling facts to me.

I found that central government employees and retired judges have special provisions those are not available to general public of India. They are getting more interest rates on their deposits in Post Office deposits.

I wrote about the same to the Finance Minister of India. *This startling revelation gave me information that there are policies or facilities or benefits created for some sects of the society of India and not uniformly available to all Indians equally.*

This drew my attention towards all those policies available under the heading of the disparity in India. What I felt that this kind of unequal benefits to the nation has created scope for creating new ununiformed policies further. *This reminded me of the divide and rule policy of old British rule.*

One of the significant benefits that is available to only either Government employees or to organized private corporate employment that drew my attention was retirement benefits. I got this from my USA pay slip where every pay slip will have a deduction for social security benefit and med claim that is useful as after retirement benefit and medical insurance program from government where all after retirement benefits are available to all US citizens uniformly.

I felt that there is need to remove ununiformed policies and create uniform policies in order to create better future for India.

What are the policies those can be called Uniform to all?

I immediately sent an email to the Finance Minister of India again on the same on both retirement benefit and medical insurance availability to all Indian Citizens. During then there was big time demand for large return on the Employee Provident fund contribution from Employee unions from around the nation that was backed by Communist Party sort of political parties.

I also wrote about the principle of premium amount in insurance sector and how it can be exploited to create unlimited health insurance to all citizens of India at ₹1 per day per head premium contribution by Indian to get full medical benefits at no extra cost under this insurance scheme.

Here I should explain about Insurance schemes. When I found problems in Medical sector, I studied the way how Insurance concept works and how it benefits society and how important it is in a Financial world and how it will be used.

I wrote earlier about my life in USA and the way how I was able to look at India and Globe. *At a macro level I started looking at India as a unit of land with human resource, industries, commerce and natural resources.*

I had never received any acknowledgement from Finance Minister of India P. Chidambaram. But later I could notice that

Public Provident Fund scheme was created in Post Office that resembles the Provident Fund Contribution characteristics and new insurance schemes in public sector insurance companies for health insurance. But the coverage by those health insurance schemes is very small amount and not complete.

In the above flow I forgot to mention one small thing. Elections came in India and Finance Minister of India changed. Now the above said intentional Rupee devaluation and related consequences were not aware to the new finance minister of India, I was afraid of returning to the same earlier state of policy making behaviour. I started rewriting again and again to the New Finance Minister of India, Chidambaram.

He appreciated Rupee to ₹38, I would say this exclusively because he has the authority and power to do that. Refer here that Rupee was not "freely" trading currency in forex market.

# 11 TAX STRUCTURE

Indian tax structure can be at the top categorised as Direct Taxes and Indirect Taxes.

Under these two categories, there are different taxes. Also India has got different names to taxes. Taxes are nothing but Income to Government. The "Income" is not a right word to represent the "inflow" to Government. Income to Government is a pool of money being contributed by every citizen of India to meet their "common requirements". Government is one way a cooperative sector.

Before we get into various taxes, let us look at where are they being imposed. India or any other will have two economies. Domestic Economy and Export-Import Economy.

Taxes are organized at various levels in India to cover different types of transactions and entities involved.

Entities involved are Government with different hierarchies, businesses and individuals.

Taxes of India can be listed as

1. Excise Duties: Usually would be imposed at raw material level. Raw material could be from Mining or through imports.
2. Transaction Taxes: Sales Tax = Central Sales Tax + State Sales Tax
3. Income Tax
4. Vehicle Tax
5. Professional Tax
6. Service Tax

7. Municipal Taxes
8. Wealth Taxes

Now these are taxes where, the word Tax is included.

There are other taxes those are not included with the word Tax. They are:

1. Water Charges
2. Fixed Asset Registration Taxes
3. Toll Gate Charges
4. Parking Charges
5. Penalties
6. License Charges
7. Tender Charges

There could be some more taxes like this.

The Income tax and Sales tax is being considered as "Direct Taxes" and the rest are all considered as "Indirect Taxes."

These taxes play vital role in creating inflation when properly not structured. It is the responsibility of UPSC officers to look at all possible chances those might negatively impact the nations and mitigate them at core. Also should see that all India has the same impact of taxes.

Delhi, National Capital Region State has lower taxes than other part of the nation. Why? Is it because all Policy Designers live there?

When I found about such imbalances and also several more blunders, I raised the need of uniformalising the tax structure and simplify the same. This was when the VAT was introduced.

India also has the problem of several options provided for tax rebates. For example, Income tax would be at 30% but rebates will be given when "invested" in some activities. This kind of practices are only useful in complicating the process for citizen and create a situation where "convicting" a citizen will become easy and advantageous to government employees to keep the scope for manipulating the procedures.

Chidambaram, when I gave details about this, he removed all Tax rebates.

The new structure of Taxes has created new problems in the form of Duplication or Triplication or More times tax calculation on top of another Tax amount.

This kind of activities spirals the inflation. In addition, tax instead of putting through proper productive channels, have been put through unproductive channels.

# 12 INFLATION

Let us understand Inflation before we continue our journey.

To understand inflation we need to go to the fundamentals of the economy.

*Availability—Demand—Consumption*

Any variation either positive or negative result would be inflation and results into loss in financial world. It sounds illogical but is the fact.

Say we have more availability then what will happen, results into un-utilization which results into waste or rotten. In terms of numbers, falls the price and overheads of storage or cleaning the waste will increase. Inflation rises due to waste management. Here, please do not get carried away by a conclusion that over heads of storage results into Inflation hence bad for economy. Inflation means opportunity for birth of new economy.

Say we have large consumption then what will happen. Short of availability creates price spurt and prices rise and inflation rises.

Both sides, there will be more negative impacts.

In real terms, there is another angle to this. We can only eat 250 grams per time as food. We can only in take consume average of 1.5 litres of liquid in a day. Beyond this it is waste.

Most of you start tagging the bus journey with flight journey etc. I am giving fundamental examples to show you the difference.

Let us see how Inflation is in terms of Numbers as Prices at economy level.

| Txn No. | Date | Description | Debit | Credit | Txn No. | Date | Description | Debit | Credit |
|---|---|---|---|---|---|---|---|---|---|
| 1 | 1/1/2001 | Product 1 | 10 | | 1 | 1/1/2001 | Product 1 | | 10 |
| 2 | 1/2/2001 | Product 1 | 12 | | 2 | 1/2/2001 | Product 1 | | 12 |
| X Selling | | | | | Y buying | | | | |

| Txn No. | Date | Description | Debit | Credit | Txn No. | Date | Description | Debit | Credit |
|---|---|---|---|---|---|---|---|---|---|
| 1 | 1/1/2001 | Product 2 | | 10 | 1 | 1/1/2001 | Product 2 | 10 | |
| 2 | 1/2/2001 | Product 2 | | 14 | 2 | 1/2/2001 | Product 2 | 14 | |
| X Selling | | | | | Y buying | | | | |

For Government, the matter is the Transaction. In sequential manner.

| Txn No. | Date | Description | Debit | Credit |
|---|---|---|---|---|
| 1 | 1/1/2001 | Product 1 | | 10 |
| 2 | 1/2/2001 | Product 1 | | 12 |

| | | | | |
|---|---|---|---|---|
| 1 | 1/1/2001 | Product 1 | 10 | |
| 2 | 1/2/2001 | Product 1 | 12 | |

| | | | | |
|---|---|---|---|---|
| 1 | 1/1/2001 | Product 2 | 10 | |
| 2 | 1/2/2001 | Product 2 | 14 | |

| | | | | |
|---|---|---|---|---|
| 1 | 1/1/2001 | Product 2 | | 10 |
| 2 | 1/2/2001 | Product 2 | | 14 |

For Government the difference between prices, between two transactions is matter.

Here Product 1 is inflated by 20% and Product 2 by 40% which will be averaged and taken decided as Inflation.

This is inflation. One more thing to focus on here is Y has gained by ₹2 more than X.

Inflation in income to Y and inflation in expenditure to X. However, Government calculates its inflation figures in a fixed time frame hence it only reflects the inflation in a fixed time frame and between two time frames, inflation could be different and larger amount.

Inflation here is imbalance in income levels. Usually, such imbalances get settled naturally unless some external force supports the rise in prices to abnormal levels in the society. Inflation usually calculated on items those impact 80% to 100% of economy.

How such imbalances get settled. Y may get advantage at one point but X also gets advantage at some other point. Seller can only get the abnormal price, profit benefit, only when buyer is able to pay it. If there is no affordability in the society, prices cannot rise. If X pays more to Y, X will not keep quite but has to earn more to meet such gap in expenditure. The money Quantity availability with one person due to more profit will become even later to maintain balance. This is interdependency, recall here what I said earlier about farmer, cobbler, barber and many more those are interdependent on each other for their needs.

Here let us remember the water bed. If pressure at one point will raise the water in other side. If pressure is compared with Expenditure, Water rise in other place can be considered as Income. However it will become even later and water bed balances the liquid and maintains equal level.

If money is supplied more only to some individuals then there will be liberal spending by such individuals which may trigger to inflation and abnormal rise in products.

Now, usually we see RBI tapering interest rates or related instruments in order to deal with Inflation.

Let us assume that there are 10 members in a room. Whenever one person takes loan from others, interest will be paid. Interest will be income for one person, and expenditure for another person at the same time.

Interest rate or Repo rates or related ones will be usually virtual income on money without any real economy. What is real economy is explained later.

With respect to interest rates there are different dimensions—Lending Rates, Deposit Rates, Repo Rate, Reverse Repo rate.

By Raising the Deposit Rates or by reducing the Lending rates, individually, the virtual expenditure or virtual income can be controlled.

Also since banks play vital role in the economy on finance, repo rate or reverse repo rates will be adjusted.

However lending rates always be greater than deposit rates. Similarly repo vs reverse repo.

RBI and market analysts always use funny phrases and abbreviations in order to confuse people.

The gap between deposit interest rates and advances interest rates is the income to Banks. Similarly to RBI difference between repo rate and reverse repo rate.

Now this is how interest rates impact inflation.

However, the actual fact is that interest rates do not impact inflation in any manner. Inflation is a term related to real economy but being used in virtual economy (it is not actually economy) created and run by money and numbers left and right. Now judge yourself if they are doing right or wrong or they are really able economists.

In real world, if there is too much production than the demand, it is Inflation of Production, Inflation of fall of prices, inflation of losses, etc.

If the production is less than demand then it is inflation at prices, inflation of demand, etc.

If the production is equal to demand but if the money supply is too much then also inflation will be there in terms of price raise.

Just by adjusting the supply of money, inflation can be created but cannot be controlled. Whatever RBI does is only to cover their blunders that they commit in the form of rise in money supply into the economy to cover the inflation figures in the form of numbers on paper and nothing else.

# 13 PRIMARY RIGHTS

Today the situation in India has reached to the level that "Do you have money? No, then no water."

Water is a natural resource and is primary right of human. It is not primary right but natural and birth right. If any act that is causing the harm to the natural rights of human is supposed to be the highest crime, however it is not the situation in India. Gandhiji fought for salt, now here we reached a point where foreign/domestic companies are selling drinking water and we are buying. What a pity situation?

Let us go back in the time to know more about different other issues.

Since my childhood, I happened to live in different towns and cities in India and also had got exposed to both low standard life to high life standards. This opportunity of living gave me the opportunity to understand the local living styles, society behaviour, that societies beliefs and understandings, customs, traditions and several more.

The acknowledgements from CM of AP that encouraged me to start looking at the solutions those may help in improving the state of India has become a habit and could not stop though not yielding any benefit to me.

I started analysing the key sectors of India where I had some involvement from my childhood either as my grandfather's family activities or from my father's fertilizer sector job or my initial business in the same trade. There was huge uproar about the lack of returns to farmers.

This made me to focus on the problems of Agriculture sector. Several Coastal villages in Andhra Pradesh had converted their paddy lands to fish ponds for more and more income. I started talking with farmers those are cultivating paddy, mango, grape, flowers, dry crops, vegetable crops, oil seed crops, etc. and many more different crops. I put my focus from different angle.

As I mentioned earlier, 80% of Indian Fertilizer demand was being met through import of fertilizers. Also farmers do not have enough guidance on the pesticides to be used. I myself witnessed the incident of selling large priced pesticides or plant growth promoters and several other chemicals by fertilizer and pesticide dealers. Farmers those depend on the debt of that dealer has to listen the word of that retail dealer who was not expert in anything but a trader. Also farmers used to suffer from lack of understanding about their land and the characteristics of that soil.

The lack of knowledge and lack of support made the farmer lonely to fight against all the odd against his profession. When this was the situation from the supporting sectors, the situation from finance was not better at all. Farmers were made to mortgage gold in order to get loans for their agriculture purpose. If Gold is not available, loan will not be given by banks. Whatever loan will be given by banks will not be sufficient to the day to day rising costs of their needs. Banks were giving less loan amount on gold towards agriculture loan at low interest rate and used to force them to take large loan amount at higher interest rates. One more pathetic situation was, every other sector in India gets loan on inventory and fixed assets of their business but not the farmer. He has to sell his produce immediately in order to repay his debts. Government policies were not giving any support or relief to farmer. Especially some of the crops cultivation has become a lottery sort of activity where farmer is just gambling against, such as corn, tomato, grape and mangoes and many more those yield once in a year and the prices during the crop harvesting season and the characteristics of those crops lead to fast spoiling and results into wastage of crop and huge loss to farmer.

I also noticed that all those entities such as agriculture research centres, universities, professors, scientists are far away from the sector and they are not seen anywhere and their involvement or visits to the place was also not visible any time.

Also farmers were facing the challenge of identifying right crop at right time that is required to the market. Farmers used to choose crops based on the price or information published in newspapers articles and neighbour talks or some other middle men talk. No proper concrete information was available from any department of government whose existence is meant for it. It means they are completely ignoring their responsibilities and their salaries or their income source is made independent of the sector to which they are supposed to serve. In addition what I found was several unqualified fellows with some knowledge have become consultants in this area. Even qualified, though qualified only by certificate received from the universities are not at all skilled to understand the problems.

Farmers have become a football in between all other players.

I wanted to correct this to the extent possible. I wrote several emails about all the problems suggesting several solutions for the same. One of them was lower percent of interest rate to farmers because loans to vehicles were being provided at lesser interest rate than that of for farmer. Also about the need to recognize the yields as valuable "inventory" that should be qualified to give loan to farmers. Also about cold storage requirements, food processing unit requirements and many more. Soil testing labs were also suggested. Also display of information about the water availability, crop acreage in the village and what else is in demand at state level, collection of crop acreage from village level to district level and thereby to state level and to see the gap in acreage to let farmers and investors know about the gap in production and demand so that there will be proper confidence developed in the agri society of India.

Chandrababu Naidu acted very well on all of those suggestions.

Later I also analysed the systematic blunders those have been victimising the farmers and wrote an article about the issues that are hurting farmers which is available in Appendix–II at the end of this book.

Apart from this, I happened to focus on several different sectors such as health, roads, education, electricity, water, women and many more.

Hospitals were being managed by Doctors. Doctors have become a more complex issue to deal with. Doctors always want to get more and more remunerations and always prefer to have everything as per their will and wish and profitable to them. Service is not their motive but money earning has become their target. Hospitals were becoming poorly managed. I started focusing on this sector in USA and how they managed to bridge the greed with service.

USA has medical services that mostly go with health insurance system. Insurance works on one simple principle. What is the Probability of Risk? That Probability of Risk converts into percentage of Premium against benefits offered. In USA, US$2 million worth of Health Insurance is possible for just a premium payment of just US$65 per month per head. This is possible because of one more reason that number of subscribers to the Insurance scheme. This is between Service Seeker and Insurance Company.

Now in the side of Insurance company to Service Providers. Service Providers could be of Doctors, Hospitals and Drugs. Doctors and hospitals, and drug stores have to enrol with Insurance companies as registered service providers. Insurance Companies negotiate their prices for their services. This way the patient need not worry about the amount that he/she pays for his services. Insurance Company also does one more thing. All the claims and medical transcripts sent by service providers will be anonymously given to some other provider to examine the validity of the illness, corresponding services, medicines and many more in order to make sure that there is no fraud being committed by any service provider. In case of found any fraud, the service provider will be blacklisted and the service provider will not have any more future prospects. Any such fraud acts would be suicidal for Service providers. Patients are well protected here by such system as Patients need not worry about financial matters when he/she has card in his hand.

Also Hospitals to be managed by Proper Management Graduates. There also exists proper norms to maintain a hospital as per the guidelines of the Government. Also IT infrastructure plays a big role in Medical Services sector in USA.

I have written all details about the need to restructure the existing system in India for better future in Government hospitals sector. Especially the ₹1 per day per head premium for a full time Insurance scheme was developed based on that. I wrote the same to the CM of AP and Finance Minister of India.

Like Medical sector, I focused on the education system. I studied in Government High School at free of cost and so several of my generation and earlier generations. But the education system and quality in government schools were being degraded. I found an incident where School teachers were more interested in the local village politics; some teachers were not attending schools, irresponsible towards their responsibilities, and found to the extent that, since they are one of the election booth monitors, were trying to negotiate a deal with elected leaders on their irresponsible behaviour and claiming that nobody should question them and their irresponsibility.

I was shocked. I felt that there should be every necessity to bring in discipline in this situation. I wrote about the need for constituting the Education Committee and Parent Committees in all schools officially. Parents of School Children, only present students, would be the members of that committee along with teachers, district education officer as members. Parents themselves will monitor the quality of the education and also attendance of the teachers. This was constituted by Chandrababu Naidu, then CM of AP but the committees were later dissolved by his successor. Of course the Education committees have become venues for political leadership which was a blunder. The committees were supposed to have members whose children are presently studying in the school.

Education systems were further spoiling by themselves. Nobody would be ready to take the responsibility.

When we see into electricity department, there were huge pilferages in electricity department. The CM of AP did a lot to improve the electricity production. He was closely managing the electricity sector to bring in change. However there were huge transmission losses. I could see him not able to control this transmission losses. I wrote him the idea of implementing meters at every junction point from electricity department till the electricity transformer at customer location and auditing on those meters to figure out who is helping to pilferage of electricity. The CM of AP himself personally replied as working on implementing the Audit system to control the Pilferages.

Hope all remember about the kind of long line queues that we used to stand in line for paying electricity bill. I wrote about the same to simplify the complexity. This was implemented right away throw e-seva.

I also suggested about minimum norms that a chicken shop or mutton shop should be in order to be hygienic. This was also implemented.

Today I don't have evidences of those emails but those emails, if taken backup of CM of AP Email in Government of Andhra Pradesh, all my emails can be found.

Earlier I had experience in dealing with departments like Sales Tax for my business. There I was supposed to pay money for every small work in the department. I used to be very frustrated.

Every disorder of such incidents above said are all having one common point, "need more money" Or "need of More Money". For that purpose, just utilize the opportunity of power available with, to take money from the citizen.

I started comparing the reason for development of such behaviour in Indian Society. Why people are trying to make more money and money? Why expenditure is rising every day?

What is it triggering such rise in expenditure? Everybody wants to be good but the bad being performed by the same. Why?

One significant fact that I found was Constant Cost of Living in USA. Established life needs at cheap cost. You are born, grown, educated, worked, retired and died. At every point of time, your fundamental needs are available at the affordable prices. How is it possible?

Indian used to have free education.

Indian used to have free health services.

Only some Indians have Retirement benefits.

Apart from all these, rising cost of living was a major concern. Everybody was becoming greed because of consistent rise in the cost of living.

I started searching for answers.

During my search what I found was, elected members are just watch dogs and the actual signature power is with bureaucrats.

What I have a gut feeling is that the top layer that is visible to us is only an icing appearing to be impressive and powerful but the actual fact is none of the elected bodies have any direct control that can resolve the problems of the system.

I am 100% sure that there is a global conspiracy behind such organisational structure.

Then Government in AP and Central Government of India was changed. I was not receiving the acknowledgements any more for my emails.

# 14 COST ACCOUNTING

Earlier I said about the exports and imports logic. Let us go back to that.

Some of the content of this book seems to be irrelevant but the complete subject is possible to be understood only when all dots are put together to understand the big picture. As I said, every point of feeling is very important to get the 360 degree vision in 3D world.

First I started looking at the reasons for why prices are dropping in USA always? The same is in UK. Why?

USA imports lot of goods from around the world. Especially products those require huge manpower involvement. *USA even imports 75% of its Fuel as similar as India*. But USA $ and its value has become a basis for the world global trade. How the heck that became a global currency for export market?

India has 80% dependency on imported fuel and fertilizer. One is for its economy to run forward and the second is for food production. Now India requires US$ to import both of them.

First I figured out that the fall of Rupee against US$ is making import of both fuel and fertilizer more and more expensive which is the reason for rising cost of living inside India.

But new questions arise inside me.

Why RBI has been choosing the devaluation of Rupee?

India does not import fuel from USA but Middle East but why would India require US$ for that?

India doesn't import fertilizer from USA then why is it tied itself to US$?

While searching these questions I came across one more major development on this globe. The collapse of Indonesia economy. Indonesia has huge large oil production. Still its economy was suffering like anything and one of its leaders was murdered. Its Rupiah was devaluated to large extent. However, the same was not the situation with other OPEC countries. Some of their currencies were anchored to US$. Why this difference? If India has weakness in its currency so much due to its imports and food production then why Indonesia that doesn't have the need for import of large fuel still has problem of currency weakness?

Fuel and Food are input costs for every sector. When both of them are becoming more and more expensive then input costs are rising to all sectors and their production cost is rising across all sectors. Then industries will have to sell their produce for more price but the buyer should have the capability to buy it.

However, the industries those are exporting are able to make their profits due to US$ realization and sometimes about get Rupee money for their exported business revenues.

Let us look at for more clarity.

Every product will have the following components in its price.

1. Material,
2. Processing cost,
   a. Man power Cost—Food – **Fertilizer**
   b. Utility Cost such as Electricity etc.
3. Transport—**Fuel**
4. Taxes
5. **Money Transaction Charges**
6. Profit.

**Figure 2:** Product price components

Before we proceed further, focus on the points that bolded above. The above figure made me believe that there are some forces working to destroy India very strategically in a very planned manner.

They are fundamental costs. If they are large, their impact would be multi-fold on the entire economy.

Look at the following graph.

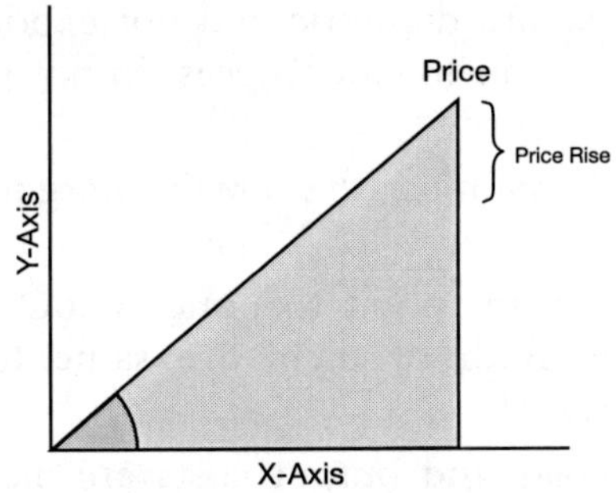


If we consider the angle as Rupee value against other currencies, variation by one degree is enough to spiral the prices of the products in an exponential manner into multiples.

*These are not errors but for me they appear to be very carefully arranged conspiracies against the nation of India. What I noticed is, even experts were not even talking about them till I raised them.*

When we organize them in sequence as follows

Input >>> Process >>>> Output

When Fuel cost and Fertilizer costs raise, both man power cost and transport cost raises. The rise in fuel cost would directly reflect as more cost of production.

When all the input costs rise then automatically, profits will squeeze. Because profits are dependent on the buying power.

There are two types of Industries or commerce in India. It goes by the market they live and operate in.

They are domestic and foreign.

We know from the fact of 80% fuel and fertilizer imports, India has Input costs dependent on its Rupee value against US$.

The output costs in India after process are prorated on Rupee value against US$.

At the point of sale to customer, the industries those export and sell in US$ gets realization based on Rupee value realization against US$.

Industries those are domestic and not export oriented but sell in Indian market in Indian Rupees do not get that chance of variance.

This has been denting the profit margin for domestic industries.

Here one important point to notice about the input cost and output costs. Both of them are same for export and domestic industries.

When Input costs and output costs are increasing due to fall in Rupee value against US$, where is the scope for Competitiveness in the export market for Indian Exporters?

The competitiveness was Selling More Products for Less Price in terms of US$ was being projected as Competitiveness.

*Products are becoming cheap in terms of US$ but becoming expensive in terms of Indian Rupees.*

This is increasing the Capability of US$ and USA economy. USA is able to import more and more products at less and less cost.

Since I am Indian, I am getting impacted. I am considering it from the angle of India.

The consistent fall of product prices in USA economy was because of US$ value in Global Market.

Exactly opposite has been happening in Indian Economy.

It is not with Indian Rupee alone but every currency around the world that is trading against US$ was having the same situation and the corresponding economies as well.

My question was, is RBI and its intellectuals not cognizant of this and adopted the intentional devaluation under the name of Competitiveness?

I am not sure why and how, but all incidents always happened to me only in my life for the subject that draws my attention. I came across one more startling revelation while watching an interview in 2004. It was "Walk the Talk" with

Manmohan Singh, who happened to be a key position of Government of India since 1973. He said that he had chosen to devaluate Rupee against US$ frequently in a gap of three months frequency by 16% and more. He also said that he used to inform that to then PM of India, P.V. Narasimha Rao, who said to him, do all that benefits the nation. What P.V., who was not an Economist, would do when a person who was considering as expert telling something as required. I was surprised. A person who was considered as saviour of Indian Economy was the person who participated in the intentional devaluation of Rupee.

I went through his bio-data for more details.

So far I understood the Finance, Numbers, Currency, Currency values, import-export market, and global market and now it took a new turn and new questions are in my mind about what is happening!!

Are people aware of the currency concept well enough? Are the experts that this nation is considering as experts are really experts? Are those media columnists or specialists who write columns in newspapers are really having the skill of understanding economy based on Currency Systems?

Please recall here that I wanted to create awareness about this currency based conspiracies through emails. I used to send emails to all media houses editors. Later I started a groups in yahoo to create awareness. Groups in internet world was first generations Social media. My group was rated as group with best discussions.

I wanted to explain the economy in simple way that can help even a common man to understand what is economy! I created the word "Indianomics" to brand my group and my effort. I started including the Members of Parliament of India, President of India, Prime Minister of India, Central Ministers and Chief Ministers and media heads.

Here reader should know one thing, when somebody likes me writing about issues and sending across to top chairs, there is a system, where all power chairs of political and administrative reside. They maintain close relation with media as well. Intelligence forces will start working on inquiring about me. This was the same senior journalist, Pathanjali, who was with TV9 then, was saying.

They gather IP addresses and many more.

If you believe or not I happened to write an email about steps to be adopted in order to resolve the issue of naxalism, then it was a major issue. It was immediately Cced to Detective department while replying to me.

I was the one who said that Naxal problem is not Law and Order problem but a problem of social disorder because the person who is "stamped" as "naxal" is an Indian who is born to live in India as similar as the Government employee or any other Indian. As long as the social disorder is not addressed, the problem cannot be resolved.

I started writing email on several policies of Government. However my emails were having reactions from government those I can see through government acts and media statements but not able to receive any acknowledgements. Of course, I even asked explicitly about my acknowledgement in order to have some link between the developments in real time and my email messages. No use.

I never shared any details about this effort to anybody except to my wife. I was afraid of ridiculing by my friends as well.

My effort continues.

Here are brief points to understand, if Rupee falls

1. Indian Resources will become cheap to USA, UK and other economies against Whose Currencies Rupee has become weak
2. Foreign Resources for Indian will become Expensive to India
3. India loses more Forex both at Export side as Income and Import side as Expenditure
4. Inside India, Expenditure rises.

The above four points are between India and Foreign world.

Let us see what happens to India itself.

Indian Resources will become expensive for India itself.

Indian margins will be crunched.

Since, Resources have become expensive, refer the product price component Diagram above. Here I should mention about the perspective of Currency in the Global Market and in Indian Market.

In Indian market, Money is considered as Asset/Credit Instrument/Income. This is a Common man Perspective which is not right from Economy Perspective.

In Global Market, Money is considered as Debt instrument/Liability/Expenditure. Quantity of Money is representative of Expenditure.

In this regard, I need to explain some more details which I did in later chapters.

# 15 BANKING

I started continuing towards finding reasons which may cause the fall of Rupee currency in forex market. One challenge that I have in my effort is, when I find a flaw, I need to prove that it is a flaw. Now that proof or hypothesis should be down to ground and easy to understand. I found this as required for even people who are considered as "Intellectuals."

Fundamental purpose or role and responsibility of banks is facilitating money movement through the economic system. However, banks are in the operation mode of Finance Companies due to poor framework of Government due to poor knowledge about fundamentals of currency-based economic system with top chairs of Reserve Bank and Finance Ministry.

In my effort to correct the Indian Economic Policies, I started looking at options related to finance burden on the nation.

I came across another major flaw in our banking systems related to banks, and their transactions in the form of Money Transaction Charges.

I used to send money from USA to India through wire transfer, irrespective of amount, the transaction cost would be US$10. After the money reached India, I used to pay more money towards money transaction charges in India than between USA and India.

Earlier, as we all know, that there used to be, unlike now, bank accounts specific to a single branch. Even with in a city between two branches, money transfer used to be expensive and time consuming. The options available for bank transactions were Demand Draft, telegraph transfer, Cheque.

Cheques used to be either outstation or local cheques. Within a city or town, banker's cheque used to be there for movement of money through banks. Banks used to charge 0.0125% with min. ₹50 as cost of demand draft. In case of cheques at local station, there used to be minimum of 3 days to 5 days and max unlimited time to get transfer of funds from one bank to another bank. Also the same way, if it is outstation cheque the transfer of money used to be minimum of 15 days to unlimited days. Banks never used to take any responsibility of any instrument and its fate. In this entire complicated crooked process, account holders used to be the sufferers.

The same aspect when analysed from the dimension of economy, movement of money from source to destination was very expensive in two ways; first direct charges of 0.0125% and second indirect charges; interest on the money in suspense for long time that is not available to the actual business owner.

I will explain this in a real terms. I was doing a business with an investment of ₹1,00,000.

Current Account minimum balance was ₹5,000—means 5% of my money is not in business, and interest is also a loss to me.

My each invoice amount used to be ₹10,000 for which I used to have Bank Cheques. DD charges used to be ₹50, for that ₹10,000 which is 0.5% Money Transaction Charges.

When I have cheques for that amount, each local cheque used to take 5 days to get cleared, if it is out station, 15 to 45 days was clearance time.

For local Cheques, clearance charges are 0.5% Money Transaction Charges.

For out-station cheques, it used to be up to ₹110 which is 1% as Money Transaction Charges + loss of Interest on the investment for 45 days as Money transaction charges.

I used to operate at 10% margin, it means I was making ₹1,000 for each transaction. It means, I have expenses of 5% to 10% of my income as money transaction charges.

Also I would have losses of minimum balance amount requirement, etc. The total was coming to 40% of my actual investment in a year.

The total of it when calculated against the investment in a business, number of rotations in a year that the business investors are able to rotate his investment in this complicated clearance system, interest loss due to delayed transit of transaction from source to destination, direct money transaction charges, resulted into 40% of investment as burden on the business. This 40% is indirect burden on the business. In order to meet such large burdens, business owner has to keep at least more than 40% margin in his business transaction in order to meet his expenditure and profit, after that which would result into beyond the prevailing interest rate.

In addition, I should be able to earn the bribes at Government offices. I should be able to earn Business expenses. I should be able to earn my family expenses.

This means, in a year I should be able to earn at least three times of my original investment in order to be successful. The Money Transaction charges were major Income source for Banks. There were no rules or commitments to their customer as service.

I wrote about such huge negative impact due to bank's old processes and procedures, and expenditure burden on the nation's economy which led to introduction of computer systems in banks, and single bank account that is accessible anywhere in the nation.

Due to such large income from money transaction charges, banks were least bothered about their primary business of rotating money by funding the needs of the nation through lending money and earning interest as return on loans. RBI was least bothered. RBI employees were also least bothered. At the end a politician with large commitment has to do this which Finance Minister of India did this well after lot of hurdles. Chidambaram was FM of India.

This email of mine led to the introduction of core banking, at-par cheques, NEFT, RTGS, etc. In other words, changes towards this kind were initiated in government only after my email to the Finance Minister of India.

However here, one more fact should be put on record. Since banks were finding this as a large jolt to their income source, they did not stop adopting techniques; corrupted techniques of making money as outstation deposit of money into account, minimum balance in the account with paying least interest to money owner.

Reserve Bank of India was supposed to have all this understanding. However, even today, it is easily noticeable that none of the top fellows of Government of India have no clue about how to see the Finance and its impact on the nation, which is the reason why they always hang themselves to Interest rates.

Especially the minimum deposit without any interest pay out to current accounts was another loss to business owners. Later introduced the ₹2 per cheque leaf, etc. charges. Also contemplated on introducing service charges to bank customers for operating their accounts in the bank.

Indian banks operate at profit margin of minimum of 6% to 30%. Indian bank employees enjoy such a large benefits that nowhere on the earth would any bank employee makes such comfortable secured job with large income. This is fact.

The changes in banks created scope for creating margin for businesses by reducing the transaction charges, interest rates, more rotations of their investment in quick time. This creation margin was later evaporated by other blunder policies of Government of India.

I returned to India and did not stop my effort. I found one more flaw which was about taking loans by Indian Government and related entities taking loans from World Bank, and IMF. I was surprised about why loans are being procured from foreign source. What about the impact of Rupee devaluation? Is RBI not cognizant of the consequences of foreign loans in Indian public sector?

Indian Government and its subsidiaries were taking loans left and right from World Bank and IMF. I was shocked when

I saw the amount of loans took by them. An average ₹12,000 per head were taken as loan when per capita income was around ₹26,000.

Not sure, if reader notices this or not, the loan amount per head is equal to the amount calculated at tax percent.

The reasons floated around for such foreign loans were, the loans in forex currency are cheaper than that the funds in Rupee terms. And also one more problem was, banks are not interested to fund any government requirements.

Nobody was bothered about calculating the money conversion factors in those loans. RBI intentional devaluation was making those loans more expensive at principle and as well as at interest rate calculation. Loans taken in US$ when Rupee was ₹20 against US$1 became doubled at principal amount in terms of rupees and also in terms of interest when Rupee became ₹40 against US$1.

The pity part was, even after my repeated emails, the CM of AP from Congress Party took ₹57,000 crores of loans from World Bank.

The state of Andhra Pradesh tried to procure loans from local fund sources but could not as banks do not want to take risk. But why would a World Bank or IMF risk by lending money? What is it that India has to lend so much money to India? Where from World Bank is able to get money? These were unanswered questions.

However my search brought me new facts about World Bank and IMF.

Both the organizations were constituted after IInd World War in order to fund the nations of Europe which were devastated due to war.

When I saw the information from the websites of the World Bank and IMF, I started getting the details that they have been involved in several different nations in several different programs in public works. I also found the programs being conducted by World Bank and IMF with the participation of renowned economists, not sure if they are really renowned, but persons in the key chairs of nations around the world in several nations.

World Bank and IMF periodically conduct training workshops to all top chairs belonging to finance sector of all nations.

I started looking at the people of India who have occupied the top chairs of Finance departments of India. They all some or other day were part of World Bank and IMF. This includes Manmohan Singh, and several others.

Also what I found was, world-renowned economists are only those who were acclaimed by World Bank and IMF. What I understood is, in order to be renowned world economists, one needs to be part of that World Bank or IMF chariot. Otherwise, he would never be renowned. Also one should be able to speak their language and in their terms.

What is the purpose of loans in US$ to all nations across the world? Why these training workshops to all world nation's Government top finance chairs?

How the heck the foreign funding validity became a law in India was cleared from the close ties of top so-called renowned "no clue if really" economists.

I got the answer, but what I understood was that World Bank and IMF took the simple management principles always in order to achieve their goal or agenda. They just identify some catalysts for their purpose and use them to get the results. For this, they identify some dumb heads and provide them utmost importance and success to make them important and highly regarded among the dumb heads circles; and the rest of the drama will fall to their advantage by these dumb heads at the second end where they want the results as expected. They provided the same to Manmohan Singh and others as best capable people, the rest happened in India.

However here, we need to focus on one more thing. When were the gates opened for foreign funds? Under what conditions those gates were opened? Earlier to that, what were the conditions? What happened after the gates were opened?

The gates were opened for foreign funds when India did not have any forex reserves. Why did not India have any forex funds? What are forex funds? Is US$ alone considered as Forex fund? If yes, why US$ alone is being considered as widely accepted Currency around the world for Global export market? What benefit that brings and to whom?

Let us recall the time when India was suffering severely without forex. US$ or UK Pound/Sterling was considered as Forex. Why was India in need of US$ of UK Pound/Sterling for importing from Gulf Nations. Because Gulf nations were having the oil fields where USA and UK and other Europe nations had technology investments. Why I am saying "technology" as "investment"? Because they have invested in inventing new techniques in exploring oil, and provided the same to the Oil-rich Gulf nations and made them obey their terms so that the skill-less gulf nations became rich. Everybody knows all the details about politics around the world for Oil and OPEC nations.

Here what we should recall is, during the second world war and later around the world in the nations where Europeans were migrated, there used to be government funded, military guarded technology innovation programs where all experts were made to work at gun point.

Here let us recall that crude as commodity whose prices were controlled by exchanges in London and New York.

Here some more questions arise. OK if it is the case in Gulf why not with other nations? Why India could not do anything with other nations where US$ is not required?

For this we should look at the developments inside India.

Here let us recall about other avenues where lot of finance activities happen.

One is stock market and the second is investments in companies. As you already know that I had experience in both Indian Stock Market and foreign stock market. I was looking for foreign investments in India.

I found foreign investments into Indian companies as Participatory notes, American Depository Receipts and Global Depository Receipts.

First one about Stock markets which were consortium of stock brokers have become companies with share holdings and SEBI as regulator from Government of India. Stock Markets, small markets around the nation were closed and a part of the stock market investor holdings were sold to NASDAQ. I was surprised. A stock market is an always profit business which is sold to foreign investor. I found it very strange. How Government could do this?

Then coming to investments in Companies as ADR or GDR or PNs, Investors shares are being sold to foreign investors and money is being brought in to India. This also has several blunders. Aren't Government of India or Experts in top chairs aware of the consequences? These were major questions to me.

Foreign Investments in India, means Indian stock market is accessible to foreign investment but not the foreign stock markets to India.

This again means the profits made out of Investments will be converted to non-rupee currency that will hurt the value of Rupee in stock market which will increase the cost of imports to Indian economy and it will impact the Indian economy with more expenditure. I was shocked. I felt something large going on than anybody else is able to notice it.

I started looking for the places where foreign investments are being encouraged.

What I found initially was ADR, GDR, PN, World Bank Loans, IMF loans. To where they are going?

ADR, GDR, PNs are into Industries.

World Bank and IMF loans are into Infrastructure such as drinking water projects, road projects, irrigation projects, electricity projects, etc.

Then the disinvestment into PSUs were promoted. I was completely in confusion. How on the earth this kind of antibenefit to Indian economic policies are being proposed by Government?

Then after sometime more PSU's disinvestment and more proposals for forex inflow of funds were started. They were FCCB, ECB, FII and FDI and many more different routes to bring in forex inflow into India.

Another major forex inflow was Credit card Business.

I wrote several emails about the above said repeatedly to Finance Minister of India. This is not stopped here itself, the inflow forex was supposed to appreciate rupee but Rupee was not appreciated due to which more forex inflow was becoming into more rupees in the economy of India.

All the above clearly reflect that there is either lack of skill with top chairs of Government of India or something else is wrong somewhere, that is the top chairs are working for their self-achievements.

Remember here that World Bank and IMF have formed a network of Individuals, a club; unless one is part of it, that one individual will not have success in his activities.

How did I come to know about this?

As you know that I was not "formally qualified" to talk about any of these things. Formally qualified means, I am not a graduate of economics or finance. I tried to meet the professors who would be the right point of contacts and right persons to handle such issues and take them to public platform.

I met a professor through a known media person. I explained him the big picture of above and gave him the facts about the consequences. He said that he cannot involve due to his career as per his KPIs in his profession in the university; he has to write white papers and need to get at least two invitations as spokespersons in a session from foreign universities or other platforms of foreign origin, participate in book writing, etc. He said that almost all the professors/scientists have the same commitments in their career and they may not support me directly but he offered his indirect support by giving references to me. I should appreciate him for this small support that brought a big leap in my effort.

Because Social Recognition and acceptance is a major requirement for an effort that I have been ambitioning.

As I said earlier, I had been sending lot of emails, one per day or more per day about latest developments or proposals of Government and consequences—both negative and positive. To further explore the chances for creating more public awareness about what is happening around, I approached several media houses and explained about this that I will give you facts and you create programs or articles on your own on the information that I have given, and publish them to create awareness in public about several economic issues.

There was some hidden help from media which supported me in my cause and participated in live TV debates twice. Kommineni Srinivas Rao was the first person who gave me first chance of a live TV debate.

Until I got professor's reference, I did not get acceptability of publishing my articles in any newspapers. I approached several other media houses who deprived me which was a major insulting feeling inside me as I had set the base of knowledge to those media houses through my emails continuously for at least five years before I approached them in person.

Earlier to this media participation I have some more findings that I would like to give to you.

On professor's reference, my articles were published in Andhra Jyothy. However, every time when I gave an article, I would not have any confidence until it is published. I had to pursue several times.

# 16 INDEPENDENCE

From here on, please bear with me as some of these may sound to you very imaginary but whether you consider them meaningful or meaningless, read through, understand the angle of interpretations; at the end of this book, you will agree with me that whatever I said, makes sense and you agree with me that you have 360 degree understanding in 3D world from the information that I am giving in the 360 degree using 2D world, that is this book.

Let us walk back in History and see the events happened around in India and around.

India got independence in 1947.

When India was in trouble in 1990, the top most media talk was "Indian Economy was a closed Economy."

What was that "closed" in Indian Economy? Foreign investment was not allowed. Is this true, if yes, then how the Bhopal Gas incident was there in a factory where American Investment was there? *That means, Indian economy was not a closed economy.*

The actual fact was, several multinational companies those had been doing business in India since last 6 to 7 decades and have been milking wealth from Indian market, were restricted from taking profits to their mother land and they were asked to spend the money in India itself and if at all want to expand business from foreign resources, bring those resources to India and do business in India but nobody will be allowed to take profits to their native land or economy.

We can see around and find that even today we use products being manufactured and supplied by multi-national companies, which were transnational companies earlier due to closed market of India that was not allowing profits of India moving out of India.

This was propagated as "Closed" economy when Indira Gandhi nationalised banks. Who propagated it? Most of them were all associated to such professions those get benefit only when they speak the language of those transnational companies and make them do business in India.

Those transnational companies were having large stock market investments and activities and also the top chairs of those transnational companies were being considered as nation's renowned achievers.

We need to look at the significant changes which are related to Global relations and which are successful even today.

Earlier to 1990, in reverse chronological order, Telecommunication reforms by Rajiv Gandhi. The technology was mostly from foreign source. The closed economy was not a right place to do business because profits cannot be taken back to their nation.

Several industrial development programs were introduced inside India to develop industrialization during 1960s and '70s. Several Small scale sector industries were started during 1970s.

Several promotional programs were introduced for food production sector such as dairy and poultry farm, groves plantation, food processing sector, and many more different sectors so that India can grow on its own and become self-reliant.

All technocrats were given opportunity to develop on their own by starting small scale sector units.

Several subsidies were introduced to benefit Indian internal economy.

Banks were nationalized by Indira Gandhi. Everybody stated that this one "Closed" Indian Economy and prosperity.

Indira Gandhi participated in several UN and Commonwealth nations opposing several unilateral global policies by

USA and UK. She was instrumental on global platform in order to benefit India.

When she nationalized Banks in India, contemporary effort on the global platform was establishment of US$ as world globally accepted currency in Global Market.

Does the above said sequence of events ring any bell about any conspiracy under execution mode from global platform towards India?

The above said were only a small number of visibles to common eye. There could be many. I also do not know. Only those in the top chairs of India would know.

Most of the media was mostly engaged against Mrs. Gandhi. People who continuously spread information about "Closed Economy" were media persons, analysts and all those who had short sighted understanding. This spread of information, correct or wrong is a different issue, but would be like wild fire through media.

Media fellows' objective has always been sensation for more readership or viewership. Also several Media people due to their profession gains a value that is far larger than the power of any other force in the society. They enjoy this a lot. They do work to gain personal profit from this.

Also one more incident rings in my brain. That was the acts of Motilal Nehru, the father of Jawaharlal Nehru who used the currency notes to make tea.

Motilal's time was the time when the currency in India being regularized as widely acceptable transaction instrument by law of British. When I read the details, what I understood was, during then, currency was considered as VALUELESS paper. It is equal to firewood. People in India were having different understanding about wealth and did not respect or value currency that was either Metal or Paper.

Let us recall my time which is *almost 100 years later the incident of Motilal's time where I found people in Villages who were still practising Barter System* where the commodity as the exchange of their transactions instead of Currency which was nothing but barter system. So people were having different other systems in their society in Indian villages, and more valuable than those papers with numbers.

From the information that I had gone through, *leaders of India were not aware of the twisted tales of currency*. It means, there is something else that Indira Gandhi, being the daughter of a leading family of India with access to elite western world, knew and had different understanding about Currency systems than any other leaders that she gained from her access through her father's PM position, and was very well aware of the style of how global forces make their moves.

What I felt was Indira Gandhi was afraid of global forces entering again through the route of financing the nation into India. She nationalized the banks. This was a big jolt to USA and UK movements on global platform.

Government had constituted Public sector units in several different sectors and also private small scale sectors were encouraged in order to develop internal technical capabilities. *All those industries became sick due to two reasons. One was rapid rise in costs, and the second, lack of innovative capabilities in Indians*. This was later completely overridden by rapid rise in the imported technology. Import technology has two colours. One is related to knowledge and the second is the technology that is ready to use. Public sector units were not able to perform well. The so called talent recruited into jobs did not yield any expected results, and science and technology was not developed well in India.

Of course, *Employee Unions* and the agitations by those unions and political party backing those unions etc. also played a role in the failure of PSU units. I will explain about this later in this book. However at every given point of time, money and costs played larger role than any other issues in the failure of the industries and created unrest in the society and in the citizens of India's life.

Here we must recall the forgotten or buried deep in the earth fact that there was a vision about Self Development, development of technical savviness, vision of creating new technologies within India and industrialization, thereby achieve economic progress.

When I started looking at different incidents since the year of 1960s, what I found was across the world in several nations, several leaders were killed by the same nation's people. Latest Syria or Lebanon or other nations' rulers. Their deaths have always been after social disturbances. Especially, in Asian Nations, there were big size disturbances such as Punjab Terrorism issue. I read somewhere Bhindranwale was close associate of Indira Gandhi but why and how did he take the route of dividing India, and create Khalistan? Similarly, Punjab issue during Indira time, Tamils in Sri Lanka, separate Kashmir issue in India.

I met a Professor in Bismarck who happened to be from Kashmir and who was proud to move to USA leaving India. He was appreciating me for being there in USA. I felt very sorry for that inside me but that triggered me different thoughts. Why am I saying this here? *There are people who like hatred about their own nation and society. They consider as intellectuals but useful for nothing to India. Most of them chose to migrate showing the local problems as reasons.* Most of the places such hatred played top role in creating disturbance that lasted for years together hampering the economic growth of the nation.

What I learnt then was, there is a provision in first world nation immigration that if somebody belongs to a geographical region, such as Kashmir or Punjab or Assam or Jaffna, etc. places on earth, where terrorism or other types of problems exist people from those regions can approach immigration of first world nations to move to first world nations and settle there as refugees.

Remember here that there were people who were in favour of British Rule when they were moving out of India considering that it was not good for India. Several of the details of administration transition from British to India were not properly documented and explained to this nation's youth which is another reason why Indians were not able to gain knowledge and expertise of several different ruling, administrative and management capabilities.

Recall here the British political tricks during Indian Independence and the issue of division of India and death of 1 million people during then just because of one simple disturbance created by British. British or Global Forces use the local differences and also individuals those are on two sides of that differences and utilise the situations in order to create disturbance.

My cognition process and my study was always on different topics to bring the dots together. I found information about the way how British encouraged the cultivation of Hafeem in Afganistan and used it in big way in China for their political benefits.

I started looking at the level of international movements and international political moves. What I understood was, as per the principles of politics, *take advantage of differences at local level and use it as weapon to keep the region always in disturbance*. This can be done by identifying IDIOT who is good orator and provides hidden support to him to make him leader and the rest will fall in place on its way.

One important fact to understand is, British or Americans, play with fluid systems of society which are run by people's interpretations, understanding and conclusions. They are mastered in that because of their global exposure.

Some of them are

- India is a poor country
- Indians are uneducated
- Indians are not capable
- Indians are inefficient
- Industrialization is not there
- India is over populated

First to remember here is such bad propaganda used to be by those disciples of Dracula who were receiving benefits from those global organizations.

This may lead to a question that why British or Americans would want to create disturbance in the world? To understand this, still more information is required. But keep this question always on top of the stack of all other nations. However I had the similar question, why India has been failing while UK and America are able to be successful?

My search brought me more and more details. The History Channel programs on slavery in the world gave me more information about how it was used to be in those old days in Africa. It was such a inhumane, since Indians do not have much information around it, never had the clue of what is real hell on earth while living.

In Africa, Blacks/Negros used to be treated by Europeans as equal to animals. On this earth one human did trade of another human as commodity.

Negros from African continent used to be transported like cattle. This is similar to the way how today cattle is being transported by stuffing in truck.

Europeans used to keep Negros in stock yards where the Negros will be stocked in such a way that in a room they used to be chained and kept without place to have even knee bend, for hours together or days together and used to be fed like animals and washed like animals. Just imagine the kind of cruelty that was there. Those slaves used to be transported to America from African nations in the same similar conditions.

The Negros in the stock yard were in the mode of "Animals" where their natural calls would be as similar as "Animals". This was treatment by Europeans to African Tribes who were innocent.

One more shocking news that I came to know was, during those days, about 200 years ago, the Europeans in order to win over competition in African Slavery trade, used "Biological" weapons. Those biological weapons were "Bacteria of water-born diseases such as measles or chicken pox etc." Europeans in order to win over their competition used to mix such bacteria in water reserves of African tribes, consuming such water they used to get sick and die due to those diseases. I was shocked. Just imagine the tribes and their day to day living hell, and cluelessness why their tribes were victimized by unknown disease that none had ever witnessed in their known history and used to pray God for relief helplessly. Also notice that such incidents will start developing the disorder in the society, such as "witches" or "praying for pacifying the angry of gap" or "evil forces have been taking their feast," etc.

Why I am writing this here, as long as we can't figure out the reasons and understand them, they sound very unbelievable.

This raised doubts in me, if the plague epidemic in India was similar effort by British? Here I remembered write-up once published in Eenadu newspaper, Telugu Daily, about a Biological Killer Bacteria generator, at the size of a domestic house hold water boiler which can produce a quantity of bacteria in less than an hour that can wipe out a city of 10 million population in just less than a day. One thing is sure that Indians are way behind in many things from western world.

I also remembered that experiments were conducted to create cross breed of creatures by mixing the sperm like lion with tiger, human sperm with others etc. from newspapers. I also watched several History programs about how medical experiments used to be conducted and how they resulted into major medical innovations. That sounds pathetic but was real, and Indians are not having any information about such experiments.

I also found one more interesting news that, in Hindu Sea, UK used to have an Island which was sold to USA for its scientific, military operations from where all the Island aborigines were forcefully vacated. It is very near to Indian Subcontinent where a fighter jet can travel in just an hour to the shores of India.

I was surprised.

Such shocking information led me to conclude that on this earth every incident has an invisible origin or trigger point and I must start looking for that origin.

I started believing that the incidents of Punjab terrorism or Tamil Elam issue or Assam Bodoland issue, or even present Telangana issue will not be natural local developments.

Definitely not. There will be some forces behind them. They are not easily noticeable.

However it is the responsibility of IAS, IPS or Intelligence officers of Government of India to figure out all such activities which could be a Salt Particle in Milk. Such salt particles are supposed to be eliminated even before they are conceptualized. But our union civil service executives are not at all capable of any of such capabilities. It is evident from our Government operation.

The reason for such in capabilities is "the organization being part of government" that is maintaining the system of Union Civil Services.

I started believing that Indira Gandhi who was instrumental during 1970 and '80s on international platform, was working against the Global Forces moves, who could not directly attack her, so in order to eliminate her, situations need to be created first to kill her leadership, second create the situation that will succumb her capabilities, and create a direct hatred on her from her own land people, create unconducive situation that will make her move towards placing herself to a situation where she will become a target to everybody, and at the end she will be ended as required.

The lack of understanding of the currency based political moves with Indian leaders became a major advantage to them. Also they waited till all those old fellows were dead and new jokers who believe and follow their Economic and Finance theories appropriately were developed and occupied the top chairs.

We need to see here the role of individual psychological and behavioural characteristics as well. They need a person like Manmohan Singh who does not speak and is not even expressivc in any manner. Not only Manmohan Singh but also several others, as Economists. They got right candidates in order to carry on the economic and financial political games. They projected him as Expert, providing him utmost importance to show him as the best, so that others' words will not be valid anywhere.

The reader may conclude me as targeting Manmohan Singh, but no, I am not targeting him and I am only trying to bring out the hidden angle of conspiracy for which I need to be candid to make the reader understand the fact.

However I should mention this here that what I don't like about him is he still disguises as "Innocent."

When talking about Leadership, we need to focus on "killing the leadership (not leader) of India", we must also recall the mysterious death of Lal Bahadur Shastry in Russia. Was there an effort towards killing the leadership of India? I have strong doubts on this from Global arena.

Global forces work on creating situations. Creating situations is very easy in any society, especially in nations like India. This is where the nation's administration system is supposed to play a vital role in killing all the means or killing all the developments even before they start those that may create situations and may cause severe disturbance in the harmony of the nation or hurt nation's welfare in any manner.

Now the reader may get doubt, the above said are all imaginary and impossible. I also felt the same way and started focusing on all those which may support the moves of Global Forces. Facts are as follows.

Today the world where we all are living, there are natural systems and rules that we need to follow in order to live on the earth. For example, breath, eat, drink and sleep etc., all by nature. At the same time every human is today made to live in systems that the man created. They are law, money, ruling, administration and security systems.

The present structure of Ruling, Administration, Police, Revenue, Legal, Military, Number System, and many more systems are all established by Europeans. Pay more attention that we are made to learn what they have decided as Education. Please recall here that we are being programmed by the education created by them and have been adopting the behaviour based on that education. Since they were the creators of the present systems across the world, they also know the limitations of them and also know what to do where in order to get expected results.

Here one important point to recall is, our freedom fighters were all Legal Experts. Because, British introduced the system of Law, rules to the society, revenue systems, documented ownership claims and many more. However they have created all of them only till the point they created differences between the entities of society. Even after 66 years of Independence, Indians are not able to find the completeness of them to organize the rules for their society to avoid disputes.

Now one more doubt may arise that how can anybody estimate the results for their acts especially by global forces. The answer for such doubt is simple, the right target would always be very narrow and tough to focus and achieve. Everything else won't be narrow as target. For Global Forces, disturbing the target of others is the goal hence distraction and disturbance is all that they need.

Also one more thing which needs to be looked at is, minute by minute thoughts of an individual may not be predictable but when it comes to the society level, the behaviour can be predicted and the types of behaviours available for an individual would be limited for being a member of a society. Management Studies mostly talk about the same.

One more fact that supports my conclusion said above today major petroleum suppliers are in the control of USA. The war that USA did on Iraq which was supported by UK was another evidence of their association. Everybody knows about this. But how did they achieve success is the question that needs to be answered. At the end of this book you will get the answer.

The rock phosphate is largely available in Jordan, a small nation having feudal system. The prince of that nation studied in USA and UK, and I happened to see a program on him and his family life and ruling with American supplied latest fighter jets and helicopters. The prince himself was demonstrating, how to operate them. The entire episode clearly reflects that America gave him some toys (real time ammunition) to that prince to play and they have been exploiting the world's richest

Rock Phosphate resources that is a core raw material for fertilisers. Like that they have kept Jordan in their control.

One more major evidence for such indirect acts are the "sanctions" that USA and UK, and other nations impose on nations those come across the way of America through UN.

Let us now look at the world's top most organizations. UN, UNESCO, WHO, World Bank, and IMF. These are five forces of any political system.

- UN – Political and Administrative
- UNESCO – Science and Technology
- WHO – Health
- World Bank and IMF – Finance and Economy

The power chairs are weaved together across the world through these organizations.

Global Forces also use Media a lot for their purposes. India has one more setback that is half knowledge with Media analysts.

Let us recall here the old fact of propagating negative image write-ups and images on India in European nations in good old days as India is a land of Black Magic and sorcerers during the start of 20th century just before India was gaining its independence. This was to create fear in the global trade and to hurt the Indian Economy.

Here I will take you back to Stock Markets. Earlier I wrote about having every bank its own currency in USA until Government constituted its Federal Bank and bringing in Single Currency. I saw a program in History on how stock markets were started and how the stock market trading information used to be transmitted to distance places through Morse Code sort of communication facilities. The concepts of Mutual Funds were started and how they gained momentum in USA and how those Mutual Funds became Venture funds to develop R&D in USA.

Let us recall here the incident of Titanic Ship that was the largest ship and imagine the kind of industry required to build such a large ship. Also Ford Company in USA, where Ford was given facilities to create an industry that takes in Iron Ore or other related Ores as Input and gives out the finished goods "Cars". Every day one ship carrying workers required for Ford Companies used to reach the port of Detroit to replace the existing workforce that may not be "Profitable" to Company. This was where the Labour rights moment was started. Earlier I said about the heavy earth equipment with Steam Engines.

There are very limited significant incidents that occurred in the last 66 years in India from the angle of Economic Development. Irrigation Dams, Public Sector Units, Private Small Scale Sector development, Food research, Science and Technology development centres, Nationalization of Banks, Lack of Forex reserves, Collapse of Indian Economy, Sickening of Industries, Agitations by Employee Unions, Liberalisation of Indian Economy, 100% Export Oriented Units, Pollution, Telecom liberalization, IT business, loses in Agriculture, conversion of Agriculture land to non-agriculture purpose.

When I had gone through such information, I ended up with questions.

Did Indians win Independence from British? Or Did British leave India strategically based on the change in the Global Economy?

Until early quarter of 1900s, India and surrounding areas on the Globe used to be tropical and rich in natural resources. Let us recall the Silk Route. Silk Route was there for ages where Spices and Diamonds used to be transported from India to Europe Region. Europe was mainly dependent on this region of earth for several different resources required for them in Europe including clothes. *India was globalized by then itself however Indians were not.* Export market used to have Gold as Exchange of medium for Export Trade until the currency systems were introduced.

The early quarter of 1900s changed the global economy due to Tropical areas identified in the other parts of the world. The Global trade that was mainly around clothes, spices, sugar and other food related requirements was changed.

The Combustion Engines and industrialization made the crude as one of the top world trade.

Then the chemical fertilizers and related ores.

Then the new most valuable one was Cocoa for chocolate, coffee and tea etc.

Now British did not find it meaningful to hold India and face its day to day troubles rather leave it to focus on new development areas as the migrant Europeans have more places to live lavishly in Australia, USA, South Africa, Canada and South America and other parts of the world where tropical atmosphere is available and also better resources than India are available.

Now, Did Gandhi win or Did British win is Egg and Chicken situation. I would say Gandhi won his war because he started the fight. But as per my understanding, India did not get independence. It was only freed away from direct control. It is still in the Control of Global Forces through finance and other markets route.

Also we need to focus on one more point in the last 150 years. Whatever the systems in which we have been living today were established by British. British were able to conceptualize the systems. The social, administration and ruling structures were established by them. When systems are formed and organizations are formed as subsets of systems, immediately a new culture will be created in that organization which will become the immediate connect of the individuals living in that organization.

Remember here that the education system around the world everywhere have the content based on the systems developed by those global forces.

That is why even today after 66 years of independence, the culture created by British is still continuing in every nerve of the Indian nation because of which the Actual Ruling system do not have direct control on the subordinate or subset systems or organizations. Indians failed to establish a controlling connection between them.

Today in the time line of Indian history, IT is at limelight. Earlier to this, it was 100% export oriented units of bulk drug manufacturers, clothes, sea food and many more. Earlier to that were stock market and finance market. And if we go back to last quarter of 19th century until Indians gained independence, legal practice, since British had initiated the legal system, a documented and structured one to define the rules and regulations to be followed by people across the world, in their local societies. This was the reason why Indians found their career path in Legal sector. Science and Technology was not in swing.

However, one must also focus on the significance given to currency system by British.

In every act of British, two things are very evident, a concept, virtual and nontangible one, will be created and implemented. The formation of orgs. or rules will program the human to follow them strictly. Similarly currency is another one. Very powerful concept.

I wrote earlier, a human may change his options to anything as long as Currency is not in scope. When Currency is brought into scope, human behaviour needle always points towards it like Magnet pointing to North Pole.

This kind of direct relation between Human psychology and Currency Numbers made them use it as much as possible.

If we see the last 150 years of India, though its society at root level was still having close relation with barter system, the educated or rich were more attractive to currency. Even Gandhi was aspired to be Barrister and to make his career as wealthy lawyer practicing on disputes of human society. Today also similar social psychology still continues, get Graduate at highest score in education courses those have demand such as IT engineering and become an IT professional to earn more, what, Money.

Hence all the above clarifies one fact that British who established organizations, created systems on concepts those control the human, were not dumb enough to leave the profit that easily.

Global Forces earlier were in the form of British and today in the form of America and its pets, World Bank and IMF.

Here we must also analyse Gandhi. We all know Gandhi lived in South Africa. Why did Gandhi return to India? He was an immigrant in South Africa, where one Immigrant (with power, British) warned him about his immigration status and imposing more restrictions on other Indian Immigrants.

Being an Immigrant for sometime, I am able to understand the Immigrant life which usually people who live in one nation and die will not have that experience of Immigration life and will not have that angle of exposure in thinking pattern.

When Gandhi returned to India, he travelled around entire India to assess India and to see what the social psychological state of India was recognise that I am referring Social Psychology and not individual Indian Psychological state. He was able to use a strategy that could attract the attention of all Indians and able to drive to a situation where he could win against Global Forces and make them to retreat. However he was able to do only that much as an Individual. Until Gandhi entered into freedom fight, everybody who were considered as leaders then were like labour leaders for British who entertained them to keep the situation under control and use them as catalysts for establishing systems that they want to implement.

Today the same state of behaviour of old leaders is visible in today's political leaders, bureaucrats and experts.

Even those days, as similar as today, farmers used to be encouraged to cultivate some crops that were required for European market. I found that today also we have the same social and economic conditions and characteristics as we had 100 years ago. This is the bitter fact. However, one major thing that Indians could not be able to understand so long is currency and its impact.

What I figured out is India and Indians have been failing in understanding the currency system which is the core reason for its failure.

All this information made me to confirm myself that all that is required to disturb a nation is just a need of "STUPID" conflicting issue and an IDIOT who wants to benefit from it.

Human has peripherals and networking connectivity as similar as Computers. Every human on this earth are connected to each other wirelessly through currency system.

A decision made at USA, Washington DC can impact a tribe in Andaman or Bushmen in African continent or tribes in South America who have no clue about how to wear clothes.

Here I should mention one thing, let us say that, this is a tribe of 100 people and have been living in a place very happily, say that they don't wear much clothes. Now we have clothes, do we consider those tribes as impoverished, backward and illiterate and make them corrupt or we respect them and only provide such help where they find better living when faced some problem like health problems etc.

This is the clarity which is missing. We are happy with what we have, but we are made to believe that we are not happy and we are poor and we are idiots because we don't have clothes, though we don't require them and had never used them till date, still we will be made to believe that we have all those problems as I mentioned above as, poverty, illiteracy, etc.

All that I am trying to say by above details is every incident that is visible to eye will have an origin at some place that is invisible.

The intentional devaluation of Rupee that was initiated by Manmohan Singh in this nation continued in this nation for 10 years until 2000. Indians who are not exposed to global level do not have the idea about perspective from global dimension.

Entire India was in a belief that Indian growth is in the devaluation of Rupee against other global currencies only.

Here before we proceed further we must consider looking at the reasons how and why Gandhi was successful? This is my interpretation after careful study.

Gandhi had enough exposure and experience in those societies where the persons in ruling chairs of Africa and India belong to. He might have understood difference in understanding of societies and the advantage of understanding with the persons in the British Ruling chairs. He has idea about the pulse of those British.

He knew that he was initiating a fight against organization and system. He knew that nation was under severe stress and they were not in a position to listen to him. He was in need of a tactics that can attract the people, attention.

If one explains the prosperity of west and aspires to grow like that, none was ready to listen. Moreover the so called feudal powers were not at all interested to change.

He might have found that acts close to the life of Indians and drawing "Sympathy" would attract the attention of the entire nation.

He chose the route of Simplicity and Satyagraha. This was really a nice strategy that made him win.

However in order to understand and create his strategy, he travelled across the nation to understand the pulse of social India.

The same studies usually will be conducted by First world nations through different voluntary organizations and through university study tours. Even today they are there. I wrote about them to warn government of India.

*Indian, since independence, did not get chance to conduct such studies, in other nations.* This opportunity was deprived through the route of promoting corrupted finance policies through properly positioned economists.

Through immigration system, Indians or other nations were not allowed to enter into the first world nations which led to create a "Black Hole" in the knowledge of Indians about the present multi-dimension world.

Watch this video to learn how they come and learn about our systems today.

http://www.youtube.com/watch?v=MFsFm4XkNhk

This is only a reference and not actual example about how we have a difference in our understanding, learning and objectives.

# 17 CURRENCY VALUE ECONOMIC SYSTEM

Hope everybody knows Marco Polo. If not, briefly, I will mention here, he was a businessmen who travelled across Asia and found the use of paper money in China way long back in 1200s itself. It means this currency system has been there for centuries.

However earlier days, from the ancient books, it is clear that Gold used to be the Exchange in Export trade. Several merchants from European nations through either Sea Route or through silk route, used to bring lot of Gold for Export Trade.

But Currency valuation system was not there. British who entered India and ruled India for 200 years have been using Currency either by paper or by coins as valid exchange of business. Currency valuation system means, different values in between different currency against each other, introduced only during late 19th Century.

Here we need to understand one thing, entire development of international trade, some sort of understandings or norms formation happened very informal and casual way and based on situational benefit and understanding. A formal process has never been in place to formalize them. Later the first world nations have started implementing formalized processes however they are in favour of first world nations.

This later came out as WTO.

India as a place on earth has been having relation not only with spices but diamonds, gold and other precious materials as export from India to Europe other places, let us not call them as wealth, where demand has been there for ages for such products apart from spices and food materials.

However Indians lost their connection with foreign land as the importers from those land came to India and became Rulers. The ruling of India by British has started creating a system in India that is to the understanding of foreign rulers.

The rule is one thing, the intention behind rule is another thing and the projection to public is another thing which always have created two dimensions to the same rule of the game or society. Though British had left India long back the system and the ambience created by those systems have been programming Indians behaviour as I said above, human is a natural computer that gets programmed by the environment where they live by their experiences.

This is the major reason why Indians could not figure out the pulse of the currency accurately. Always the meanings are manipulated to the convenience of the power chairs which is still continuing in India.

One significant fact that we should focus on is how currency systems got established? How the currency quantity would be decided?

For this we must start looking at this from the beneficiaries of the concept. As we all know that British or Europeans who were ruling the world and maintained different currencies around the world or confronted the local demands by local rulers for their own currency, were the major beneficiaries of Currency system. Because they were the Global Trader or Business people. They were in need of establishing a system that is convenient for Global Trade and simplified means of carrying wealth instead of Tons of Gold or Precious gems or diamonds.

When currency was conceptualized, around the world, in order to make it accept by all the nations, the first to answer was the above said quantity of money. How to define that? Thc same usually referred as Liquidity.

For this, if we delve through the social psychology of rulers of those days and the internationally acceptable wealth representing commodity was GOLD. Since barter system was main in use in the respective local economies, since GOLD was the mostly acceptable uniformly acceptable wealth representative at international trade, it was suggested as the basis to represent the Quantity of Gold with the ruler as the defining factor for printing money.

However all currencies are equal to each other. The Value System was developed later on. The value system is not an economic concept but a mathematical concept, which is purely a number game. This is not a concept that represents economy in any manner.

Here the points need to focus is Money—Wealth—Gold. This is a triangular relation.

Before moving further let us understand the liquidity and Liquid which gives better understanding about multi-currency world and value of money.

The economy with money as Liquid can be compared and understood using Milk.

Today we have different milks in individual nations as similar as Milk from different creatures on earth.

An economy with currency can be compared as pure milk from which we can have different benefits. If you mix anything else to it, to any fraction, you cannot get the results as required.

Adding foreign currency to the existing money quantity is nothing but mixing milk from two creatures.

Adding more and more liquid will dilute and pollute the original milk.

Consolidation in Economy means, Milk becoming curd. Can you make good curd/yogurt with corrupted milk?

Can you mix two creature's milk and drink? We don't get the taste and other characteristics.

As we know Milk if contaminated will be broken. Similarly, our society can be considered as Milk with us and our thoughts as particles of Milk. We as solid component of

Milk and our thoughts could be liquid component of milk. That milk could be broken when contaminated.

Contamination could be by anything, as simple, as just a difference in understanding of a small point.

When milk is in good condition, it can be made as curd and cheese can be made out of it and many more. Milk can be consumed to gain strength. Here strength in Milk represents the Unity of the Society, when unity is there, anything can be achieved. It means, we are consuming the Unity of our society for our benefit.

Currency either Paper-based or Metal-based or other type of technologies is not available to all nations. USA that has understanding on the currency concept always stays, vigilant about all the developments in the area of currency and related field.

I will give one example how lethal this currency value system is.

I already told you about the impact on petroleum product prices due to currency value system. RBI will do devaluation, will rise the price of imports which reflect as price rise in petrol.

This will result into fight between Auto driver and Passenger of that auto.

Here Auto driver might be forced to use Kerosene in his Auto instead of Petrol and committing "Crime."

Now this Currency value system is moved to Global level. Imagine yourself how a no where related activity will impact your personal life and you will be forced to commit crimes.

# 18 MONEY–WEALTH–TRANSACTION

The moment Money was born and became a universally acceptable currency, the hidden meaning behind it was Money is representing a "Transaction". Money is a paper with a Number but that is meant for carrying a "Transaction."

We must define here, what is a transaction? A transaction is always with exchange of a tangible Product or Service in exchange of Money.

We need to recall here one major fact, the relation of Money—Wealth—Gold was purely surface level relation. Gold doesn't have to be in reserve of Ruler. Gold could be anywhere in the geographical region with anybody in any form. It means, a currency that is representing, usually a nation, where people of different kind live in. However, a nation is mainly represented by its political power. Earlier political powers were in the form of Rulers/Kings and now Governments. Earlier it was defined against the Gold Reserve with Ruler which was not the right representation of the wealth because common people also possess gold, or there could be Gold ore. So the relation of quantity of money and quantity of gold is not accurate.

Now let us look at the relation between money and wealth. Wealth can represent Gold but Gold cannot represent wealth. Wealth is a larger matter than Gold. In a nation, wealth could be in different forms.

They are resources of different kinds and capabilities. Resources could be usually natural resources. Capabilities usually represent the human capabilities like knowledge and skill.

Now Money relation with Wealth has a broader perspective and it lost the limitation of representing only against the quantity of Gold.

So Gold is not there in Picture at all. While searching the facts about understandings the quantity of money and factors those define them, whomever I could interact with, has this impression of Gold Quantity in reserve as basis for printing money.

Here I need to explain about something else in order to make you understand the prevailing understanding with all those EXPERT ECONOMISTS having DOCTORATES.

For example, two persons made tea individually. Both have the same resources. One has made a very tasty one with accurate use of ingredients and the second is not good. Now the taste of Tea tells several details about the expertise of people who made it and the process if we post-mortem and analyse all facts.

Everybody on this earth is a Taste Expert by Birth, everybody has to agree with this.

Similarly, the behaviour of the so called Economic Experts in India and their proposals, statements, decisions and many more reflects their understanding and expertise in the subject that they have been dealing with.

The fact is, whomever India has been having at top chairs as experts to control their economy are not at all economists and they don't have any expertise in that area.

Just about one month ago from the date I started writing this book, there was a proposal in papers that Government is looking for Gold deposits from temples to Government reserve. The objective was not told to anybody but the only purpose that government can use it for is printing new money.

Printing new money is right or wrong? You will decide at the end of this book by yourself.

The above said lack of expertise with the experts, is not their fault, it is the fault with the education system of India that has been inheriting very wrong understandings since ages.

So now the new relation might be understood well now. It is Money—Wealth—Transaction.

Here Transactions need to understand again in detail.

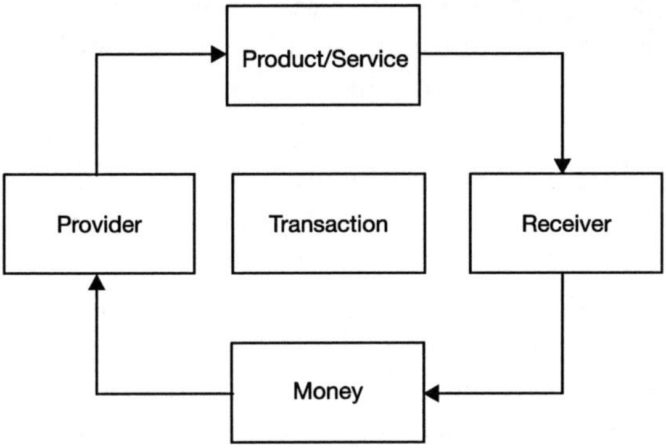


Look at the arrow flow above to understand more in detail. One significant fact to notice is Money can only be in the transaction against a product or service and not by itself.

Now here let us focus on two important aspects of Money. One is Quantity of Money. Second is Quality of Money which is value.

How to decide the Quantity of Money?

I may have to take you through a hypothesis. Let us assume that there is no body on this earth and there are only two persons and they are using Money as Exchange for their transactions. Let us assume that there is only one transaction per day between them in alternative direction. Then how much money is decided by the Transaction "Price". Say it is ₹1 then, Rupee one is enough or equivalent Change in Coins. And now I leave this here for you to expand this by yourself. Don't worry, I know you have some idea by now about how to look at Quantity of money.

India has 120 crore People. As per the calculations, these 120 crore people do transactions of around ₹200 per day. Means, how much money in quantity is required for a person to keep in his pocket per day. Let us say ₹200. So India requires minimum of ₹24,000 crores of Money in Quantity per day.

In Economic terms, this Quantity of money is referred as "Liquidity" which is as similar as Water. We know that human may be able to live without food but cannot live without Water for long time. Similar Properties are there in the present world where everything is transacted by Money. Symbolically it is to know that life cannot move forward without water or money equally.

Our body transacts using water to live in this nature. Our life transacts using money to live in this world. Now let us see the value of Money. Value of money has multi-dimensions.

First, Value of money is related to the price of the Transaction. To understand this better, let us consider our daily life. Say we are buying 1 Kg Rice. If Price of 1 Kg Rice raised from ₹1 to ₹10 then Rupee value is rised or fell? We all know that Rupee lost Value. This is known to everybody.

However, when Price of product rises, we see raise in profits so we are happy to see the price rise as good sign. There is a reason for this. India has been always having rising cost of living since ages. And nobody has a clue about the reason for continuous rise in prices. The price rise has always been attributed towards several different reasons such as rise in population, poor product availability, inefficient practices of production in India and many more. But the fact is different.

The fact is the introduction of money and not understanding the concept associated with it that has been the major reason for all problems in India.

One more fact that we must not forget or remind ourselves now is Money is Number/s and not real but imaginary.

One pity part is Indians are not able to understand it even after 200 years. For Indians, those have been practising barter system even till 1980s, were not familiar about this imaginary concept. Those got educated in finance also do not have proper understanding of it which is clearly reflecting in the society of India everywhere.

Due to this, rulers, leaders, economists, finance experts, stock market experts, educated, uneducated and common man, everybody has the same understanding. This is the reason why they always speak about the quantity of money, and not to the quality of the money.

More Numbers are representation of more Wealth is the belief of Indians.

There is a reason for why Indians are not able to understand it. The society of India is more familiar about the visible and tangible ones and not familiar with intangible and invisible ones that requires more brain, imaginary and thinking capabilities. If we look at the society of India it is clear that since ages, Indian society has been giving preference to quantity of cattle at back yard, quantity of paddy bags, quantity of land, quantity of everything is matter. The same continued to consider that quantity of money as right understanding because quality of money is not in their hands. Quality of money is a result of several issues and such issues are usually in the hands of Government. Government was in the hands of British. Transition of power to India did not transit the knowledge, understanding and perspective of the money.

*Since this has been the understanding in Quantity, Indians could be able to understand only Quantity of money but not able to understand the concept of Quality with respect to money.*

*Similarly, the great Sensex joke in Mumbai Stock Exchange and the associated media and market analyst's comedy every day. There has been predictions around that reaching 40,000 mark, how funny is that?*

The kind of means that Indians have for gaining knowledge is the Accounting education in colleges and universities. Even knowledge about banking system is not being provided in schools or colleges. Whatever is able to gain through accounting subject will later be used in the professional environment and to gain the knowledge of some different perspectives required for the job. Even people who are responsible are not able to gain that knowledge. Who are those responsible people?

The responsible people are economists, administrators and rulers. What I am able to find from the contemporary to historical information, even economists after 1970 have lost the sense of economic thinking.

Administrators also failed to understand and demonstrate Administrative capabilities. Rulers are not different as several ill qualified got into the leadership roles due to several different reasons.

However, what I figured out was, the collapse of Indira Era that was the start of the deterioration of India. The conclusion that I arrived from the post-mortem of Indian Economy that leadership of India was targeted and certain means were adopted to do it, when I found that Manmohan Singh's act of Intentional devaluation of Rupee against Global Currencies under the name of improvement in Global Competitiveness, one thing was confirmed to me that there is much larger picture of activities in execution mode across the world, knowledge about which is not in the reach of awareness of Indians, though experts have global exposure and are renowned internationally.

I started analysing the developments in the present world. I always used to find proposals or policies that works against Indian welfare. I used to wonder why and how such thoughts born in India!!

Take the case of Food Security Bill.

In a human life, Food is the primary requirement. Food Production is the Primary requirement. If transactions at Food Production level is completely destroyed then what would be the fate of the nation.

# 19 EMPLOYEE UNIONS

Indian GDP if is ₹100, ₹30 of it is the budget of both central and state.

Out of this ₹30, 85% of it is equal to ₹26 is going towards Government employee salary and other infra expenditure.

Total Government employees are hardly 3.5 crore population of the nation approximately which is hardly 2.5% of the nation's population.

2.5% of nation's population is consuming revenues equal to 26% of the GDP as income.

Only revenues equal to 4% of the GDP being used for public works.

Government employees are taking the route of unions in order to blackmail the ruling chairs for increasing their income.

This kind of distribution of revenues to individuals creating dent in developing facilities common to all nation.

It is the responsibility of Bureaucrats to see that such situation of blackmailing should not arise but they are not doing that. They are taking advantage of these agitations for their personal purpose ignoring the purpose of tax system.

One major threat is that the income of Government employees is delinked from the status of Economy and its success which has made the nation more complicated.

Since all Government employees are educated, it is their individual common sense that should make them motivate to change the situation in nation, especially Union Civil Service Executives and experts of Government of India.

One of the incidents caught my attention was the demand from Government employee unions for pay review and hike in salary in tandem to the expenditure rise. Until that point of time, pay revision was at the mercy of decision of Government Ruling. There were huge agitations around the revision of Salaries by government employee unions. Ruling bodies were not in a position to raise the salaries because the tax collection was supposed to be adjusted for salaries and maintenance of the nation, and welfare schemes. Since Ruling bodies were not taking decisions to raise the salaries, a new proposal popped up. It was constituting Pay Review Commissions. A commission that comprises of Government Employees. The Pay Commission is constituted by employees and reviewed by them and approved. I found the "committees" technique very strange because there was no democratic body representation. This is to avoid all elected ruling bodies from the ruling of the nation and its subordinate systems. This is threat to the nation's economy.

After the constitution of pay commissions, changes were brought into the pay review structure of Government employees, first thing happened in the nation was disconnection between their income and to that of Indian Economy. Even if the Economy doesn't have enough income and not doing good still salaries are being paid by taking loans from foreign sources. Policies are amended to that effect frequently.

The broken link between employee salary and local economic condition led to the point where government employees are completely ignorant of their duty towards the nation.

Today, Government employees receive 150% of the basic salary as dearness allowance as compensation to the inflationary effect in terms of prices. Also that Dearness Allowances will amalgamated into basic salary when it crosses certain percentage of the basic salary. From there onwards, same DA will be calculated on the new Basic Salary.

For example: Original Salary is ₹100 and if DA is 100% then DA is ₹100, when both are amalgamated, total basic salary will become ₹200, from here onwards. From here DA will be calculated on new basic.

Such policies are supposed to be not allowed by Union Civil Service Executives belonging to Finance Department of India but here Politicians are being targeted as Villains. Everybody has been contributing to the situation of destroying the nation economically.

Let us recall what I said earlier about Rupee Value falling, intentional devaluation. Also I referred about World Bank loans. I raised alarm about the foreign loans to India and foreign investments into India. Around then huge criticism started in media about World Bank involvement in every government policies. World Bank has been actively conducting different surveys, preparing data points, and have been suggesting different solutions that benefits.

I wrote several emails to CM YSR of AP. There was news article about his approach for local loans where there was no hope from any local body which are cash rich such as LIC or Banks or other finance institutions. They were asking for surety for their loans. They were not trusting the legal system to safeguard their investments. This was a surprise to me. An Indian companies that are having the investments from Indians are not lending money to the Government of India, state government, PSUs and other public companies for the betterment of India, but World Bank has been encouraging and offering loans left and right to every project in India. I found it strange.

Also at the same time, I used to find cooperative behaviour between several different entities starting from Central Government, like Finance Ministry of India, department of economics, CAG, state government departments and administrators to the tune of World Bank. Ruling chairs used to propagate them as Loans at Cheap price, obviously that is the understanding provided by all the workforce of Government with proper qualifications.

The World Bank involvement, capability of influencing the Government policies led me to focus on the operations of World Bank and IMF. I reviewed its history. World Bank and

IMF were constituted by USA and UK after World War II from the same building in order to provide assistance to the devastated nations in second world war. They have been actively involved in training the top chairs of government in all along with top economists and professors.

World Bank has been engaging Indians in their operations in India. Indian individuals who are highly scored in education. Even politicians in ruling chairs are trying to maintain close relation with those employees of World Bank for funds as similar as an industry owner with banks.

The media news and tandem behaviour in Government and no response from concerned Government departments criticising the World Bank activities are clearly showing the indicators that World Bank has been using influencing tactics in different ways. It was showing "paths" as CORRECT "Solutions". But the fact is that Indians are there to provide all such "corrupted suggestions."

This has cleared me two things.

World Bank has been doing the following things.

1. Conducting several different surveys and studies on India, and its social and economic systems.
2. Set an agenda as that is Funding for Economic Development.
3. Appoint local talent
4. Use them to influence local government
5. Rest will be assured:
   (a) Local talent in order to have their personal career benefits work for the Agenda of World Bank.
   (b) World Bank never gets exposed.
   (c) Purpose will be solved and attained.
   (d) Foreign loans to local projects.

In the projects that Government has been executing as projects for development, material would be Indian and manpower would be Indian, but Money would be foreign one.

Unless foreign money is taken as loan, nothing has been starting in India.

Here, what happened to the capabilities of IAS officers is another question.

The objective of World Bank Loans around the world by USA in US$ terms is to expand the transaction power of US$. Recall here earlier what I said about the Money—Wealth—Transaction. The more transactions in a specific currency represents the strength of that Currency. This strength of the currency is nothing but Value of Currency.

USA has strategically used World Bank and IMF to establish US$ into other economies.

How this impacts India?

Let us say India has ₹100 Quantity. You know now about Quantity of Money.

When foreign money comes into India from World Bank in US$ form, that money after transforming into Indian Rupees will be added to the ₹100 that is already existing in India.

Let us analyse the developments due to this foreign fund inflow.

The new foreign money creates new rupee money.

New Rupee money creates new transactions.

New transactions demands for new resources.

Rise in demand for resources is creating pressure on their prices which is leading to rise in prices.

Now you have to focus on one more point. The existence of Currency is nothing but representation of Expenditure and not Income.

However, Indians consider money existence is INCOME representation. Of course, a person receives money as Exchange for his Services or Product. However that money is actually an Expenditure coming to him for spending. This is the economic angle of it.

For Human, individually, coming in money appears as income.

*For Economy it is exactly opposite. Money represents Expenditure and Consumption.*

Here is a catch to understand more importantly.

Money that come inside has to leave also. While coming in, Rupee doesn't get appreciated against US$. While Leaving, US$ gets appreciated because Rupee income will be used to purchase US$ by World Bank or by RBI while returning the money.

To understand the impacts of such foreign inflow let us see the following scenario.

Assume that there are 10 members in a room with ₹1 in each hand. Each one of them has been buying or selling only using that quantity of ₹10. As long as Quantity is not changed their activities will not be impacted. However the Interest rate will add both Income and Expenditure to them.

Now a new person is allowed to join. This new person has come with US$. Now assume that 1 US$ = ₹50, then what will happen to the transactions, and money and people in the room.

Similar thing started happening in India due to Foreign Fund inflow into Public Projects of India.

The new money will create new Liquid and new liquid will disturb the existing people life.

When Money is flowing in, RBI should pay more attention towards controlling the rise of the existing liquid. But RBI has completely ignored this.

In the room of 10, the product prices will rise due to large money with new entrant. This will result into rise in prices. Rise in prices rises taxes so government reserves appear to be rised with income. Income levels will rise with people in the room due to rise in prices of products.

But.... But pay attention that in the hierarchy that I said above, about Product Cost Structure, except Profit everything rises, Profit is a probable element and everything else are non-probable components.

When Profit is probable, your income is probable. So you will always be with insecure psychological state.

*The "negative" impact of this liquid inside would be Unlimited. To what extent your imagination could go is not sufficient to understand it.*

Let us first start from entry point of World Bank or other foreign funds for infrastructure. When the tenders are called for, the money will start flowing to Government contracting companies, those usually will have intense participation of Politicians, Bureaucrats, Contractors, and many more.

At first level, money will stay there with them so that they can be rich and control the economic condition of the nation. Also Money will be made available to them as and when is required by World Bank. If we carefully look at the behaviour of Politicians, Bureaucrats, Contractors and many more, they always play safe with World Bank because whenever they need money, it is the only bank that has been providing money to them.

The availability of money or supply of money to those powerful people directly helps in impacting the Elections of India as well.

When Product prices rise inside India, then what will happen? When the products are becoming unaffordable, technology development will become more and more expensive and when existing practices are becoming obsolete, when new technology development is becoming impossible, then what would be the result? We have in front of our eyes, we will become incapable persons when compared with fast growing world in all aspects. Our knowledge, creativity and many more will be dampened. We cannot perform.

When the prices are rising, industries or businesses would be unable to maintain their balance sheets? They will be in tension of meeting their ends and would be in frustrated state and in hurry hasty decisions would be taken, and they would be committing severe blunders; and to cover those blunders would be committing more mistakes. Here I am saying mistakes because their blunders are on "assumed" causes. But the actual cause is in the form of large liquidity due to foreign fund inflow.

Is this all? NO.

In the product cost component hierarchy, there would be one significant part, which is related to Man power. Man power is the only place where some compromises can be made by employers. Man power also would be the resource that can change its behaviour based on needs. Like stretch beyond capability, eat less and perform more, suffer but try to improve performance, frustrate still laugh and stay calm. In the same lines, Adults could be replaced by Children in order to do the same job. Hence committing the unwanted mistakes of engaging child labour. Using Women for wrong jobs. At the end to be competitive, employer has to do all sort of nonsense.

The same impact results into black marketing, tax evasion, thefts, bribery, and many more.

Now there is one thing that we must focus on. Is the loan from foreign source a valid one? I would say NO.

Taking loan from foreign source is an invalid one. To explain this I may have to take you to the core of the issue.

Whatever explained in this chapter is one aspect of price rise. After completion of reading entire book you would understand all the reasons for price rise.

# 20 CHANGE MANAGEMENT

The world has different currencies in different nations. Each nation's currency is meant for transaction within that economy.

Register this in your mind that "Economy means Transaction/s."

Successful economy means, Profitable transactions. This sounds simple and known topic. Trust me, it is not.

Transactions could be of two ways.

Assume that in a Room, a pot of water is there and 10 members in the room are consuming 1 pot in a day, 100%.

The availability of water and Consumption are equal.

Variation in Consumption could be:

1. The same 10 are consuming same quantity of water in lesser time due to environment or wastage
2. One additional person gets added to the team.
3. Added some flavour, means flavour is addition to the water that is causing more attraction of consuming water.

What I am trying to say here is rise in number of transactions creates new economy. As long as the new transaction is from native resources, not imported resources, required new money that can be added to the system anytime at the will and wish of that nation's administrators.

However, adding liquidity should be adequate so that excess money may lead to unnecessary rise in prices as I explained above.

The foreign loan, as per the established guidelines, when each nation wants to maintain its own currency, no currency is allowed to enter other nation's arena. It is invalid hence the foreign loans.

However, foreign money inflow is projected as right choice and only choice available to India by renowned economists and columnists. Not only limited to that, flow in of forex money will be converted to Rupee money at Trading Value in forex market.

Now the question needs to address is, is the trading concept valid? Before we look at this, let us just look at ourselves and laugh at ourselves about this concept of "Importing numbers."

Before that let us see the foreign money. Foreign money is equivalent to foreign body to our body. Let us say, we need water to our body, 5-litre a day. Do we drink water or something else instead?

Water cannot be replaced by any other Liquid. Every other liquid may be tasty and that sounds reasonable to consume but side effects will always be there.

Rupee currency for India is pure water. Adding anything to it is nothing but polluting its water. It means, our economy is polluted. We know what blood is. Similarly, blood of Indian Economy is Rupee. When that blood is added with foreign liquid, say we are injecting water to our body using Syringe then what? Will it create problem or not? That similar disaster has been happening to India.

Here, please refer the skill and capabilities of Economists or other specialists who are being considered as specialists or experts. Are they really so?

Now let us focus on trading of Currency against each other.

When we are talking about Currency, what are we talking about?

Numbers.

What are numbers?

Imaginary figures.

What if imaginary figures are trading against each other and generate new set of numbers? How funny is that?

Money—wealth—transaction relation is completely wiped out.

Money is trading against each other. No productivity. Only gambling is happening in terms of numbers and such transaction is creating new money/numbers as profit in one currency terms and at the same time reducing the money/numbers in another currency terms.

When money is not related to any transaction with tangible product/service is involved, money existence itself is invalid. Because the existence of money is basically to simplify the complexity of carrying exchange medium such as metals/any other as under barter system. Now when the transaction is not involved, money is invalid. Money cannot create transaction against itself. However this is corrupted by world renowned economists and started committing crimes in all the economies across the world to favour some currencies.

Are all such concepts being created by public demand or they are being evolved and implemented from unknown source? No.

All such corrupted systems are being properly conceptualised carefully after proper effort with great mathematical scientists and economists and are being propagated properly with logical reasoning and are being properly promoted as legitimate practice, and are being established across the world in every nation.

All such activities are being carried out using "Highly Intellectual Platforms."

Remember here the World Bank/IMF programs of conducting training sessions and other activities to all top finance and economic chairs of every nation across the world. This is the starting point. However, this effort is not limited to here to achieve results as expected.

Here Proper Management techniques are being used in order to implement such concepts. In Management, we all know about Change Management. For this they are using different tactics.

The old change management principles of India were, Start with conciliation or gentle persuasion (*Sāma*). If that does not help, offer money/material wealth (*Dāna*). If that still does not change the status quo, use threat or cause dissension (*Bheda*). Use punishment or violence (*Danda*).

These were the old tactics and they were considered as part of Politics and ruling. They were suitable and valid in feudal systems. Then Management was not considered as Significant Subject. Now the world has Management and the tactics are different.

The significant new management principle of the present world is Change Management. Global Forces are mastered in this due to their global exposure and understanding. How change management would be implemented by Global Forces, let us see.

Let us assume that a policy is required to be implemented in India or anywhere on earth. Assume the FDI into Retail.

For any policy to be created, starting point would be "existence of a problem", a problem that is considered as Significant and mammoth in nature and existence of it is the core of all other problems.

First step is creation of the problem. Now, Problems don't get surfaced easily. Existing some failures or some understandings or perceptions should be studied and used them to build a problem. Problem and existing perception should be mixed well like milk and water. When the problem is properly conceptualized or conceived in the society, then propagate debate for reasons, make sure that reasons are very well matching the problem and at the same time provides a meaning that our final objective would the result of those reasons. All reasons or majority of reasons should appear that they are targeting the objective as solution.

The first work here is, creating and spreading information that projects the "Problem" and its "meaning."

The above said is the story. Now we need actors and stages to where the above said story would be played as drama in real time.

There are several different stages for this drama. Not only that there will be different sub parts played at different stages.

First let us focus on different types of stages. Stages could be private or public. Private could be of general or niche. Niche could be of experts. Public could be of Newsprint, TV, social media etc.

Now actors need to be identified. Actors could be of different types as

1. Tier 1 or Tier 2 or Tier 3 Direct Beneficiaries
2. Indirect beneficiaries
3. Brokers
4. Catalysts
5. Jokers
6. Loose talkers
7. Side trackers

In order to carry forward this exercise, there required a third party contract hosts (TPs).

Throughout the exercise, the actual beneficiary or sponsor who is the core of all the drama will never be exposed anytime to the public.

The TPs will choose the participants very carefully for Catalysts or Influencers. Now these catalysts and influencers are not identified just like that. They study the understandings and perceptions of the individual and their aspirations and then they choose them aptly and provide them opportunities through different forums to show them as VALUABLE ones. For example, please remember here the professor and his KPIs in order to keep him successful in his personal career. In such requirements, there will be a platform created in order to maintain such VALUABLE ones handy when required. Sometimes, such large exercise may not be feasible, so identify one and prepare one in short time. During FDI, a professor started tossing caste system and backwardness as one of the reasons why he has been supporting FDI. In any case, catalysts and influencers are properly identified.

Here, I would like to mention about the creation of caste based reservation system in India. That might be written by Ambedkar, but we need to focus on what might be happened to bring up such system as solution to a social problem.

What was that "information" and "thought" that brought out by this "backward castes" into light and led to a division in the "thoughts and understanding" of nation at the time when Indians gained independence on "All Indians are equal", and "united India" and "unity in diversity", just try to answer the question, when such unity was there in the nation, how this "Caste-based reservation" took birth, what were those seeds that led to this system of caste-based reservation. This resembles the Indian division on religious grounds, trick played by British that divided India to form Pakistan.

When I consider several different policies of Government of India, our nation builders had created all such systems which provide equal opportunity to all citizens of India equally. They all categorised as Primary Rights.

They are, as far as I remember, from childhood, free education, free health, freedom of expression, free drinking water and many more as Primary Rights.

I am completely convinced by such policies of Government that everybody under the constitution was provided with Equal Opportunity to work and excel.

However somewhere some seed was implanted as "Socially deprived", hence "Eligible for special Treatment."

Such Seed has become a major weak point of inducting "Poor Capability Persons" into "Highly Efficient Jobs."

Now, all those so called "representatives of weaker section" might think that this is against their welfare or something else.

I will give one of my own experiences here as example what is the Complete 360 degree of this issue. I am a forward caste person with no support from Government in any manner. As far as I know, I or my father or his father's family never used any benefit from Government or from nation. However they paid all their liabilities to Government and the nation.

I lived as Immigrant outside India and found that my life in India as citizen of India is not different from that immigrant life in foreign nation where I don't have any rights.

This inequality is a major "divide and rule" principle where a person like me always think of others whom I feel that they are getting benefited unreasonably.

Now it is our call to put stop for this or we still continue as "FOOLS OF EARTH" playing for the tricks of Global Forces. Also living with reservation equivalent to living at mercy of others, living without pride, living without capabilities.

Why I am saying Global Forces here, I am 100% sure that their role is there in seeding such ideas in the nations. Because they are mastered in doing that without leaving a trace of their plot.

Now using the above they will create situations in the nation using media. News spread through media will create proper environment and create some jokers and loose talkers. At the same time, Brokers will be used in Media in order to create positive news spread through arguments.

This will create an environment that will project the objective as the one and only solution available for solving the problem.

Now one question may arise. Who is going to fund all this? The actual beneficiaries will fund this. However one important point here is, let us focus on the US$ and Indian Rupee Conversion rate. As much cheap would be the value of Rupee against US$, that much cheap would be the effort cost in terms of US$.

Let us recall here my earlier statement about export competitiveness and related US$ vs INR conversion price and its impact. The stronger US$ and its daily rise in strength against other currencies, has created a situation that around the world resources are exported to USA at cheap price. This is a kind of twister that has been sucking in all resources from around the world to USA.

The cheap resources around the world has provided not only import capability of USA but the opportunity CHEAP EXPENDITURE in other nations for all its political plots. The daily strengthening of US$ has been creating more and more profits in terms of US$ while at the same time leaving the expenditure or losses into other economies like India.

This is equivalent to, we are taking losses and expenditure in order to create profit and success in USA. We all know the "Baali" in Ramayana who sucks up the energy of opponent. USA is like Baali of today's world. The more US$ gets strengthened that much more; its efforts will become cheap in other nations and opposite will be for other nations.

We have come to the point where we have completed our understanding about Money, Finance, Numbers world and Virtualization with numbers. Let us move forward towards the understanding of a mammoth disaster due to some small changes on a paper projecting them as for the good of people and welfare of the nation.

Now there could be a question that because of trade deficit or current account deficit and many more jargons will be used to explain the reasons for US$ strengthening against other currencies.

Global forces have created some useless fellows who live and survive on numbers written on paper as experts and have been fooling the world. These are human bombs.

The conventional human bomb impact could be limited but these human bombs impact is such a viral one, identifying it itself takes longer time and proving it takes even more longer time but the damage will be done by them to the extent that is equivalent to asteroid hit on earth.

When I found this, I started my effort.

Most of the participants in the exercises of global forces would be very common people. Their aim is to send the word to the world in the dimension they want it.

The same approach I also took with leaders. I need to send counter information to the Global Forces anti-biased information.

Identifying the Biased information is the skill that I have. That is what made me to put my effort and started writing this book.

We all see several advertisements in our life everywhere around us. Propagating information is also one of the powerful tools of change management.

There are different ways to propagate such information. By proper framing of "frames" of different information, Gandhiji also can be projected as "Bad Man" of the world.

We know the most popular medium of propagating such information. It is Media.

# 21 GDP—CAD—INFLATION

I wrote about the unaffordability due to fall of Rupee. Also I wrote about the vision of the leadership of India during the first 30 years after independence to build a knowledge society. This knowledge society was not discussed then but the same is being discussed a lot after 2002.

I wrote about the stopping of Intentional devaluation by RBI. I wrote several emails about the currency value concept to Chidambaram, Finance Minister of India asking him to appreciate Rupee in order to keep the input costs lower. There used to be huge uproar everywhere about strengthening rupee value.

Now is the time to further focus on Economy and understand it better.

There are two types of economies on this earth. One is Virtual one made by using Money and other is Natural one. The real economy is the activities we do in this world using tangible materials. For example, farmer does cultivation and produce food. Tailor sews clothes to give them a shape. Farmer may use 1 bag of paddy and nature gives him back 10 bags of paddy as Product. A tailor sews cloth to give it a shape as service. Product or service are the only two types of transaction usually here on this earth.

**Maslow's** Hierarchy of needs 3D

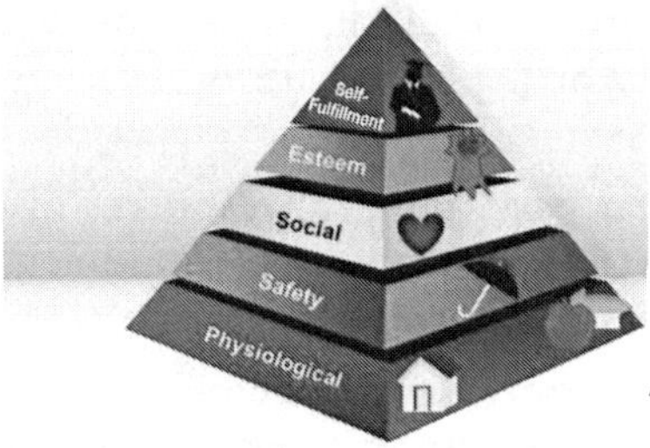


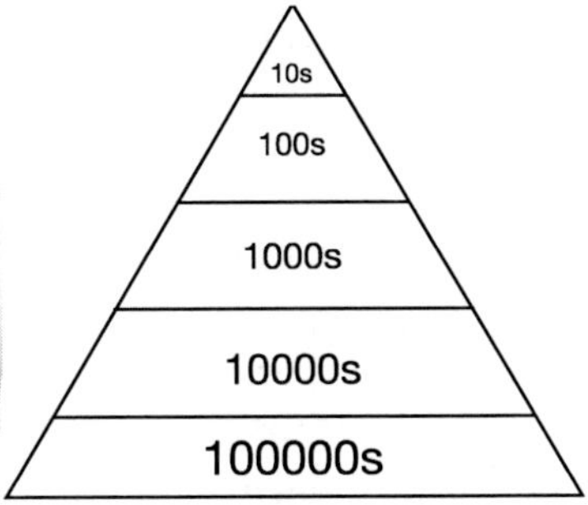


First World Values

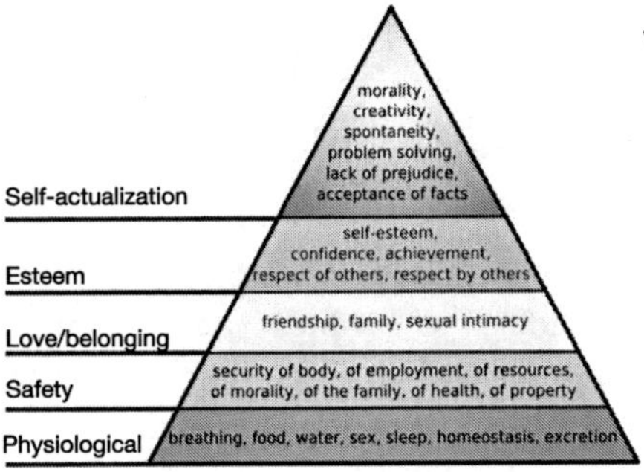


Indian Values

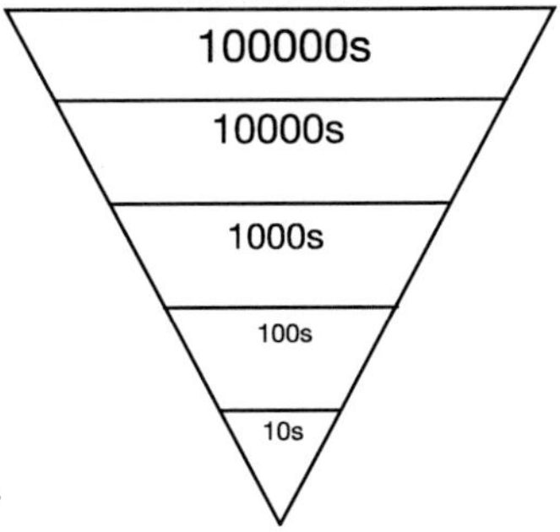


The above is a world renowned Management Theory called Maslow's Hierarchy of needs.

The value/worth of resources being produced required for physiological needs are being reduced in India and the same has been opposite in the first world nations.

The Physiological Needs are the Real economy which is fundamental economy on which the world is based on. Every other economy above that layer is supposed to be within the limits of the real economy in order to be a successful economy together.

The rest of the higher levels in the hierarchy also creates economies that are virtual. As long as the virtual economy lies within the limits of real economy, every economy will be successful. Unfortunately, all other economies except the first one at the bottom are made to go beyond the boundaries of bottom one.

This is one fundamental error of Indian Economy. Indian Economies Physiological Needs have become valueless in the world. All the physical resources of India have become valueless to the world. All the world physical resources have become valuable to India.

In the similar lines, the world psychological resources also have become more expensive to India and the same with respect to Indian psychological resources to India.

In simple words, Indian Economy is made upside down due to poor economists who are not economists but just simple useless fellows.

While writing this book, I need to recall several of my earlier analysis from different angles which are usually get triggered from the live incidents of life because of which the book sometimes appears to be unorganized thoughts.

I would say that this is not a linear subject. Since it is multidimensional in 3D world, the topics are written sometimes to relate the incident and to provide you the perspective.

Throughout my effort, I found two things and concluded that the following are facts. The so called experts of India as Economists, Finance or any other related field with doctorates and in significant positions are not experts at all. They do not have a clue what is the job they are doing. Just because of their situational advantage either by position or by immediate success or acceptance have got the opportunity of reflecting as experts. One example I will give to prove my statement or conclusion here. Every activity or policy of India developed in this regard has always targeted towards more quantity of money but not a single one has ever been made any time targeting quality of rupee. This explains the rest. Not only that but also the statements and the language or bias of activities every one of them always reflects the same.

Let us look at the trade deficit and current account deficit and understand how they are being created!

What is trade deficit? The difference between Import and Export.

What is Current Account Deficit (CAD)? Government requires say ₹100 for all its needs (Government will not have needs, Government needs are nothing but our common amenities) and if Government gets ₹60 then deficit is ₹40 and if it gets ₹110, then it is surplus.

Let us first focus on CAD. How Government gets money? In India, it gets money from Taxes and Investments. In India Government strangely does business. Due to this, Governance is imbibed with Profit expectations in the top chairs.

Also there is one more thing, since British had ruled this nation for longer time whose motive was exploitation of resources for their benefit as a foreigner, and profit from resources as corporate, their ruling was not actually a "Social Political Governance Ruling" but a "Corporate Governance Ruling."

Government of India and its operations and understandings of its participants even today after 66 years, due to lack of capability of identification of such differences of what is difference between social ruling and corporate ruling, has that old British system psychology in its entirety. Hence many times, Government of India policies are concentrated on Income from nation. Government never loses/gains money from its own system. Money in the system of nation rotates through, and Government only picks up some part of it to put through right means and see that money rotates through all systems in full cycle without clogs.

How CAD gets created? To understand CAD, one needs to understand the per capita. What is per capita?

I wrote an article about CAD which was published in Andhra Jyothy. It is available in Appendix–II of this book, it is mentioned as payments Deficit to Government.

This is only a simplified version.

Let us look at 10 member in a room for example. We assumed that they are transacting with each other.

Each member is doing transactions for two times food, it means in a day they are doing two transactions per head, for 10 it is 20 per day; in a year, it is total of 7200 transactions.

Let us say each transaction is Rupee One. It means total of ₹7200. Now when this is divided by 10 members that will give per capita which is ₹720.

The above is equal transaction and equal price scenario.

There will always be variations of any kind. Say for example, the variation is making the total to either ₹7500 or ₹7000. But the total will be accumulated and will be calculated against 10 members equally to derive per capita. If per capita is ₹720, the actual income of one of them could be only ₹100. But per capita is a totality figure.

The total is GDP which is gross domestic productivity. Here in example it is ₹7200.

Here consider only Products and Services between them as Transactions. This is not turnover. This is simplified version of giving you a feeling about GDP.

*Gross—Domestic—Productivity*: Productivity is taken as the individual persons OUTPUT in terms of Money here, which is obviously his/her successful transactions in a year. Pay attention here that One Debit will have Credit with other participant in the transaction.

The GDP of India of 120 crore people is ₹110 lakh crores and per capita is around ₹90,000.

Back in example, out of ₹7200, there could be common things to all 10 members for which they want to contribute some amount. Such amount is TAX. Tax is meant for mutual benefit.

Similarly Government of India collects money from public as TAX and uses that money for public works. Tax money would be collected at different levels of starting from village till central government of India. How to figure out how much is being collected? Sum of budgets of all levels of Government in India will tell the total amount of tax required for Government which is usually will not be accurate.

Here one important point needs to be focused is Transaction and Transaction amount, they are the only matter. Let us focus on the kind of transactions happen in this world.

Transactions could be either between two persons or between organization and person or between two organizations.

However finally, all of them will result into some income of a person only. This is the fact.

Tax collection could be usually either on transactions or on income. However, the income tax is also a transaction tax. As we understand above, tax is for common needs of all the people.

Now if some of the transactions are not resulting as income to government but government spending money to them, then what? This is what exactly happening in India. It is CAD.

Where is it happening and how is it happening? After the so called economic collapse or economic stalemate in 1990, Government had come up with policies where 100% Export-oriented units will not pay any tax to Government in any manner. However they will consume the resources of India and export the resources of India at cheaper price.

In Product component structure that I mentioned above, in every product or service, majority of the percentage would be Tax component. For example, if that component is 20% and if that tax component is removed then what? Product will be 20% cheaper.

When products are exported to USA or Europe or Australia or other places, products in those places would be cheaper than India.

Let us consider the situation of Bulk drug units, established in India after liberalization or economic collapse. They started polluting the nation, and were not contributing any tax money to India to clean up that pollution. Here I should mention one thing with respect to such industries. If Rupee One is required for actual production unit of the bulk drug manufacturing, ₹2 is required to clean up the pollution created by such units. There used to be large pollution due to such units in first world nations who intelligently shifted their needs to nations like India. Indians who were stressed for forex income, felt that as an opportunity to utilize and started bulk drug units and became polluted. Here one more thing that added fuel to the fire of establishing export oriented units, those had connection with foreign land were able to establish the industries left and right. The 20% tax rebate helped the industries use that margin for transport or other purposes from India to far distant lands.

So CAD started getting created due to imbalance in the income and expenditure of Indian Government. This imbalance was attributed towards "it is due to large subsidies being given to Fuel and Fertiliser and food items at different levels". For this we must understand what is subsidy.

As we learnt Government gets its income from several different sources, it has to maintain balance in its economy, for this what it does is, it puts its income in some areas to balance it. It is as similar as in a house with different size people with different levels of needs. Some eat more and some eat less and mother or father will eat less to compensate the food demand. Father and mother subsidized their hunger for kids.

Similarly, Government does not have to "subsidize" but adjusts its money flow to maintain balance. For Government money comes in and money goes out and rotates in the nation of India. Speaking of subsidy etc. reflects the immaturity of the persons and lack of understanding.

Money, that is usually referred as Liquid by all around the world, from that dimension, let us assume it as water. We know water cycle on this earth. Water in ocean gets evaporated during summer to form clouds that rain on land during rainy season which will flow through rivers to reach sea again. Similarly, money always flows through the systems of the nation in circles and reaches Government kitty and comes to flow through again. Meanwhile, Government just adjusts the flows or directs flow of water or money to balance the system. Also economy with Money is like a water bed. When pressure is there in one point, water reaches the opposite side. Balancing is required.

However here with respect to subsidy, the idea of showing Subsidy as major dent or bend in the system is a major CONSPIRACY implemented in India very easily through media and fooled the nation. This was successful because of lack of proper expertise or corrupted fellows in Bureaucracy and Media.

So Subsidy is financial adjustment by Government and nothing else. However, some industries such as Oil Public Sector units gained a lot from such policies of Government and in fact for decades Oil PSUs and their top management had cheated India like anything and ate lot of money from Indian Economy. This was supported by Bureaucrats of Government of India. In order to cover their blunders, they used to give wrong information to the nation to mislead the nation. At one point of time, Govt. called to pay ₹35,000 crores to oil PSUs towards reimbursement of subsidy. This explains the size of the cheating.

Coming to Trade deficit, it is difference between Import and Export. India has been exporting several of its resources at cheap price without tax income to Government One part of loss or burden on the nation is here in this form. Another form is, recall the above said Rupee vs other currencies. We export at devaluated price. If we give 10 items for ₹10 at last year, this year we give 15 items for ₹10. However, on import front, if we get 10 items for ₹10 last year, this year we get five items for same ₹10. Like this we have been losing lot of resources at cheap price and loosing income also.

The situation has led to the point that the purpose of sacrifices done by all those freedom fighters for the welfare of the nation and who formed the nation are completely defeated. Today we are exporting by ourselves at cheap price and also getting fooled by our own fellows. Who are those?

Before I tell you who are those, I need to explain about such persons and their capabilities to make you understand how dangerous they are to the nation of India.

# 22 REAL VS VIRTUAL

To understand who are those, let us look around us.

On this earth there are two kinds of professions. One is the skill that is related to Tangible world and the second is related to Virtual world. For example, a carpenter whose skill is tangible. A lawyer whose skills is only words and expressions which are not tangible.

In Technology Management course, a subject "Technology Creativity" explains about the "Stages of Cognition Process" which I could brief it as sequential steps of:

1. Pre-awareness
2. Awareness
3. Familiarity
4. Experience
5. Mastery
6. Replicate
7. Create

The real time tangible skill requires to have this cognition cycle. What I believe is that Indians have misunderstood, were misled to misunderstand, their old epics due to interpretations by some half knowledge fools. This is the reason why all those belong to real time world are being considered as belonging to virtual world.

The cognition cycle stages explained above are similar to the way how it usually would be written in old epics of India where you attain the capability of "creativity" only after all the earlier stages. This attainment of "Creativity" is nothing but MOKSHA.

One example that I give is, Electric Motor. We were familiar of it using for water pumping in earlier days, later Food Mixers, later vacuum Cleaners and many more. Behind all, only one Fundamental Equipment, Electric Motor. The stage of attaining the state of repurposing the same technique is nothing, but can be said as attained "Moksha."

I somehow was able to relate that the actual meaning was related to the real time tangible world which lateral interpretation made it as "spiritual (non-tangible useless skill)" one in order to kill the capabilities of India.

Do you agree with me? Read till the end to answer this question.

As an example, the above said is similar to "Cooking" at home. Compare yourself from the level of maturity to the level of cooking and mastering it and leading yourself in creating new recipes.

In parallel to the above said stages of Cognition Process, a person would have the same stages which can summarized as:

- Prospective User
- User
- Technician
- Expert Technician
- Engineer
- Expert Engineer
- Scientist

The reason why the above said became the phrases of Non-tangible world could be, Majority of human are not "Leaders" or could not pass through the cognition process of "Leaders", hence can't understand it. Who is a leader and what is his/her cognition cycle? Reader will get the details when he completes the reading of the entire book.

But the society usually has more "non-leaders" or "common man" who would or could only understand all such things as extraordinary things hence the subjects of tangible worlds have become intangible world skills.

Every human on earth has the same brain power with gradient of analyzing skills. Why is it gradient? Some people take longer time to understand and others are able to do it fast. Between these two levels, there will be gradient scale.

A person with good Tangible skills will take slow time to understand, he will go through all the micro-points before coming to a conclusion. A person with large analytical skills will be able to grasp fast but will not be able to achieve excellence in the tangible skills.

The above what I said sounds illogical but I am writing my conclusions based on my observations. Don't conclude it here. I have to assume some dimension to put forward the perspective to understand better. Now the world is believing that the virtual world established by human is very complex one and all those analytical skill fellows are intelligent fellows.

Now such fellows are very much required to exploit the world. This is what has been happening on this earth. Such people are being projected as "leaders". These leaders are not political leaders. These are manufactured leaders from prominent colleges. We can see such fellows today as Administrators/Managers/Supervisors/Monitors/Lawyers, etc.

Contextually, I would like to give one mind-blowing information. In America, tangible skilled persons get more remunerations than nontangible skilled fellows. It means, Technical skills have more value than supervisory or manager skills. This is the fact.

Now the world of Finance is a Virtual world. It is non-tangible. Before finance, we had other systems which are not tangible. The most important one was Legal System.

The Framework of Laws and need for every human to follow such laws as rules of life is there in order to live in a society. As far as my knowledge goes from the information I had gone through, may be right or wrong, not matters, British had introduced the documentation of "Laws of Life for human society" in India. Until then, Indian social rules used to be situational and mutually agreed, and disputes of understandings were resolved by a powerful person in the society, may be by village leader or king that we usually read in our folk tales.

Law that needed to follow was never documented till then.

The introduction of documented law started creating confusion in the society of India. There are several reasons for this, such as:

1. Laws are biased towards power chairs
2. Laws are limited
3. Laws are documented without proper definition
4. Laws are open ended.
5. Laws are misinterpreted
6. Laws are not properly implemented
7. Laws are exploited
8. Laws are taught to general public
9. General public society was having different structure and understanding
10. Lack of literacy and many more.
11. Lack of different dimension of understanding due to limited exposure to distant societies.

I need to give you details about the last sentence here. For example, we in Andhra Pradesh believe that Full Moon is good day and no moon day is bad, which is opposite in Tamilnadu. Some societies allow the marriage between cousins from mother side, and some from father side as well. So such understandings are there, we usually refer as Traditions. Traditions were laws of society until British introduced the LAWS.

This new law created a big opportunity to generate disputes between different sections of society starting from the level of individuals to larger groups. Such disputes have started providing big opportunity for making money for Barristers.

Here one major thing that we all must understand. By drafting the laws as rules of living in a society or nation or state or region, the creators or drafters or inventors of creating laws found that human behaviour can be controlled by some sentences written on paper as laws or rules or conditions to obey.

Also similarly, they found that Money, related profit and loss also impacts the behaviour of human.

A person's behaviour depends on his situational reaction but at group level, group psychology and behaviour would be different from individual.

Human cannot behave as he/she feels like when among group. The laws/traditions will control the understanding and behaviour.

When it is found that Human is more tied towards virtual things than tangible ones by those global rulers, they found it is easy to establish systems comprising of laws, money and human. It is not that they are intellectuals because of which they are able to do it. It is because of their exposure to different societies.

They identified that people who are good at virtual systems, especially who we consider as analytical and manipulative skills, are useful in controlling the local population. If they are provided with the opportunity of income then they will work for the employer.

The introduction of Law and money had started new professions. They are like, lawyers, financial specialists, administrators, managers, supervisors, writers, speakers, astrologists, analysts, and many more like that. The virtual professions were started around the virtual systems.

Since we are talking about law, let us focus on lawyers. Please refer the chapter "Law" for more details on law in India.

Here we need to focus on one important point, though they are having skills of virtuosity, they at the end need all tangible materials such as food etc. to live and survive which they are not mastered in. They have to depend on others for tangible material skills to survive in their life.

Earlier days, when money and numbers were not considered as valuable by human society, such skills were not successful then. The evolution of money with numbers as concept of wealth representation, the virtual skills have become more valuable.

Now one of such skills is related to Economy and Economists. Economists are those who look at the world through numbers and measure the world with numbers. Here is a tricky point to remember that is how individuals interpret numbers.

Economy with numbers is such a tricky subject, Quantity of Money will have different meaning and Quality of Money will have different meaning.

From Economy angle, Quantity of Money into Individual hand is equal to rising Expenditure. From individual person angle, the same would be equal to Income rising for Individual.

From Economy Angle, Quality of money is Income rising. From Individual person angle, Quality of money is less income.

We need to enlarge this more to understand this better.

Let us go back to the same 10 members in a room example. If all have ₹1 in each hand not more than that whatever the transaction happen between them would be in Paisa terms. If the same ₹1 is made ₹10 then the transactions would happen in Rupee Terms. Means, providing bigger numbers, raising quantity of money, rising price of products which is nothing but rising expenditure.

Please pay attention here. In case you have not understood this, please read again and again.

If I increase the money with all 10 equally in the room then the prices rise evenly.

If I increase the money unevenly, like I give ₹10 to one person, say X, only X will transact with Y liberally, X will not mind to pay more to Y. This leads to increase in Quantity of Money with Y. The change may be any extent but it increases money quantity with Y. Now the rest of the people are still having the same transactions in Paisa terms.

Whoever is able to get that new money at increased quantity in their transactions will be wealthy and rich and the rest will be weak, and will be in Poverty. In reality, people who have got forex income will have the power of transacting ₹60 if US$1 = ₹60. People those work with in India would be having their life transactions at ₹1. In between whoever is able to get the income at better levels than ₹1 level will be having better "capability" to meet the risen expenditure. However, the net effect on economy would be the Expenditure is set to ₹60 level when US$1 = ₹60 with varied levels of Income in the economy.

Quantity of Money availability is defining Expenditure and then poverty.

Let us go back to Virtual Skills. The new Virtual Skills with New Virtual Wealth have picked up more and more strength and such skilled fellows are getting better and better day by day. Majority of the times, wrong will always cherish as similar as the present Crony Capitalism being referred by everybody is an example to it in this virtual world.

Since there is more importance gained in Virtual world with Virtual wealth, people in India or other part of the world who are not familiar with the concept of currency have been negatively getting impacted very severely. This skill of Virtuosity has become more important and significant than real skills. Real skill fellows have become more and more working class fellows without leadership qualities.

Since Indians do not have the capability of finding such impact, they have been struggling as similar as any others.

However, those global forces who have exposure to different part of world with different understanding and different perspectives had figured out that the world can be controlled in directly using Laws, terms, conditions and money. More exclusively with money values.

Now you have understood how to create poverty.

The result of this poverty creation is not limited to financial loss but loss of lives as well which is visible as suicides of farmers. Two Lakh fifty thousand farmers committed suicides and those families became orphans. The virtual wealth started hurting the real wealth. The virtual knowledge started hampering real knowledge. The virtual knowledge started killing the real knowledge.

Over and above this, they figured out that the combination of these components will create systems and human behaviour would be in some definitive formats and using money controlling them is very easy.

They started focusing on forming the Entities with Systems.

What are those entities with Systems?

# 23 GLOBAL ORGANIZATIONS

Entities are nothing but organizations and the participants of those organizations. A confluence of more than one person would create an organization, either formal or informal. Such organizations will have their characteristics based on the needs and objectives. Usually such needs and objectives together will lead to formation of a vision for existence of that organization and a mission to achieve that vision.

The one major advantageous thing with the formation of organizations is the vision, mission, objective, agenda and activities could be different from each other and it does not match but the difference can never be able to be noticeable or questionable or suspicious. Let us see how they would be. In order to understand, let us start from the point of understanding organizations. Agenda never dies as long as organization survives.

Organizations' life times are longer than Human. Anything those are associated with organizations sustain for long time, hence agenda. This is one more reason for the success of the first world nation on this earth.

Indians are in dark with respect to several historical knowledge. If that is not the situation, Indians' understanding could have been different, when that is different, then their thinking pattern could have been different, that difference could have made them come up with right solutions to their problems.

In the history, Indians had Systems but not organizations. British also came here as Systems like individual business units for profit. Later British started focusing on the formation of Organizations as part of their effort of taking over the control of India, especially in the form of Military units. Military controlling units of British can be said as first form of Formal Organizations on this earth. Forming organization gives shape to system.

Why I am saying this, organizations are autonomous units.

The evolution of Organizations and their establishment in India and around the world with rules and regulations provided them the opportunity of understanding the benefits of Creating Organizations in real time gives shape to a System and thereby taking control of existing or poorly organized systems.

Indian systems had always been related to then ruling power, religious and social circles that we can see even today.

When organizations were started forming, the organizations require some structure to maintain the power in order to control the organization and its behaviour and some medium to bond the participants together. First one is Law and the second one is Money. Money, numbers, that work as glue to bond the human together.

I wrote above, the documentation of law was introduced by British. One more important thing to understand is, British always used to give utmost importance of documenting about all contemporary developments that the organization goes through. This tells that they figured out the value of data and information about 300 years ago itself. There is a reason for it.

The Globetrotting of Europeans made them to record everything on ships and in their caravans while travelling in order to keep themselves familiar with the places where they had been passing by. This used to be helpful in those days itself because such information could be useful to others as well, and can be sold at price.

Power of information is not known to Indians even today. This is the reason why Indians could not be able to figure out the value of history and they have always been destroying their history which destroys several facts, including techniques and technology. This is another reason why Indians could not be able to be innovative. There are other reasons for Indians not be able to be innovative.

The formation of organizations, creating systems and controlling the human behaviour by those systems have given them the realization and skill of formation of new cultures and behaviours and more accurate expected results when compared to only system. Every organization when formed will have a unique culture. Every organizational system will have its own unique behaviour.

There is one more thing that they are able to figure out. The world has four pillars.

1. Political, Ruling and administration (UN)
2. Education, Knowledge and skills (UNESCO)
3. Wealth, Money and Resources (World Bank + IMF)
4. Human Resource (WHO + UNICEF)

For this the global forces had formed different organizations and started establishing them to closely bond with other organizations around the world.

Here two important points need to be understood.

Systems without organization could be in fluid form and cannot be formally expanded and establish formal bonding with other systems to closely knit and merge each other.

If the same systems became part of an organization then the expansion and merging or bonding with other organization and its system would be more formal, convenient and very tightly bonded. The relation also would be very smooth and uninterrupted. The participants of the organization become the actors of that system who will be very dedicated and committed and will have goals to achieve.

The same has been there in the above said form where—

1. UN is able to establish a very formal and tightly bonded relation with other political and administration organizations and systems across the world.
2. UNESCO for tightly bonding with all education organizations across the world.

3. World Bank and IMF with all Central Banks and economic departments around world.
4. WHO and UNICEF with all the formal health and HR departments around the world.

The most important point needs to be understood here is that they work to influence other organizations and their systems. How they influence other organizations and systems? They use all Change Management tactics for this.

**Secret of USA success**

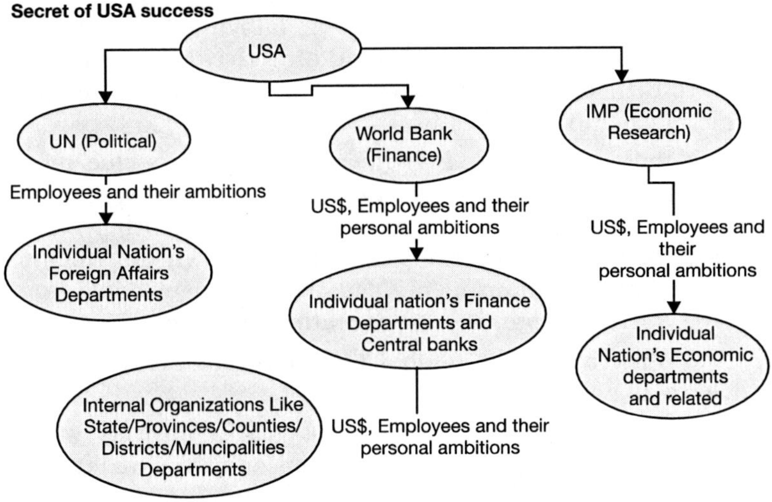


**Individual nation's Employees could be**

1. Bureaucrats (Civil Service Executives)
2. Professors/Specialists/Experts/scientists/economists
3. Media Analysts

**Characteristics of Employees**

A. Individual who live with Greed of Achievements and Strive to retain their control on the situation for their superiority.
B. Least bothered about Social/nation welfare.
C. Love to give charity but do not contribute unless have some returns to them contribution.
D. They Strive hard to corrupt systems to keep them beneficial and in control and for selfish benefits at the cost of nation.

To understand this, we need to get into their operation mode.

Every organization will have a Vision for its existence. However, every organization could have several objectives and associated agendas to achieve its objective with corresponding activities.

They create a project for each objective that they want to achieve. Sometimes objectives could be large and those objectives will be further divided into sub-objectives and individual projects will be created for those objectives. When such projects are formed, the main objective will not be known to everybody except to the top person or somebody who created the Main Objective. Also Main Objective and Sub-Objectives are never put together to give complete picture of the outcome of different projects together.

In this entire exercise, there will be individuals involved at appropriate level with their jobs and objectives of their jobs in return to their personal objective, which is income to them for their survival and social status.

One funny part is that individual will not have a clue about the Main Objective that might be against his own welfare or threat to him and he would be working with a belief of his personal benefits however working for his own destruction. The global organizations mentioned above engage people from the same society where they are executing the projects.

The objective of the Global Organizations would not be known to all participants.

Like this, individuals will be engaged in projects where they could be analysing the other systems and their weaknesses and work to corrupt them. I will give an example here.

I came across a person who works for an organization in India which is a global organization. Global organization is voluntary organization funded by Global firms on charity basis. The objective of global organization is to study the local land ownership traditions and practices in India and also around the world. They operate globally in several different nations. Across the world there will be different practices and beliefs in different regions that are based on that areas living conditions and social understandings.

Now the work of such organization brings in information in several different angles to one place. The top chairs of the organization are collecting such information and they will gain the knowledge of strengths, weaknesses, opportunities and threats of that locality. When such individual deals with that locality, he can use all his other external knowledge and confuse the local understandings.

Every locality will have some weaknesses, this individual with larger knowledge can take advantage such weaknesses and use them for advantage and win over that locality and society. Now that organization is creating framework for Indian land ownership system which is at present in a horrible condition. Also that organization is proposing a new policy that adds fuel to the fire which makes the bad situation lead to worst situation in India, and people will fight each other.

The organization is working closely with Government authorities and other stake holders about creating a law as every person who does not own a plot of land for house is entitled to receive 10 cents of land from Government of India. Does this make any sense? I do not analyse now but you do it by yourself.

Such entire exercise never be suspicious to anybody. Even now probably you as reader may not be able to completely understand the negative consequences of the above policy being created by Government of India.

I got introduced to this fellow through media person who could not find anything wrong with that organization and its activities until I explained with detailed analysis. They were finding it as required for nation. And the new policy was also not found to be bad at all.

Several Government employees of India aspire to be in positions which give name, fame, power, influence and many more at international platform. Same is true with many intellectuals such as professors and scholars etc. Such people always aspire to establish and maintain good relations with such global organizations and consider them as achievements of their life. Also media journalists and analysts aspire to be in touch with such large global organizations in order to excel in their career and get globally acclaimed scholar or achievers.

Remember here that "Employee will do anything for his benefit because his benefits are immediate and tangible ones". If his benefits are hurting the nation, such harmful policies will never surface easily to prove that they are committed with intention. However, the immediate benefit to employee will not be harmed. He is least bothered about any consequences. Exposure of his involvement and proving his malicious intentions behind working on that also cannot be proven. Exposing the blunder itself takes years. This has become advantage to IAS and IPS officers.

Here I should draw your attention towards one more powerful medium. Great Gandhi also used this for his great success. It is the way how Global Forces use it and exploit it. It is MEDIA.

Also here one should notice that Mahatma also adopted a Concept for his freedom fight of India. One major difference between India and global forces either British or America or others that are influencing the world to their dimension is that Global Forces constitute organizations in order to create and carry forward the Concepts. However, in nations like India, concepts are more of person centric. Hence even Mahatma's concepts though popularised well but could not be sustained along the timeline of the human era or Indian nation's timeline for long time.

Media has different forms such as Leaflet, newspaper, books, novels, radio, TV and now latest Internet, social media. Having its support was considered as major strength in ancient India also. It is visible in the form of epics of India such as Mahabharata, Ramayana and many more. Media spreads of Information through ages beyond timelines.

Remember here that writing is also a Virtual skill. Such career in historic era was not feasible and helpful for surviving unless some wealthy fellow recognized such activities and provided them livelihood. Here we need to recall the era of Ashoka, and Universities of Nalanda during prehistoric era.

It means virtual career has been there in India for ages.

Was it prehistoric era? I don't think so, based on their traces available even today but Indian history had always been destroyed by invaders, their history had been losing the fundamental inheritance of heritage of knowledge from history. When history details are not properly maintained, even 100 years old would become 1000's of prehistoric rock age era. The end result would be tangible world and will become a world of illusion.

Using Media anything can be achieved and manipulated with the help of Information. This is not something that I am trying to tell you as I invented it. But there is one thing that is to be understood here.

That Manipulation is the secret of the Global Politics.

Before I tell you that I should mention about one major Management tool which is called "Cause and Effect Diagram" or "Fish bone diagram" or "mind mapping diagram" or "hierarchy diagram". This is a major tool that would be used so extensively across the world in strategy designs.

The same are usually called as Plan of action and alternatives plan of action.

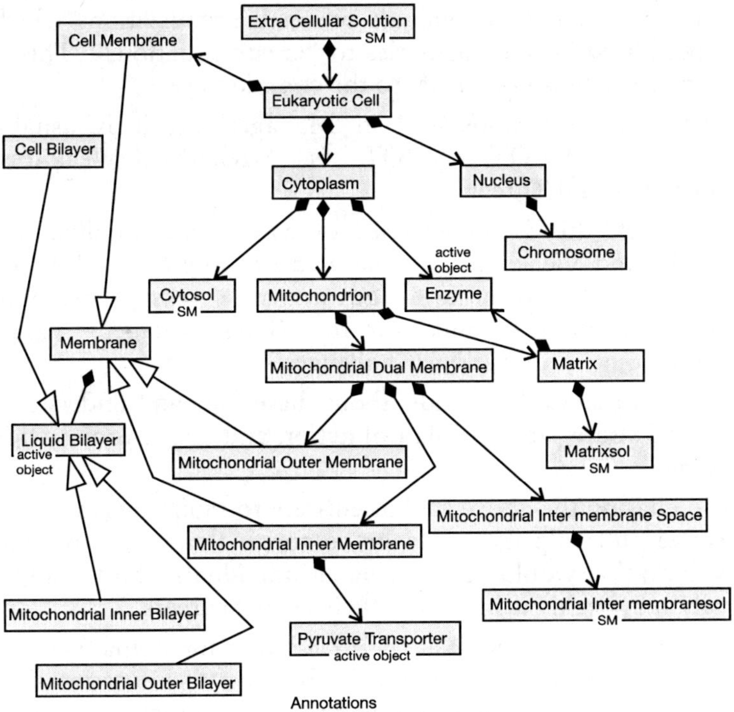


Annotations
SM: contains small molecules
active object: has rules that act on small molecules

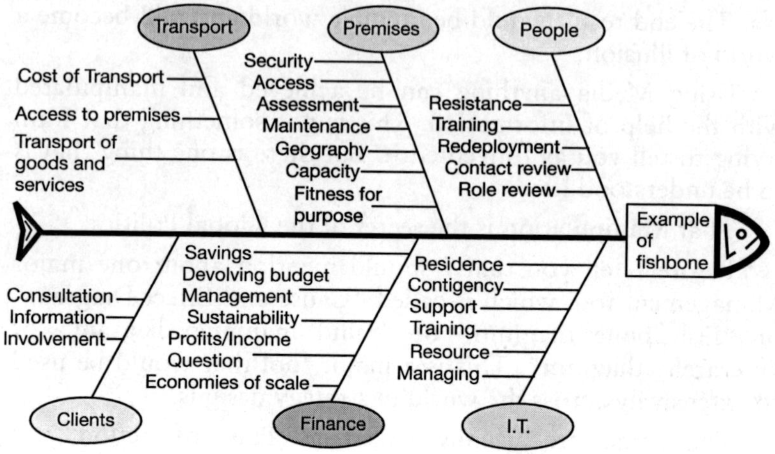


The secret is "creating situations". Global Forces create projects and engage individuals or small organizations which are specialized in some activities to "create situations". This is the secret which is not visible to the common eye.

There is one more tool in Management, it is usually referred as SWOT. SWOT is Strengths, Weakness, Opportunity and Threat.

In brief, this is an exercise of assessment. Finding out Strengths and Weaknesses of the area of "interest". Also List out of Opportunities (advantages, easy winning points/propositions.) and threats (Disadvantages, tough winning points/propositions/Challenges.)

Global Forces do a study about these four and understand them and strategize their plan of action and create projects for the same.

So chasing the above said at entirety to figure out the main objective and culprits would be so tough that anybody who tries to do that would be fingering at individuals who would be usually very highly achievers in their virtual careers.

Here we need to look at the foundation for virtual careers. The virtual careers foundation is in the form of Education that we are being put through since childhood which is nothing but the information being given to individuals based on which the individual considers it as "Correct" to accept and follow and adopts to behave as Good Behaviour.

Government employment is also a virtual career.

Here one needs to understand an important point, nobody on earth can survive without Tangible needs. Also creating tangible products is not that easy. It requires scientific and technological skills. It is innovation.

Creating Virtual Concepts is easy and doesn't require any skill but just some saleable story.

Such concepts are being created left and right in financial world to fool around the world based on Currency values for several decades. For this they are creating some Pseudo Experts who are really half knowledge fellows and do not have the idea about the fundamentals of concept of money with numbers and different things working on the society. This has become an advantage to Global Forces. They have been using such fellows in order to create policies that work against India and create more and more troubles in India by Indian Government itself with their own political leaders by using their systems.

Here you may have understood, why British might have left India! They left India because their systems were here. They were confident in that controlling them using several other means, one of it especially is the "Currency value" System. Also remember here that America and British are not different, but only different by name.

By using the Global organizations, you can see the word often in papers "sanctions" against specific nations.

By means of these sanctions, the so called puppet economists around the world will be made to implement procedures in such a way that specific nation will not have any import or export operations with any other nation. Such confiscation established through trade transactions will create a kind of choking situation inside the economy where people will not have any option but look for options to survive.

Recall here the recent incidents in North Korea or in Iraq or in other nations where sanctions were imposed through UN route, where people started becoming cannibals for survival purpose due to lack of food which was purely because of sanctions.

Such situation will be written in newspapers and spoken in different platform, criticized or debated, but nothing stops.

No body questions or challenges the right or power available with the entities which are imposing them.

It is because the Employees in the individual Governments are in the mode of agents of those global powers.

Around the world and especially in India, moves are being made and changes are being brought up in order to strengthen Bureaucracy system and weaken the ruling system.

This doesn't mean destroying the Ruling system but only weaken it so that it is not effective at all. Recall here the way how ruling system is just a wrapper on administration system of India. This helped in manipulating several systems of India and blame every blunder of "effectless" ruling system of India.

# 24 GLOBAL POLITICS

Global politics work around corrupting the understandings.

Objectives of Global Politics:

1. Government should not have income from its sources—100% EOUs, SEZs etc.
2. Disturb the income sources to Government
3. Allow Government to have income only till the point it maintains the Government employees
4. Create insecurity in Government employees
5. Create restlessness in Government employees
6. Make sure that Government income is put through waste avenues that includes excess pay benefits to Government employees.
7. Use local differences as weapons
8. Create unaffordability in the society
9. Maintain differences in understandings of society
10. Mislead the education system
11. Propagate wrong information through media
12. Government structure should not be same for longer years
13. Government should not have trust from their people
14. Bureaucracy should be out of control of Ruling
15. Bureaucracy should be stronger and long lasting
16. Margin in Economy should not be there
17. Large Expenditure in the economy.

18. Over lapping tax structure for injecting large expenditure
19. Disconnect the relation between Government employees income to the success of economy.
20. Destroy interdependency between all entities exists nearby together.

How Global Politics works on earth is very much important to learn and understand in real time.

Global politics works around Society Understanding and not around Individual understanding.

Following will explain how they implement their politics in real time.

Some time ago I saw a TV program in Discovery channel. This I am taking as example from real incident.

It was all about the families of old Feudal Rulers and the information around that era, especially portraying very carefully with a balancing message in such a way that there were good days then, and those families are today living without that charisma and their kingdoms are having problems due to corruption at Indian Government. There will not be any direct references to any of them.

After that I saw a big news article in newspapers about a crowning ceremony of a prince belonging to an old feudal ruler's family.

Now Government cannot do anything about it. But this has sent a message across the communities and society that would start developing a new kind of colour and mood in the society.

Many incidents would be at local level and will not be exposed to public every day but several programs of activities in support of this new, not new, renewed old mood that was killed after Independence of India, will be in progress and such developments would be boiling in the local societies as Lava and one day it will burst out as a major issue or wish from society.

This is how Global politics work. At the end, the local society will be having disturbance of at least 10 to 30 years which will hurt the growth of the local society and its knowledge and economy.

Spread the information appropriately to corrupt the thought pattern of the society is the principle of Global Politics.

Also one more thing to be called here is, Global politics is closely related to Immigration system. Immigration systems are to create ring fences, virtual ring fences in the human world. This is to restrict the cross culture exposure. The control of cross culture exposure restricts the understanding of other part of the world which in turn restricts the scope of versatile understandings of the same situation.

This restriction is nothing but restricting the scope for all that impacts the capabilities of "Creativity".

The immigration systems and restrictions created blackholes in the knowledge of Indians due to Lack of entry into first world nations.

As an example about how understandings will be corrupted, recall the sunflower crop and oil Introduction and Promotion by ITC and bad propaganda about groundnut oil. The fact was groundnut is very good for heart.

# 25 POLITICAL PARTIES

Today the mode of Indian Political parties is in the form of corporate bodies. The earlier Political forces were in the form of Kings as Feudal forces.

In the olden days, the wealth and power were mostly based on the geographical boundaries due to the kind of economies then. It was mostly Tangible Economy. Everything was counted on Quantity base.

Quantity of land, Quantity of Soldier Forces and many more.

Small size Feudal Forces would "obey" the comparatively larger size feudal forces.

The introduction of Democracy and introduction of Virtual Systems and Virtual economies have brought in new structure to the old Feudal Forces.

They took the form of Political Parties. The present virtual world has many different versions of virtual kingdoms.

They are in the form of Political Organizations and Corporate Organizations as Formal Organizations.

As informal organizations, they are in the form of clubs and unions.

The political organization's wealth and strength is their support from public and funding from public either through quid pro quo or any other means. Here "Profit" will be in the form of "Power" or "Favours."

Corporate Organizations are profit organizations. The geographical boundaries are not limited to Corporates.

Elections system is today an event of "earning opportunity", whoever wins will have that opportunity during the five year term. Earning opportunity for "non-skilled" "daily labour". An Economic activity created due to expenditure or consumption or utilization activity of Political parties and contestants.

Political parties compete each other in their promises, ignoring the limitations also. In this Congress has gone beyond limitations to the extent of focusing on administrative scope items such as benefits to Government employees and promising them an increase in the retirement age to 60 years and five days work week. Since last two elections, Congress manifestoes have been focusing more on the Government employees and their benefits where the voter strength is so much that they can influence the election outcome.

Take the case of State of Andhra Pradesh where there are 12 lakh Government employees with voting right and dependents with voting rights. Similarly at Nationwide Government employee voter strength, including direct Government employment and PSUs and their Dependents, it is almost 2% of the Indian population. This Vote bank is enough to severely influence the outcome of the election. By giving more and more benefits to exhaust the income levels of Government and ignoring the Welfare schemes has been damaging the nation's economic strength to an unbelievable extent. Publishing misleading information to public for this purpose can be easily figured out from the information coming out of latest exercise of division of state of Andhra Pradesh. The actual income level is around ₹80,000 crores but budgets are being prepared at the range of ₹1,70,000 crores.

Government employees are also demanding more and more benefits at unreasonable levels ignoring all their facts about affordability, responsibilities and duties towards the nation by lobbying through their Employee unions.

This corruption has gone to the level that the meaning of "Welfare Schemes" also changed. This phrase was originally defined to address the "services" to public in return to the tax paid by them as "responsibility and accountability" of

Earlier Feudal rulers used to have ownership on all th resources within the geographical region. Present da ownership doesn't require such physical presence. Corporate can own resources anywhere on earth with money power.

The present day human is having different citizenship based on their involvement in the organizations.

Human has to obey rules or laws of that organization els he/she will lose that citizenship.

We may call it citizenship or membership but at the end ( the day the end result would be one and the same.

All the organizations have their own "constitution" as we as similar as a nation and its governance.

Since human has more immediate returns on his/he citizenship in the individual organizations, the importance more for such of their citizenships. The importance ( Citizenship by region or nation is not a matter now. It matter because we are living in that region.

In case we are living in a Township owned by corpora then that nation citizenship impact on the person is almo zero.

In India, cities such as NOIDA is already developed whe democracy influence is almost Zero and bureaucracy influen and power is Ultimate.

SEZ sort of regional hubs are created to keep th Government and its power out of scope in those regions.

It is the responsibility of Bureaucrats to see that suc disorders should not be developed but bureaucrats due to the poor capabilities are unable to keep situation under control ( Government of India and have been blaming Ruling Partie and they started mending the situation into their powe control.

Here one thing to be cleared is Bureaucrats of India ar bookworms who always look at the world through books an would like to control the society with virtual expression written in book and always live with "lack of practica understanding."

Government. Those services are Equal Opportunity of education, Drinking Water, Medical services for Good Health, Sanitation facilities, road infrastructure, clean air and many more which are common and required to all the people of the nation. This is over ridden by the "quid pro quo" promises and policies by political parties due to failure of creating a proper framework so called "Economists and administrators" of the nation. The pity situation is, all those used to be under the category of "Primary rights of citizens" during earlier days about 30 years ago are now "being reiterated" by present political parties and their leaders as "will be newly introduced and implemented by them now for public welfare to alleviate the public poverty".

Political parties have been repeatedly uttering "poverty" and "Employment" wherever they go.

However, none of these really address any core issues. Everyone of those parties try to project as all the good happened because of "I" all the bad is due to "you". All the Good in your lives is due to "King's Golly" and all the Bad in your lives is because of "Your Sin", henceforth go to temple and pray God for your "good fate".

Fifty crore young population of India got "educated (awareness which is developed due to reading and remembering information)" and their brains are stuffed with lot of information but how to apply that "information" is not known to those naïve youngsters and to the "teachers" also. This is due to one simple reason, policies which are supporting the import of Technology by rulers, administrators and "subject matter experts (SMEs because of having better awareness than others)". Technology means, Solutions. Solutions are nothing but our skills to our Problems. Problem is nothing but needs/wants. If we don't know the "problem" then can't create a "solution". So far, if we look around, every "needs/wants" of India are being fulfilled by "imported technologies".

Every political party and leaders have been promising the schemes related to imported technology. In this import of technology couple of things are very evident that so called "leaders" and also along with "administrators" have been working on establishing "global relations". When those technologies are in utilization in India, they can have global relations with large global "agencies" of those technologies that is not visible to common public.

If the same project is developed from scratch of "technology", employment could be at least five times of present employment potential being projected. Not only this, such scratch start development could lead to generation of new techniques. Such import of technology for quick money has been leading to killing of inner strengths of Indians which is leading to "poverty" and "unemployment". Because of this even small thing of life like "common sense" also became 'speciality' skills. There is more damage being caused due to this.

India is completely wiped out of science, technology and engineering skills. This clearly reveals one fact how much damage can be caused to the nation due to "lack of proper leadership in ruling chairs". This kind of "poor" leadership has become advantage to several 'traders' operating on the same lines and "required" for global agencies those are Original equipment manufacturers (oem).

Such 'Traders' are backed by 'global oem' and influencing the Government in bringing up policies of Government of India in such a way that they get benefit and traders of those oems.

This has led to the point that focuses on 'Indian economic (core skill)' strengths which are completely shattered. The wrong policies are reached to the point that "Indian if working with Global OEMs benefits will be profited, both in the businesses of 'imports and exports'". The lobby of those traders also effect the "Rupee" value in forex market. Since they are operating for "Global OEM" benefit, they are making profit from loss of Rupee value. This is evident in the statements by Narayana Murthy, Infosys chairman and its balance sheet and share market price due to "loss of Rupee value in currency market". The crazy situation has led to the point where Government of India started projecting "number of cell phones (imported ones benefiting USA, China and Taiwan markets) as representation of Development and economic growth" through Media campaign programs. This is added by "SEZ" statuses and tax rebates.

Since Global OEMs are developing the complete technology, they only require persons with skill levels of "operators/mechanics" of their equipment. As I wrote above, "Skills of person" also has a life cycle, during it, the person with experience will change his strengths from user to the level of "creator" of new technology. But such improvements are being killed by Traders of OEMs whose focus would be only "ready to use" resources for immediate trading activities and quick and easy money.

The entire exercise reached a level where Indians are being exploited to provide "cost effective services" to produce a product for Global OEMs and the same product will be sold to Indian in India at "expensive international prices". This is similar to farmer's situation, yields will be there but cannot eat the yields. This kind of situation used to be visible in aqua culture earlier.

In this exercise, what other things are happening is persons with 'non-related' education background are being absorbed, this is as similar as dog doing donkey's job and vice versa. For example, non-computer and non-electronic graduates into computers and IT sector, civil contracts by general graduates etc., engineering graduates into finance world etc. Global OEMs requirements is as I said above, people with quick learning skills without depth of expertise. In this entire rapid changes, depth of expertise of Indians are being wiped out and Indians are being faded out Indians are becoming "out dated". The undue yields to companies like Infosys, TCS or any other companies have been resulting into "deficits" in Indian Economy. Not only in IT companies but in several traditional companies and business units, IT operations are being headed by person those are neither from the same background nor having enough experience of "develop indigenous solutions within India".

These deficits are not limited to "finance" terms but to the level "skills". Due to the lack of leadership strengths in the political leadership and administrative chair of nation, several technical capabilities of India are being disabled and all those experienced are being disabled and impoverished due to "policies" made to Global OEMs that created "traders".

Today, India is gone back by 100 years in its technical skills which is visible in our living standards. Whatever is being projected as poverty is not actual poverty of India but poverty is in the form of "lack of skills". Between India and rest of the world, there is a 200 years gap in terms of "time" technical knowledge. Time required to recover the damage is monstrous.

We say India has knowledge society and expert engineers but we don't have at least that which would address at least one problem of India. How big wrong is our belief of having technical skills but we don't have proper drainage system, recycling facilities, communication facilities, proper designed roads, too many accidents, inundated roads when rains. All 125 crore people can have employment to improve their life standards by themselves with their own knowledge and the policies of India should support that from the present state of supporting "global oems" objectives.

Now transforming from here might take such long time probably "never" and even after 200 years from now Indians would still talk about "some vishwa karma" who built "maaya sabha" in "mahabharath". Due to this kind of murders of technical skills by traders with the support of OEMs, we have reached a point that conceding "construction of large building" though not required and keeping them empty as representation of progress and development.

We are in need of Electric power, I met a person in the exercise of establishing a wind mill generation farm. He was former colleague of "Abdul Kalam". He has 15 patents in wind mill designs those are 25% higher efficiency than regular wind mills. However, he could commercialize or I could not because of unfriendly policies. Quick money is reaching "unproductive" avenues and resulting into "unproductive" activities of constructing buildings, those are not possible to use for different puposes but not being used for "development of new technologies (solutions)".

# 26 POLICY MAKING—TYPE OF ECONOMY

One more experience of mine while living in USA, this was about the war of USA on Iraq and on Afghanistan etc. The repeatedly used phrase in USA about the need of those wars was "Freedom of USA Life."

I used to wonder, what is that "Freedom of USA life"?

Answer for that is, low cost products/resources from around the world to USA for their purpose. The other way is, leave the losses to the nations like India and yield the profits into USA as low cost products.

There used to be analytical program in TV on war in Iraq and in Afghanistan. Some of the TV media has gone to the extent to air live transmission of war. While I was watching such TV shows, I started recalling the Kurukshetra War from Mahabharata Epic and the way Sanjay explaining the details of war to Dhruthrashtra.

Of course, I need not explain about the way how USA or UK got together and did carry the war though opposition in the world. Here I must detail about one incident that really pissed me off and made me determined and committed towards doing something that revives India. During then, in CNN, Yashwant Sinha, foreign minister of India was interviewed for denying support to USA for driving forces against Iraq. Anchor and analyst in the show, just before the interview used the word "SOBs" to refer Indians and were discussing, why Indian "SOBs" are not supporting when USA saved that nation by giving H1B visas. Here SOBs means "Son of Bitch". You can verify archives for this.

This raised two points in my mind. One, there were media services ages ago in India. Second, Mahabharata historical calendar details were not known to Indians.

When I put together this with other recent history details in the last 300 to 400 years, the ruins that we find as living history in our India, like rubble forts and more, I felt that Indian history was destroyed, because European historical evidences are still there today, but not in India, this made me to conclude that the knowledge or feel or experience of History is very much required to understand the transformation of a society/nation.

One of the major reasons for USA or UK to be so successful is preserving its History and keep on explaining the transformation of it through different programs.

Anything will be used optimally in USA to the extent that is unimaginably possible levels.

In USA, FM radio stations are many owned by even school kids from home garage. This drew my attention towards the kind of hype created around Radio stations. *I found that Radio stations can be established as simple as from a Small room with Small equipment and self-employment can be generated from it.*

I found the way how Indians are deprived of even simple employment opportunities. I felt that this could create employment opportunity. I wrote email about the same to the concerned ministers of India. What resulted was, policy made in such a way that—

1. There will be close bureaucratic control projecting lot of apprehensions as reasons for such requirements
2. Large investment requirement
3. Only large investors can be participated

This taught me a lesson.

1. Bureaucratic Behaviour
2. Providing unreasonable importantce to make small things as large things so that unnecessary inhibitions would be developed
3. Controlling to gain profits by only some people

Here I will refer two more sectors in the same situation. One is Petroleum Sector and the second is Liquor Sector.

Liquor that was not in the control of Government. Later policies were created in such a way that Manufacturers had to supply to Government and Government takes care of Supply Chain Management of the product.

There are very highly micro details here to be discussed.

When it comes to Policy, Politicians are being targeted.

When it comes execution, politicians are being targeted.

The fact behind politician is Bureaucrats and Gazetted cadre and Police are in the day to day control of the entire Government and its operations at micro level.

Corporate Culture Psychology was injected into the Government of India. This was a major conspiracy. Since we have clueless fellows as Union Civil Service executives, such concepts have been promoted very carefully through different entities such as Employee Unions and media.

Government does not gain or lose.

Following will explain you how a bureaucrat thinks of himself and how common people get victimised their stupidity.

My brother-in-law, a farmer family, who used to consider liquor as nonsense business, had to get into the business of liquor helplessly for more income. When the tender system that still prevails today started, in the first term of the system, he wanted to participate but we all pulled him back. Due to this, we lost almost one crore or two crore profits with an investment of just one lakh.

Everybody became so rich by it. When he bid for a retail outlet and got into liquor business, he was people elected member of District Ruling Body. Surendra Babu, Vijayawada Commissioner of Police had one day warned him on some issue commenting as "You suck the blood of the Poor". He was very hurt, he told me this.

What I felt was, we are made to be "sinful" people due to the system. But the actual beneficiaries are those bureaucrats of Government.

My study found that the belt shops were operated by Unemployed Graduates for their earning to live. What more I found, if proper system is there in place in India, several Bureaucrats could have lost their jobs for preparing such corrupted policies and for implementing those policies as laws through Gazette order route to create corrupt systems.

I started comparing the sectors between USA and India.

What I figured out was, USA also had large fight on liquor for decades. Hope all know the name of "Al Capone" who was a big liquor mafia leader during the ban of liquor era. He lived in Chicago area then.

What I figured out was, USA found that Liquor ban doesn't yield any benefit. And also they figured out that Liquor is not a "Lethal" one if properly utilized. Liquor, if perspective is changed, is a Food Processing unit.

They adopted proper policies and promoted liquor and let it go as Food processing unit and promoted several microbreweries to large breweries. In fact it was considered as Cottage industry.

However they took one measure at government level that is quality Control.

Contrast to that has been happening in India. Initial days, liquor manufacturing practices, native practices were suppressed by large industries. A native practice has become an illegal activity.

Second, administrators, bureaucrats who were supposed to work on establishing systems, have no clue what is wrong, and started implementing all that British practices on India, though India has been liberated.

Here I should mention one thing, Indian Civil Service executives are Clueless fellows of administration. This is the Fundamental error why India has been suffering for decades and centuries. Earlier bureaucrats were also idiots, hence the knowledge was not allowed to grow in India.

I focused on the liquor manufacturing details. What I found is, 1 kg Rice is enough to Produce 6 Litres of Beer.

A product that can be manufactured and consumed healthily was made as illegal and illegality is promoted and the native skills and industrialization is completely killed.

Lastly this was tied to the Principles of Mahatma Gandhi and started projecting it as some sinful activity. I did not know if Mahatma had ever spoken against Liquor.

Since Mahatma's reference has come, Mahatma talks have always been reflecting the need to focus on native practices of industrialization so that technical skills can grow within India and technology innovation could grow from within India.

Instead of promoting the right intention of it, cottage industries were promoted and "Mahatma"is being promoted as brand ambassador "Out Dated" technologies and concepts by Government in its campaign programs on cottage industries. This is how the great person who had spent his life with lot of vision and aspirations on his place of birth and identity has been receiving respect.

This above said para may appear to be controversial but it is the fact. We might be having Mahatma's pictures everywhere but we did not understand him at all which is visible in front of our eyes in our lives but we are not educated enough to understand what we have lost and have been losing. One reason for that could be that Mahatma did not document his vision.

Similarly, in India, several sectors were made as limited accessibility hence the employment and native skill will not be grown.

I started focusing on the native skills and education. Why India has been failing miserably?

The subjects in education and their structure also have always been to meet the changes, needs or wants globally and not to address any local changes, needs or wants.

I wrote above the Virtual and Real worlds. Since most of the Virtual world is based on imagination, our education also has been on the same grounds.

The entire education system is divided vertically into two parts, Virtual and Real. Virtual are Finance, Management and others etc. Real are Engineering, Medicine, Agricultural or other similar types.

Now, since our existing systems were more made to be controlled virtually, as established by British, since old days there has been value to such professions in terms of Money and power, we started adopting them as Good to have.

Here pay attention more to Money and Power. British has created the Virtual Systems to rule the nations around the world. They are the present government employment where Tangible skills are not the skills required but only a supervisory skills fellow with skill of "creating confusion" such skills, we call them as "Aptitude" Skill.

Skill of selling words and numbers has become an art of Management and Leadership skills. Just understand here how big fools have been becoming Intelligent and skillful fellow on this globe with skills which are not really skills at all.

The same skills are required for Multinational Companies also where technical skills are not prominent requirement but controlling technical skilled persons is the prominent skill requirement. MNCs require persons who can manipulate things to benefit them.

Also defeating the value and arrogance of technical skilled person is also the required skill of Manager. In Addition to that the manager should have Good clerical and accounting skills. Now this one is being termed as "Soft skills". The best clerk is the best manager. Appraisal system is one form of the tool to kill the personality of the individual. Manager is a Meaning Manipulator which is being termed as "skill of communication, reasoning and others."

In real terms I can be said as 'picking up on person'.

Everybody with good aptitude skill will get anger, when you understand the total book, everybody will realize what kind of skills we have been considering as "Worth" to "Pursue."

This Aptitude skill is being clubbed with English Vocabulary and is being used to insult capability of logical thinking with the knowledge of language.

The capability of communication is turned into expertise in language. In my entire analysis what I have found is that India is the only nation and the only place where we have this nonsense of English language expertise which is being considered as one of the aptitudes of the person. This explains what kind of comedy system we have and is being promoted as "Valid" one. The comedy act of considering proficiency in a language is symbol of communication skill started killing the capability of logical thinking and Expressiveness in Indians.

Several management graduates in order to confuse the debate and win over the situational advantage of the debate use long sentences with tough English words. The same was made as one method of "screening".

Now here I should write a disclaimer, I am not a successful Student and I already said this.

It is not that I am not intelligent but I am not good at read, remember and reproduce concept.

Global forces provided more protection, money and power to all their employees with virtual skills which started attracting rest of the society towards such virtual skills which is true even today after 66 years of independence.

Since the Currency world is in their control we have not been able to understand the tricks of trade of virtual world. We lost the sense of recognizing the importance of Real world.

Also, since engineering, technology, medicine or other tangible world subjects are not able to be developed well by Indians, reason is not practicing well, poor R&D, and since the study culture related to them also in the same style of Virtual, we started biased ourselves towards virtual world more.

In order to do R&D, we need knowledge base. Also one more important thing, since resources are becoming more and more unaffordable due to fall in Rupee value consistently, R&D has taken a back seat.

Science is the subject of nature. Technology is the subject of creating imitation of nature. We are not good at it at all.

USA and UK want the same and always work to defeat all that creates knowledge base in nations like India. We should recall about WTO here that is contextual and patent rights.

Here I will tell you one simple example.

I was looking to start an innovative business to invest in. I was looking for such a business which will be uninterruptable, long term and very needy to the nation.

What I found was, renewable energy source, Solar Electricity.

Not the Solar Cell one, but a parabolic trusses based heat production by concentration of sun rays and thereby heating an oil through a pipe that works as a heating coil to drive a Steam engine to run a turbine. I was searching for cheap options for this. I came across a centre near Gurgaon, Haryana. I went there and found that the centre was established in 1970s decade when USA was conducting experiments on solar energy. It was owned by Central Government of India. Since the date when experiment was closed, nothing has been happening there. The scientists were just drawing salaries since then and doing nothing. None of the scientists are able to produce any tangible output that benefits this nation in any manner till date. This is the bitter fact. Scientists were contract labor for USA operations from Government of India under the program of mutual activities at free of cost to USA.

There is one more major blunder that I observed. This is related to the quality of knowledge. I will write separately about this in a new chapter.

Because of this, for every problem of ours, we have been looking for solution from foreign.

Scientists are also on the similar mode of searching for solution that might be already invented around the world. Scientists or professors are in the mode that "learn" those may not be known to common public and they pretend as expert in the field. Now Internet is available for all information of the world. Earlier information used to be available in specific

Journals those were expensive and available to only "Scientists" designated in India.

USA has a 450 MW power plant on that same technology.

In my conversation with a scientist who participated in that USA experiments from Indian Government side being as Government of India Employee, I found that they have certain performance appraisal system with some sequence of activities to perform in a year to get appraised and receive salary hikes and promotions, they are like, invitations from foreign meets, white paper writing etc., they have been doing those activities. That is all.

Recall here the economics professor's clean and neat confession, he was very genuine and sincerely told me the way how anybody would be, simply follow the KPIs for more financial and career advancement, no care about anything related to India as a nation.

Who cares?

These all explained that the state of the morale of the nation.

At the same time, recall the "Concept" execution techniques by first world nations.

This triggered the doubt about awarding Noble prize etc. Where is the guarantee that those prizes are being given to proper achievers. Such prizes can be given to people and use the same people in order to achieve some political gains by using them.

These sound apprehensions but I was able to see some biased statements which work against India as best advices. Now how to prove them as working against India is a major task but results are such advices have always been working against India due to which India after 66 years is still in horrible conditions.

It was not the poverty that spoiled India, it was lack of knowledge and awareness but it now being moved into poverty.

Here I should mention one thing. This is regarding the retail chain of shops entry into India.

While I was living in India, I planned to start a chain of shops business in India. I felt it as a good business proposition. I did some work towards it. I myself was in favour of them. I could not start but during my effort I happened to contact several large company heads in order to support the concept. However, it did not happen. But later, several large companies entered into business.

Why I am saying this?

I wanted to be creative and would like to be pioneer of something in India. During my effort I created some new hardware + software products.

What I figured out the reasons for Indians not able to be creative is its unaffordability created due to pressure in terms finance on the economy, government and industry.

Due to this, knowledge base of India is left at level, where an engineer is qualified by certificate of education but by skill equal to not even a mechanic. I am trying to compare to make you understand the sorry situation that we and our nation are in.

Remember here, historically, Indian large engineering skills have been destroyed where evidences are there in several different forms such as historical monuments etc.

Since knowledge base does not have depth of the subject, India is not able to be creative and innovative. Means, India/ns has lost all Fundamentals. First world nations don't want to give scope to such innovation and creativity inside the nation of India. Knowledge is power in the present world. Technology is the strength. Patent rights are the legal ownership.

Indian economy has become a trading economy where "Creation" is not there at all. Understand here that *Manufacturing is not creation.*

Since knowledge and technology is not being allowed to be created, Traders are required for those Creators, hence they have been "promoting traders" such as Tata/Birla/Wipro/Infosys or any other groups.

To be further deeper, if we go, brokerage companies could be seen in the names of "Tata Honeywell" or "Tata IBM" etc. companies earlier days.

Also to be more precise, TCS or Infosys or any companies are "skilled labour supplying" companies but not technology companies.

Traders require *Skill-less Supervisors*. Tangible skills of Real World are not required.

Supervisors are Labour herders.

I have taken the risk of directly mentioning names of every entity to give accurate "fact" where India and Indians are so that there would be proper clarity which helps Indians start transforming their behaviour.

Hence a good name is given to it as "management" and it is projected as a skill and science and provided more value. These are all controlled by Money using so called dumb Economists at top chairs of India.

You can see such dumb heads everywhere around you.

India is made to be dumb for another five generations. This is the fact. Whatever the skills Indian nation used to have were also killed in the last four decades by using the continuous rise in resource prices.

The depth of damage being caused using finance as weapon and currency values as nuclear weapon is disabling the Indians at skill level.

We have reached a point or we are made to reach a point of not able to notice our problems but being made to consider as "some junk" issues as "problems" and made us to consider "some junk" issues as "causes" of those problems and made us to believe that "some junk" issues are as "Solutions" and we are completely corrupted at our thoughts.

This is the reason why Indian employment market has been so volatile and fluid.

We are all connected virtually by Finance at global level. An activity at Global level can be made as impacting the person at remote place of earth where he or she may not have any relation with the modern world as well.

Such incidents could be witnessed in several programs on those very primitive tribes in remote place of earth through new channels.

Now reader might have understood the nature of Indian Economy. It is not "Creative" economy but a "Trading" Economy.

The recent introduction of new policy into retail by Government of India on retail is nothing but saying that Indians are such dumb heads where they are not even good at trading activities.

All these are made possible by some dumb heads who are being projected as Economists and experts in Finance world.

Here I must tell one thing, even an uneducated who might be doing a small business or rickshaw pulling also will have same fundamental capabilities of those who sit in the top chairs of Government of India as experts in economics and finance but the only difference is the "span of horizon".

If the same exposure is given to that uneducated rickshaw puller, he might do better economics than those dumb heads in the top chairs of India and who are being acclaimed as experts by global forces.

As an example, let us look at "Right to Information" act. Information that is correct can only be provided only when there is correct documentation and record maintenance. In Government activities, none of those ever be maintained. Instead of focusing on all those measures which improves the record maintenance, being Prime Minister, Manmohan Singh created a misleading policy to engage people in unproductive activities.

# 27 GLOBAL SYSTEMS

Following explains the hierarchical Structure of the human world systems and how it is being controlled. Both pictures below are to represent a Cone.

The above shown diagram represents that the perspective of earlier stage will be different from present stage. Up to some extent, it looks like the lateral stage as a successor of the earlier stage, but a person who might be a good worker doesn't have to be a good monitor and above. Similarly, a Monitor doesn't have to be a good worker.

Ruling is the Ultimate Expertise.

One more thing to understand is, Ruling Chairs only strategize and Administration implements. Administration is responsible to implement all those to maintain integrity of the nation at all levels and maintain balance. But Administration of the India has completely failed in this.

Due to failure of Administrative chairs capabilities, there are moves to destroy the democratic processes inside the nation. A culture was developed in India in such a way that all politicians are being considered as Criminals of the nation.

But the fact is opposite.

In India, most of the controlling power is with government employees. Politicians are only watch dogs. The democratic system was created in such a way that elected members and elected bodies have very little control on the nation's ruling. How that structure did get created, need deep study, but since independence, bureaucratic power and associated lower government employee system has been gaining more and more strength and all the ruling systems have been disabled.

One more important fact is that Ruling System is Visible to eyes. Rest of the lower systems are not visible to eyes. The weak capabilities of incumbents in media has been focusing only on visible ones but not behind the deep and strong system because it requires more in-depth knowledge on several different subjects and media would usually not expose all of them. I wrote about this at the start of my book, putting together different subjects and giving a perspective and the associated complexity.

Global forces have been working with "strong system behind the screen" and weakening the visible ruling system.

*Global Forces are experts in establishing systems hence have worked at places which can help to build such systems.*

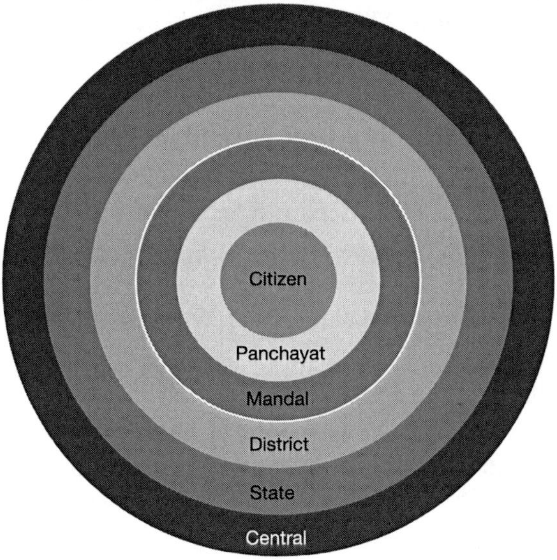

The above is the way how Indian nation is structured. Also the same can be represented in Cube or Ball shape as well.

The purpose of these pictures are to explain that there are different dimensions in hierarchy and also each dimension angle of understanding would be different from each adjacent layer.

Here we need to look at the skills of a Person. I told you earlier about virtual world and real world. In the above hierarchy, as we move from worker to top level/outer rings, or from citizen to outer rings, virtuosity will be large and reality will be less.

The above shown structure of India has the role structure shown above, ruling, administration, management, supervisor, monitor and worker at every level.

Every one of them are virtual skills.

A real world skill takes longer time to learn and become perfection. But without real world items, no human can survive.

A Virtual skill takes shorter time to learn and doesn't have any definition of perfection, "wining the situation" is the measure of perfection. The ultimate goal is to exploit others.

However, in India, such virtual skills are considered as Leadership quality.

Look above carefully, there is Leadership anywhere in the pictures above.

Contextually let us understand leadership first.

In India, anybody who attracts the attention of crowd is being considered as Leader. In my perspective, this might be developed again from the same Real World and Virtual World Difference.

Let us understand Leadership.

"Leader" first quality is having a "Vision". "Vision" that he/she"invented" as "Solution" to the "existing problem".

Leadership is "Innovation", "Vision", "No Selfishness" and "Sacrifice".

Before going further let us see what is "vision". Vision is nothing but "Divya Dhrishti". Vision is not projection, imagination, forecasting, predicting, estimation, aspiration and dreaming. "Vision" is first related to that doesn't exist till that point of time. It will always be related to tangible world. It is a perfect "output" of a perfect "process" that is appropriately designed with accurate plan that is prepared with complete knowledge and skill.

One more Quality of Leadership is accepting others Leadership.

Bharat Ratna sort of titles should be given to such persons who are Leaders.

Here we have been honouring people who are employees, gained monetary benefits as return to their services, their services are their duties paid for.

The latest trend is "projecting good workers as leaders".

This is very dangerous and an effort to corrupt the young Indian brains.

The above said is at very higher level.

At day to day level also, the word "Leader" is being used at very inappropriate places such as Team "leader/monitor", "Supervisor", "Manager" and "Administrator", which is nonsense.

Again here one more point to be considered is "Understanding the problem Right".

Read this to understand the above sentence.

A Psycho Tailgated a Woman into an ATM Center where no Security Guard was made available, closed the Shutter and injured her severely and left the place.

Police Alerted the Banks and warned for Security requirements at ATMs. Media analysed it as "Secured" Access to Glass Doors of ATM centre.

None were able to find the "Problem" right. What is it that supported the incident to happen?

"Shutter" to the ATM centre. If there was no Shutter but a Grill Door that exposes the room to outside viewers, the psycho may not have dared to enter.

This is what is "Understanding the problem Right" and "deriving" right Solution for it is Vision.

"Leader"means person in "Position" "One".

Last here to understand is, an inventor in real time world is also a Leader. Now do you consider a best clerk is a "leader"?

Hence the leader is not there in the top pictures anywhere.

Managers primary responsibility would be Accounting. Accounting an estimate and Accounting a result. The accounting primary activity would be "Questioning". This Questioning is being considered as "Leadership". Look how funny it is!!

If we look around in India Virtual skills were created by British in order to exploit the Real Skill which have become major required skills.

British may have left India long back but their concepts are still there and such skills are being used very much in large corporates which are cherishing largely on exports. Even today, many of us have been adopting systems conceptualized at foreign.

Indian society has been victim of virtual skills for ages. This is the reason why Indians have always been swamped up with lot of sentiments. The proof of it is visible as religious preaching in our nation today.

The net reflection of such preaching would be always influencing psychologically to make society believe that there is some other world which is a heaven or hell and you do not do anything in this world so that you will be happy in your lateral world. A way of disabling the creative thinking.

Earlier days bureaucrats of India were in the form of religious preachers. Those days dumb head rulers were using such virtual skill fellows to propagate the message of lateral worlds of heaven or hell through the society in order to cover their uselessness.

If everything goes well in the society then that would be because of the Ruler. If something bad then that is because of the sins of the society. Hence go to the religious place and pray God to get yourself relieved from ill fate of the life.

Indian society has been the victim of such useless skills that they are becoming more complicated and such evil systems have been passing through generations together.

Real world skill can be called as "Technical Skill". These skills also have levels.

We all usually heard a lot about Science and Technology very often together. Many do not usually have clarity around it. Science is the knowledge and expertise about the nature. Technology is reproducing the natural object through artificial methods.

Above I have showed the structure of the Indian ruling system. Here also, lower levels were disabled by upper levels. This is another disorder.

The above structure of Indian organisation structure and associated systems are disturbed and some of them are completely disabled by Global Forces using the internal systems which are not visible to common eye. This tells what kind of capabilities are being considered as "Strengths" of India.

Government employees are supposed to be working to protect the systems, they have been working to corrupt them. Following explains how.

We all know about how laws should be created in India. Every law has to be debated in Parliament/elected houses in order to become law.

Law is the one that is supposed to be obeyed by Citizen.

However laws were created by creating a Gazette Order.

Gazette order was used in British Ruling as means to create local laws which was later wrapped with Democratic procedures after independence. Gazette order is an administrative order supposed to be used for Government office purpose for Government Officials and are not supposed to be applied in any manner on Citizens. But the administrative staff have been misleading the ruling chairs and have been using the route of Gazette in order to create laws.

There is one more thing, every citizen should get a fair chance of challenging the charges in the court of law. But citizens are not getting such chances in several places such as traffic violations.

I wrote about framing a citizen by Government officials by Government rules. This situation is disabling all elected members and their privileges. This kind of misleading the nation and devaluation of Ruling system has become one more reason for major deterioration of Indian systems.

India is deteriorating. Deterioration can only be cured but cannot be treated by another methods or techniques.

By now you may have gained an idea about Real Economy and Virtual Economy.

You may have understood the organisation and system structures of India and disorders in them.

One most significant one is the top layer which is ruling layer. It is very fluid where elected members may always change for every five years.

There are some more disorders there.

The elected members do not have any direct control.

They only can direct to administrative chairs but cannot act on their own. Even Elected bodies together also have the same status.

Most of the direct action control is rest with administrative chairs.

Ruling can only suggest for action on any lower layer chairs when found problems.

Ruling bodies are also the same.

One more problem in Indian ruling system is Ruling can have people without people mandate.

*The total disorders are resulting into that India is not being ruled but being managed by all those reached Ruling Chairs through nominated Route of Rajyasabha.*

*How India is being managed?*

Recall the policy making saga of FDI into retail.

First propagated as "Government has Executive powers and has veto power with authority to create a policy" which was not true. Indian Government ruling structure by Nation builders after Independence was created in such a way that "People in Ruling chairs are only custodians or watch dogs". Organizations such as Parliament has all the power in framing the policies. Because, individuals/groups of Individuals (cabinet committee) structure was a Feudal structure and Nation builders did not want to have that to be the situation in future. This concept was carefully defeated and everybody started misleading the nation.

The main culprits in this are "Union Civil Service Executives", it is their responsibility to maintain the frame work intact.

The second major crime committed by Manmohan Singh, Pranab Mukherjee and their team was coordinating with Lobbies such as some individual NGO organizations and promoting it as they have been consulting all stake holders at every level, and have been practicing "Democracy" by taking people's opinion through consultations of NGO organizations. NGO organizations have no legal liabilities. This was second back stabbing activity of the people in the ruling chairs and again UCSEs, instead of controlling such behaviour, they did not do any.

Third major thing was efforts to bypass the nation's parliament and keeping it in dark and started managing it as personal choice of ruling body.

This was the way how entire developments were managed at different levels which they call "Lobby".

The management behaviour instead of ruling behaviour with the persons in ruling chairs is clear from the "scope for gaining personal credit (a workers mentality)" as achiever to the nation.

One more thing to be paid attention here is, India is a democracy where People Elected Members should be in ruling chairs. However, Indian Democracy has a "Flaw" in the form of Rajya Sabha or upper house where people nominated by political powers will be. Such persons are not restricted from occupying the Ruling chairs. This flaw is appropriately being used which is against the principle of Integrity and Sincerity towards the Constitution that is built on democracy spirit and respecting it as well. Taking advantage of that flaw is nothing but Corrupting system without fixing the flaw of the system and also cheating on the nation. One of the first qualities to a leader is "Openness and no selfishness and sincerity."

In fact the reason for such pitiful situation is due to inefficient administrative chairs whose responsibility is to maintain organisations, systems, processes and procedures appropriately and improve them.

All the above sounds like my personal interpretation and can be considered as ridicule. The simple answer to that is, I told you, I am a systems analyst, and I look for reasonable matching points in order to create a meaningful form that could be 90% accurate from the destroyed and distracted pieces. This job can be simply termed as "Autopsy" of economy.

Global forces have been using their tactics as suitable to the individual nation's nature of existing operating structure and have been applying different techniques in order to destabilise the local organization structure and operating systems.

They mostly use the following entities for that.

1. Opponents/competitors of the ruling chairs
2. So called Experts
3. Media
4. Government employees

Stability in a nation would create scope for thinking about development. If development starts then that hurts the control of Global forces.

Global forces always target at the availability of natural resource to their control and power and disposal for their lavish living.

# 28 (CAPITALISM/COMMUNISM/ SOCIALISM) ISMS

In order to understand more in detail, read further.

Let us look at our life. In our life, we have always been living with uncertainty. We behave and act against some expected results. Any deviation from such expectation is nothing but Risk. This risk could be loss from actions that we performed or from external forces. The risk could be either positive or negative one. In either case, the expected results would vary. In order to mitigate such risks, a mechanism is required.

Insurance is the mechanism of Managing Risks in Finance world. I already mentioned about sama, dana, bheda and dandopaya from our ancient books.

Similarly there are four ways to handle risk.

1. Voidance (eliminate, withdraw from or not become involved)
2. Reduction (optimize—mitigate)
3. Sharing (transfer—outsource or insure)
4. Retention (accept and budget)

We are insuring ourselves from our risks. Either it could be Life, health, property or casualty or other types.

When I studied the kind of Insurance businesses that exist in USA and in India, I observed several differences that helped me understand the advantages of insurance and what are the demographics of Finance system on this earth.

I worked in a health insurance company during when I worked on a system where State Government was providing Health Insurance to anybody who might be hurt anywhere in accidents. That was a 70 million US$ business for Insurance company. I was wondering why state government has been using insurance. They could easily provide free health through hospitals as similar as India. Why they are using this insurance route? It is clear that government is using money to account its activities. Recall here, in the view of Government, money is just numbers. Of course it is the money from tax collection from public.

Working on the system in Insurance Company also gave me some details about how health Insurance system works. In USA, a doctor has to get registered with one or more health insurance companies for better income. When registered with insurance company, doctor would be part of the network. Now Patient pays only part of the fee which could be hardly 10% of the amount and rest of the 90% of the consulting fee will be paid by Insurance Company. Now here is one more catch, if the doctor is network participant of the insurance company, there will be negotiated price between insurance company and doctor.

Here one more thing need to understand is, Insurance companies put doctor medical transcriptions through an investigation process anonymously in order to validate the findings and treatment given by Doctor. This way doctors will always be genuine and they do not commit frauds. If doctors commit any mistake or fraud, it may result into delisting from network, which would be the last day of the successful career of the Doctor.

However, focus here on the money part. Doctors are getting paid though patient only paid 10%. How it is possible?

As per the studies, the probability of risk occurrence would be only around 3% or less. When risk occurs then the resulting loss would be 97%. Now here Insurance companies play vital role. Insurance companies put effort in collecting that 3% amount from several different insurers in order to provide compensation of 97%.

Rupees 3 will become premium for ₹100 coverage. As the number of people increases, premium reduces and coverage increases. This is like a Cooperative society.

This way measures are taken to face the occurrence of the risk.

I used to pay only US$65 per month for US$2 million coverage of both for medical services and medicines.

Now here one more point to mention is regarding the capitalism and socialism which usually is discussed a lot in India.

India used the route of Free Health services in Government offices that is more towards real time transaction between individuals. However USA is using Finance as means for that Transaction to take place. USA is using Capital/Finance, India is using Human Feeling. And this is the difference between different 'isms.

The establishment and controlling of the systems of nation using money is *Capitalism*.

Here money will be used as a medium which we all experience in our life. However making profit is part of it. Numbers play vital role as money. The Capitalism will have two simple components. Input cost and output cost where inherent "Profit" Component is a must.

The establishment and controlling of the system using ration card is *Communism*.

Here accounting plays vital role as everybody gets equally treated and equally benefited, currency importance is almost nil.

The commonality between them is "Unique ID".

The establishment and controlling of the system through human feelings is *Socialism*. Here numbers play very little role. Most of the transactions goes on one to one relation between persons. We may call it anything, like Quid Pro Quo.

Now this is being misunderstood and is being attributed as Money, investment, profit, exploitation etc. Of course, they will be there in three societies. Let us not get into the fight of good, bad and ugly or correct or wrong.

I have faced situations where media persons gave me a brand of some sort of ism.

*I used to ask them why you are branding me. Why can't you say that I am coming with Indianism?*

Of course there is a reason for this.

It is their exposure to the world and understanding.

There are clear cut reasons why those ism are successful in some locations and not successful in other locations.

Also one more thing is none of the Isms could be exclusive from others. No society on earth can be categorised as 100% of one ism. Only one of that such Isms will surface more when compared with others which leads to assigning brand of that ism.

# 29 MULTI-CURRENCY—MULTI-DIMENSION

I am sure the reader has now reached the point of understanding how to slice dice the place of our living and surroundings when he reached this line for reading.

The difference between those global forces and Indians are, they look at the world as a conglomerate of systems. In that systems, different entities will exist with behaviour and culture created by those systems. This sounds more like theoretical knowledge right. It is not my book's purpose.

Let us look around, we have Government which is predominantly by Political and Administrative systems. Then comes the industries and then comes the commerce or business. Most importantly to understand is none of them exist without Human.

Now all these are having one communication medium which is money or finance.

We all are networked with this wireless medium. We may use our mouth, voice, sounds and words to communicate each other. However we use money to transact. It is the medium of communication.

Every one of us knows that the today' world has 180 and odd nations and each one of them has individual currencies. All those currencies are linked each other through forex market with some definite trade values based on their trading value in those forex market. It means there is a closed tight network of currencies as similar as Spider web is there in this world. Changes in one economy impacts the other economy.

Currency-Symbol Regions of the World, circa 2006

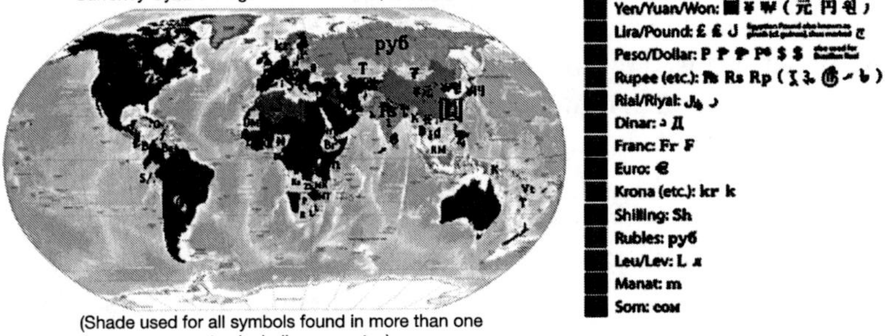


(Shade used for all symbols found in more than one country, including cognates)

Now each nation has a central bank for establishing and controlling the Finance Systems and Regular Scheduled banks to carry forward the Money movement.

Here let us recall the purpose of the money. Money purpose is an exchange to carry a transaction of tangible products. Product could be any tangible item or service.

However, Money in different forms is made to transact each other which is termed as Trading against each other. Forex trading is made as a legitimate transaction by all nations. When did this happen is a long story which doesn't add value to this book. How did this might have happened could definitely add value to this book!

Remember here the above network that I explained in a picture how Global Financial and Economic Forces and the way how the network was established with so called economists, bureaucrats and experts. It is the platform or consortium that worked to create it.

Now understand this point here, this concept of trading currencies against each other was created with proper "scientific reasons" agreed as valid to accept and practice. If one has to be better in life they will be part of this concept and supporting them to excel themselves in the individual careers ignoring the nation's welfare.

Along with financial systems, we need to understand one more fact, that is Government and its characteristics.

Government is not an Organization. Government is a system or consortium of different organizations. The organizations are comprising of rules, regulations, processes, procedures and individual human beings. Government is not as equal as Industrial corporate or commerce business entity. They both are different. Government does not make profit or loss but will have deficits or surplus.

Here I should add one important fact. Usually this is a major Management activity, it is referred as, Make or Buy. Usually, this analysis occurs in order to assess the profit or loss in terms of finance. It is perfectly alright for businesses which take birth and live for only one purpose that is financial profit. However for Government, in the dictionary of Government Profit and loss words will not have any value or meaning, money is equal to pure numbers and those are only for measuring purposes. One major problem in India is entire Government and its operations are today in the form of Business organization.

The Profit and Loss of Government lies in the form of Knowledge and self-reliance.

Government in India is Democracy. We all know about the structure of the Government of India and also about how India is divided geographically into states, districts, Taluqs/mandals and panchayats. Also you know about the political structure, ruling structure, administration structure, etc.

Here I should mention about the Democracy. As we all know that the above said structures in India are created after studying from different nations like UK and USA. Here we must remember one thing that democracy was first created in USA. When I visited the Capitol Hill of USA, and I read or watched the history of USA, what I figured out was, George

Washington, first president of USA, was a true democratic person, who was having all chances to become a Feudal ruler of the nation like dictator or a king but was First President of first Democracy on earth. One more interesting thing was, he was military leader when occupied the top chair through election and became a leader of democratic nation. This was when the society of the world never had any experience of democracy. Isn't it really amazing?

In a nation, Democracy is a system that runs under legislation, law and finance and all the systems around it. The reason for mentioning about the three here is to let know the influence of the three on individual Indian. All these three are usually implemented by using organizations. Organizations are operated by employees. Employees are carried away by the influence of money benefits and other benefits.

Persons may be impacted by the acts of the organizations. Persons may suffer. Organizations do not suffer any time. Organizations may have losses in terms of Virtuosity but not in real world. Organizations belong to virtual world. They are conceptual.

In USA, an individual person has more weightage than an organization which is completely opposite to the situation in India. This is because the organization is not a live entity that gets impacted by individuals. Also the employees of the organization do not get impacted.

In India Organizations have more value and individuals sacrifice for the success of the organization. Organization's objectives become more important than individual welfare. This culture was inculcated into the society of India. How was it possible?

Recall here that India has been under Corporate Style Governance for 200 years where British as any other organization has inculcated the psychological impressions of:

1. Organization is First
2. Organization success is your success
3. Organization welfare is your welfare
4. Organization existence is your existence

5. Organization future is your future
6. Organization value is your value

These were required for British to be successful in India with Indians as Workers. However, recall the instruments that they were using in order to bind the individual to the job and then to the organization.

These are possible when the employee/worker is provided with employment, power, wealth and social status. They established this by using the instruments such as finance (Money), facilities and protection.

British in order to protect the employees of their regime, provided the facility of "protection by law" to all their employees who were nothing but Government employees. Even today the same thing exists in India.

One more important thing here is about the rules defined by the British as Laws. British through their framework of laws and rules were able to establish a system where Indian citizens will be liable to Government means to British but Government will not be liable, accountable or responsible to any citizen. The same is true with Government employees since then till now. The net result Government employees are not responsible or accountable or liable to their jobs, roles and responsibilities.

In Government there will be laws for Social Regulation and also there will be procedures and processes with business rules for the purpose of execution of activities of Government. British had defined laws but left many of the definitions of Procedures, processes and business rules to the employee of the Government They defined the Ruling and Administration but left over the Management, Supervisory and Monitoring activities to the Employees as per their will and wish. This was not necessary for them also this was left to employee in order to establish a platform where employees can demonstrate their discretionary powers to the society which helps in building social importance to the employee as a dignitary of the society, like a VIP of the place.

Since last 66 years no effort has ever put on defining such procedures, processes and business rules, entire nation has been suffering with different disorders where evidences of crimes by Government employees has become untraceable. Lack of such crystal clear definitions at every level also created a confusion state in identifying what is right, what is wrong, who is right, who is wrong. The same is very clear in several incidences of Government actions and Supreme Court orders. Isn't this clearly reflecting if we Indians are really capable of Ruling?

The culture of "organization first" still visible in India today in several different forms that reflects that Government is still having the culture of Separate from Citizens. 'WE' and 'OUR' culture is not there but 'YOU' and 'I' culture is there.

British or global Forces are very well experienced in establishing organizations and corresponding systems in order to achieve an objective or objectives. Organizations will be created and will be destroyed after the objective is either successfully attained or not, which is usually decided by the situation that exists. When Organizations are created to carry on the activities for achieving the objectives, virtual body independent of persons will be created. Such virtual bodies can be destroyed to clear the evidences along timeline to wipe out the evidences of its existence.

Following explains better.

Say a bank was robbed by a group of individuals with different skills like a "project". None of them was given the total picture of the project. Total rob was recorded in a camera. They were caught but law could not convict them as every one of them were given a task to complete as per their specialised skills.

The robbing activity was carried out as a Project with several sub-projects. Project was sponsored by an organization that received funds from public. Public invested in the organization by looking at the organization's business plan analysed by market analysts. None of them have the big picture of the objective of the project. Now who would be convicted for the robbery?

All those participants are employed hence cannot be convicted because they did only some percentage of the entire work and have no clue about the rest of the activities.

See how big gap can be created in systems. Today such robbing activities are usually referred as White Collar or Blue Collar Crimes where every step will be properly designed and carried out carefully so that the crime can never be surfaced, even if surfaced, will never be able to be proven wrong at any given point of time.

Such Procedural activities usually carried out very carefully in Government activities especially in public works and in Government policies.

How is it possible? How are they being carried in such crisp way that they cannot be figured out easily?

First to understand here the Democracy. Democracy is a system, a system of organization where there will be further systems. Democracy, since has been new to several nations such as India, since Democracy has been imported to those nations, as nations and societies, transformation is required.

Such transformations take longer time. During this transformation, prevailing disorders in the nation will create new problems and disorders, simultaneously new disorders will take birth, during this time, the initiators of the transformation will be out of project, new brains new thoughts and new understandings and new approaches and many more to complicate the entire thing.

Whatever I said in the above para has been happening since independence in India. However, there is a twist to this. There are foreign forces involvement in corrupting the understandings in India so that India doesn't get better. Why do they do it? What do they benefit from it?

The answer to these questions is their wealth because of the poverty of this part of the world. The losses getting created in this part of the world, like in India, are converting as Profit in the first world nations. This is being achieved by means of the trading system between currencies of different nations.

Now let us see what kind of organizations we have around us which play vital role in any nation at its entirety.

1. Government and its Ruling Structure from Central to Local Panchayath
2. Government and its states, administration and subordinate offices
3. Courts from Supreme Court to local Mandal Level courts
4. RBI and Banks
5. Government Owned Commercial Organizations

In management, it is clearly defined about different kinds of organizations. Let us not get into too detailed but look at the extent that helps us in understanding where what is wrong. The most important one is that related to Governance.

Formal Organizations and Informal Organizations. Above said list are Formal Organizations of Government The informal organizations are Employee Unions. They are not part of Government but Government employees are part of them. These informal organizations have been there from top chairs of Government such as IAS officers, Court Judges, till lowest grade in the chain at Panchayat Level.

There is one more glitch in the form of Government owned Commercial Organizations. They were started to develop R&D in Science and Technology field considering the large investments required to start such organizations. Now these organizations are in the form of commercial organizations for profit. Such Commercial organizations are with Government, many administrators are positioned there in leadership chairs and working in the mode of Profit Making. Here the employees of those public sector units are Government employees and at the same time they are Labour working for a profit organization.

Here the clearly missing point is the lack of understanding with Administrators, central civil service executives, about difference between governance of a ruling government and that of a commercial Corporate.

This overlap between different organization styles in Government led to a situation where Informal organization became more powerful.

Government employees are not labour working for a profit organization. They cannot consider themselves as being exploited and cannot even participate in any organization directly or indirectly to work against the governance. How this understanding of Government employee is a labour as similar as any other industrial labour where the chances of exploiting the labour for profit were actually developed may not be known but it is a large blunder being carried out in India by Government employees.

Laws in a nation and organizations of government in a nation are meant for all including themselves. Government employees are supposed to be custodians and should use only the means that are established for general public for their problems resolution as well and cannot adopt any organizations such as unions for the purpose of lobbying and benefiting from them.

However, this major blunder was born and has been cherishing for quite long time is not known but *it is a concept* to corrupt the systems of India and not sure how long more would it survive! As long as it is surviving, India cannot get better.

This way Government employees are not in the commitment of the welfare of the nation.

# 30 SHARE MARKET–II

In the present world of Finance, investments and industry, Share Market is the place where the entire nation's ownership will be available for purchase and sale. Owning shares of Industry in share market is equal to owning the industry and associated land and resources available to those Industries. Here resources include the "natural resources".

One of the companies, Indian Company, of course funded by American Company, bought a company in Canada. It was a technology company. Canada Government rules don't agree to shift the Intellectual Property Rights of the Company beyond the borders of that nation. The company in which I was working was taken over by Oracle. It took over the IP rights from India through Global IP route.

Reader might remember the FDI and FII saga by Government Some of the sectors are opened and others not. Opened up sectors are allowed a FDI of certain percent and FII of some percent.

Let us look at the scenario of 51% of FDI and 24% of FII. What is the total foreign investment? 51 + 24 = 75%. The remaining 25% is not a big deal to control the company and to own the company or to run the company as per the will and wish of the foreign ownership.

Earlier to FDI and FII, there used to be different forms of Foreign Investment opportunity. That was Participatory Notes (PN), American Depository Receipts (ADR), Global Depository Receipts (GDR).

FDI and FII are new form of PN. ADR and GDR are different from FDI and FII. Let us say a company has a shareholding of 75% of Indian investor. Now an Indian Shareholder can issue ADR in American Stock market for his shares and collect money from there. What he is doing is, he is selling his ownership to US investor for his part of investment. He in Indian terms owns the company but in USA terms he has sold to USA citizens. USA citizens and USA Economy gains income from Indian Company's business in India.

This is the kind of schemes created to have the ownership of Indian Economy taken over by foreign resources. Here I must tell you one important thing that is hurting the nation.

There are many conspiracies in execution mode based on Stock market. New money was injected into the stock market due to which share prices of companies rise to unusual levels which is reflecting as sensex today.

Stock market due to large liquidity allowed has become a place of gambling. Stock market today in India, can be said, is a gambling house. It is as simple as it is.

There was a time when sensex was projected as symbol of Economy or an indicator that reflects health of economy.

Recall the 10 members in a room concept. Consider that there are only 10 persons in Indian stock market.

Each one of them have ₹1 and have been transacting with each other. Now let us say one of them has printed a new note in his house and started using ₹2 instead of one then what will happen. This will create new liquidity. Right? That fellow will start spending liberally because he is wealthier by ₹1 more than others. This will trigger problems as price rise and so. This is rise in Quantity.

Now the other part of this conspiracy.

In the room, there are total ₹10. This Quantity is enough to do the transactions inside the room.

Say that one of the intelligent fellows has created a new concept and has sold/mortgaged his share of property to foreign source and has brought in new money. *This sounds logical but here is the catch. Quantity of money should not rise any time as per the principle of the Economy based on Transactions.*

There are no new transactions added to the economy of the room. Then why this new money? Is that money valid?

Even if the new money comes in from foreign source, it is not supposed to be added to the economy. This intelligent fellow cannot add the new money to the economy.

But it is not what is happening.

I will explain with another example. Say that I floated a company with an investment of ₹100 as ₹1 per 1 Share. I have 50 shares. Now I have ₹100 in the company. I sold my shares or mortgaged my shares and brought in ₹30 again on my shareholding. Now what is the liquidity available in the company? ₹130.

The inflow of money from within the system of one economy and from external economy makes a difference. If it is from within one economy, quantity of money will not rise. If it is from foreign source, quantity of money will raise. Rising quantity of money will create again price rise and poverty.

This company is part of India. India has officially ₹10,000 in its economy because of 100 companies like that. Now, because of my act of bringing in more money, I added ₹30 more. Similarly by other companies. Now the ₹10,000 will become 13000. This way more liquidity is added to the economy.

No change in company or its transactions. No change in India and its economy but liquidity is rised.

This kind of addition of liquid has been happening from different directions, through different sources under different sources.

This kind of activity has been happening.

1. As shares are being mortgaged in foreign sources and allowing more money.
2. As shares are being sold to foreign sources and bringing in new money to add to economy.
3. FDI and FII into stock markets.
4. Several companies have taken loans as foreign commercial borrowings.

5. Several infrastructure companies have taken loans from foreign investors and are getting benefited from such investments which includes World Bank loans.

Such inflow of money is creating more and more liquidity in India resulting into rise in Prices.

*Every transaction of India has been yielding benefits to foreign investors.*

Since we have such large investment and large liquidity, which resulted into more and more money, prices are rising inside India for both Indian resources and foreign resources.

Such process of rise in liquidity in Indian Economy is automated through different forums such as Forex Trading Market where the more rupee gets devalued that much more money is being added to the economy of India. In fact, such a large blunder is being projected as "Legitimate and Scientifically Right" system.

Remember here, money world is virtual world and "correct and wrong" are completely related to our acceptance and consideration.

There are several questions here.

1. What is wrong?
2. Why is it wrong?
3. If it is wrong, then how did it become law/policy in India. How this wrong gets projected as Correct?
4. If it is wrong, what the intelligent Union Civil Service Executives have been doing?
5. If it is wrong, why parliament has accepted it.
6. What are the negative/positive results due to this wrong?
7. What is the solution for this?

In present time of democracy, if we look around, political organizations are also operating as corporate bodies for profit. Since Government employees are using their own Informal Organizations, all non-Government employees are adopting the political organizations as lobbying units in order to save their vested interests.

This has been adding situations to political organizations in such a way that they transform themselves to work as profit organizations instead of service organizations.

There are reason for this. One of the core reasons is the loss of affordability due to continuous fall in the Currency values.

The fall of currency values, rising prices, impacts everybody in the nation starting from the common man to organizations and including Government.

The fall of currency values, rising prices, loss of affordability is leading everybody to adopt methods of making more money from within available options.

I wrote earlier about my emails to Finance Minister of India, media, Chief Ministers of states, Members of Parliament, I used to write on several different contemporary subjects, I used to notice several different comments from different corners of Government.

Probably it was because they realized about the intentional rupee devaluation concept that was found to be the core reason in which several of the top chairs are involved in this conspiracy for several decades and have been involved against the welfare of the nation, a new concept was evolved that is Rupee Trading system.

# 31 LAW

Law when not defined appropriate enough with proper equilibrium, then disputes arise always.

Let us say, a business house wants to sell a product or service. Now, it is selling the product or service to a customer at some cost. Customer expects some benefits from it. When those benefits are not met or expectations are not met, dispute starts.

Here, the role of Government is to see that producer provides right product that meets the expectation of the customer. This is the responsibility of the law. Proactive towards supressing the disputes, requires the involvement of legal experts who review the offerings by producer and draft them in such a way that customer is made aware of what he is receiving at what price, setting the expectations proactively.

The difference between India and First world nations, I found was, Legal Experts in first world nations show their expertise in the proactive activities which do not lead to rise in disputes so that quality of the life will improve. In India, most lawyers prefer to have more disputes in order to have their earnings assured. The continuous rise of cost of living led to this kind of social psychology.

This is one of the reasons why India has more disputes. When one of the entities of the nation is expecting it as opportunity to earn for livelihood and that entity is considered as the expert then what would be the result of the nation's legal definitions and framework, is very clear in India.

Also several times, most of the legal activities in India since are not properly created, updated and refined timely, several of the judgements are becoming references of law. Supreme Court rulings or some other rulings at state High Courts in several different occasions usually will be used as references for defining what is correct and what is wrong. Several times, Supreme Court or other apex court's rulings have been mostly reflecting the nature "not technical" but "benefit of doubt" like "Maryada Rama" or Birbal judgement that is situational.

In the present situation, Courts have privileges but not authority. Courts have privileges to drive all other entities to take action in order to act on entities that are responsible for disorder. However unfortunately, courts are assuming Authority some times.

An entity that is supposed to implement law has become creator of law. An entity that is supposed to give feedback to create better laws has been misusing its privilege and has been directing and creating several unwritten illogical laws inside nation.

Such large confusion is again because of lack of skill with Indian union Civil Service executives.

Instead of conducting proper analysis and defining the frame work for definition of "Correct" or "Wrong", this kind of ad hoc activities have been leading to the destruction of the nation's legal system and leading to the confused system and creating more scope for corruption.

There is a reason for this; that is lack of skill of identifying the root cause for the creation and existence of such confused system with all the so called experts of the field.

The role of Union Civil Service executives is also very prominent in such situation of lack of proper definition of law and its framework that can be followed by Citizens.

1. Most of them are not having enough study and analysis before framing the rules.
2. Not enough debate is on the new rules.
3. Not enough debate is on existing social condition.

4. No due diligence on the present social affordability and suitability to the new proposed changes or readiness of the existing society.

Also this kind of bad practices lead to the point of creating corrupted laws or incomplete laws in order to confuse the citizens and mint money from it by using the power of the position being a Government official.

Also such laws lead to creation of weak system that leads to the point where corrupted officials cannot be convicted easily.

However what I observed was, several of the laws are being created intentionally and also its repercussions were properly being analysed and ready answers to cover the repercussions, if surfaced as intended crimes in media, and trying to provide new meanings to the corrupted or incomplete laws. But no effort is being put to correct the corrupted law or incomplete law to fix the problem.

One more Stupidity has been getting developed in such a way that it is becoming more and more cumbersome to deal with. Following will explain more in detail.

Today subjects are micro granulized such as a doctor with different specializations and finance with different verticals or horizontal specializations etc. Similarly Union Civil Service Executive system is also having different branches, such as, Foreign Service, Administrative Service, Police Service etc. Such division has created a well ring fenced areas of operations where when cross subject issues have come up or to operate as confluence of different subject as leaders; leaders are becoming weak when subject matter experts are dragging as specialization of their area of expertise. This has been creating a major problem at the nation level.

Leaders are becoming "Helpless Jokers" and Media with half knowledge have been ridiculing the acts of leaders. Whereas the actual facts are there where SMEs are over smarting and complicating issues left and right.

Such acts of Media have led since last 10 years to a new disorder that started developing inside the nation. It is the misuse of power and opportunities by Government employees.

In the history, every major human rights problems were actually created by the corresponding "Workers with Power" and not the actual leaders. The same has been started developing inside the nation.

In fact the same has been the problem for several disorders inside India like the Naxal issue, or other issues.

Several rules are created by administrative people with improper analysis of suitability to the situation. This was because of lack of understanding of the problem at right perspective. Majority of the time, Bureaucrats want to keep the power and control at their disposal only. This is a major "Anti-National" activity which has been cherishing because of stupidity and lack of knowledge with Media and so called experts participating in Media.

Also Government employees have been using their employee unions in order to gain the advantages which are actually illegal. Their efforts are nothing but conspiring against the nation. As a matter of fact, employee union system is not applicable to Government employees because they are not employees but public servants at volunteer level to serve the nation.

In them, profit thoughts are injected and they have been considering the job as their right. They have been in the impression that since they have cleared hard screening process, they are entitled to receive all unreasonable benefits which is completely wrong. For example, Government officials, including retired people have been drawing benefits which are unreasonably high as Salaries, Perks, Dearness Allowance and many more ways. All such money is supposed to be used for nation's development so that several youths get job opportunities and nation's life standards rises.

More details are given at the end of this chapter about why what Government employees have been receiving and where they are wrong and illegal.

Such thoughts are supposed to be properly cleared through proper counselling exercise by Union Civil Service Executives which is not happening today. They are using that for their advantage in order to keep their power and control on the system.

"Several laws/rules are being created in such a way that the Citizen cannot follow them hence he will be trapped in the frame of law and has to pay bribes or some other means to get away from the situation".

The lack of skill of identifying such disorders by Media analysts has become an advantage to Government employees and bureaucrats.

What are you able to figure out of above?

They are not getting developed naturally from out of blue. They are being created successful only because some hidden force has been working behind them. Those behind working forces are none other than Bureaucrats.

I have given some example later in the book.

The anamolics are being very strategically created at different levels by global forces. Unless one understands the Completeness of "Ruling (Administration + Management + Supervisory + Monitoring + Worker)" capabilities with more matured understanding of Ruling, this cannot be understood.

Trust me, this is not an Illusionary of my brain or my own world. This is part of present world which is not understandable due to lack of such large visionary.

While I hear anything from our epics as power or skill of Lord Krishna, or "Third eye" I always feel that some time ago in the history of India and human kind such large things happened hence they are being mentioned in the *puranas* and *vedas*.

This is what "third eye" is. Third eye is the vision, that is developed from the knowledge base created from the broad information related to that specific situation.

Today, in order to correct this to make India better, Government employment, of any kind, tenure must be fixed to say that 10 years per person in his life time. Only this can change the fate of India.

There are around 2.5 crore people working as Government employees at different levels in different entities of Government.

They are consuming 85% of the Government income. Only 15% is being used for development purpose. This is not my talk, as you know the reference of Rajiv Gandhi and from information from Government.

When such large amount is going to them as remuneration and not used for development of several different common facilities then that results into rise of every facility inside the nation.

For example, drinking water used to be free earlier. Now it is not. Why? Earlier, natural recycling time was sufficient for that population.

As the population has been growing, if the facilities of artificial and quick recycling are not developed for producing fresh water from drain water then people have to spend their earnings for water to sustain life.

This is exactly have been happening.

Since Government has been distributing money to each employee and wasting it by unproductive means and the money that is supposed to be used for developing common facilities to all, cost of living inside the nation has been rising and resulting as poor sanitation inside the nation.

This minimum sense is supposed to be there with all Economists and Union civil service executives. But why is it not there? Where has it gone wrong?

Do you guys know how it is executed?

I wrote earlier, there was huge demand for raising salaries by Government employees and raising salary was a decision of Ruling chairs. They were being targeted for not paying enough to Government employees which is leading to rapid rise in Corruption.

Later there was a concept created of Pay Review Commissions.

I detailed to Finance Minister of India about the wrong being committed by appointing Commissions.

Instead of Correcting the situation, Manmohan Singh raised the salaries of elected members by 10 times.

One blunder, no, not blunder, a conspiracy against the nation's economy was added by another blunder to bluff the nation.

Here I must mention this, probably, one cannot find any bigger corrupted Governments of both UPA–1 and UPA–2. The prime minister of these Governments was Dr. Manmohan Singh. However, since their corruption activities not possible to understand by even the so called highly educated with doctorates. Several more are there as economists and in other form in the central government who have been enjoying the back stabbing activities of Indian economy.

Do you guys understand now how deep we have been deteriorating?

Again I would like to remind you that these are not happening due to an UNKNOWN source as origin. They are the results of major long duration political plot execution in terms of Financial Policies and economic policies of India by Global forces using some useless fellows as Economists.

Here I must mention and explain about Committees and scams of UPA Governments.

As an economist, raising prices were supposed to be a major concern and the nation should be made aware of it as soon as possible. However he never does it. He however uses the rise in prices as symbol of PROSPERITY because rise in prices gives more MONEY in QUANTITY to individuals and such raise will be considered as INCOME by individuals.

He also misleads the nation on the same note and several others who are agents of foreign Dracula forces chanting the same in different words to mislead the nation.

One more major thing is, he always tries to create bigger problem in order to cover earlier problem. When situation is out of control, do all that to make it more worst so that nobody can figure out what is wrong.

One more thing is he uses the "creation of committee" route in order to make anti-national activities as genuine and legitimate.

Since several more in the top chairs of India have been committing anti-national crimes against India since last 40 years by being in Employment chairs of Government of India, and are still there as advisors or in other positions as "Committee Chairman", they have been helping each other in order to cover their crimes against the nation.

Their one and only effort always be would disabling the Democratic Leadership of the nation.

There are some more outside people who work in global firms or in media who works in tandem to the global forces agenda in which the above said corrupted fellows are participants.

How many of them are there? Probably many.

Hope you remember the folk tale monkey and two cats with one bread loaf, where monkey eats away the total bread while dividing the bread evenly for cats. Today lawyers are in the place of monkey.

Here I would like to give details about how big dumb heads are Indian bureaucrats and economists and even many intelligent Indians. Today we are paying toll charges whenever we get on to the road. This concept was imported from USA showing its toll roads. I studied them USA where the population is ¼ of India on Geography of three times of India. USA constructed its roads but found no citizens and can not ask public to pay more tax money. So the option left was, construct roads and collect money when people use them. The situation in India is completely contrast to USA. USA that has a clear strategy properly used great Indian dumb head economists and bureaucrats and made moves to privatize the road network to invest its "fake" money through world bank and make money from Indian economy.

# 32 FOREIGN FUNDING

After several emails about World Bank and IMF related funding activities, there started a new set of policies creation in Government of India. This is about BOT and PPP operations. Here one more important aspect to understand is after 1995, when World Bank started giving loans for infrastructure project of Government, there started a new set of millionaires whose profession is civil contract works. Most of them are MPs of India.

The new BOT and PPP is an opportunity for all those new millionaires to become billionaires and also almost private ownership of public properties. An initiation to new feudal system that destabilizes the united Indian strength and weakens the Democracy of India.

Airports were getting privatized. Metro rails are being built. National Highways have become privatized. Toll gates were introduced. The earlier issues of constructing using World Bank Loans, now are not there. But where these new PPT or BOT consortiums have been getting money from? Reader should recognize here one important thing.

What are all those occupied by such foreign investment?

1. Roads—Where India moves
2. Electricity—Where the entire nation is dependent on
3. Banks—Where Finance is used what the nation runs
4. Irrigation dams—Where Food Production of nation is completely dependent on
5. Stock Markets—Where ownership of Industry resides

6. Media—Where nation gets awareness from, it means information to individual human
7. Communication—What India used for communication.

Every activity of an Indian will fetch profits to global economies. Every activity of the Indian will weaken Indian Rupee and strengthen the global economies.

Also several natural resources of India are now owned by foreign companies. A new type of Capitalism. Actually capitalism is completely different from this anarchism under the name of Development. Did you hear the word Global tenders? Does it ring any bells?

All the resources in the projects belong to India but Money would be from foreign.

Loans from foreign land is nothing but importing money. Importing numbers, how funny it is!!

Are you finding it funny or not? If you are not then you are still not able to understand the number game. You may want to read the book again to understand the number game gain.

We are importing numbers. Such a joke is being promoted by world renowned and widely acclaimed and praised by experts and intellectuals.

Here one thing what should be understood is, in this world of multi-currency, the principle of one currency entering other currency is not supposed to be occurred and not valid at all.

Why is it not valid?

If you are not able to find it logical then that means you are just completely influenced by those corrupted reasons of Global forces.

Here I need to take you to depth of it to make you understand why it is not valid!

One thing you may agree that one nation's currency cannot be used as currency in other nations. So it is invalid but they created a new concept which is "Currency exchange system" and trading of currencies between each other. This concept can't be sold easily unless some jokers are promoted as experts.

Hence they used some jokers in several platforms to promote this concept and implement.

For this they used the route of intentional devaluation. This Intentional devaluation started yielding money to EOUs and to those MPs as contractors inside India and working on World Bank Loans.

This kind of easy money, since they could not have a clue about the reasons that are causing rise in cost of living every day, this was promoted as "reason for rise in prices is rise in population."

Since we don't have real good experts as Economists, all junk heads are considered as Economists and promoted as experts inside nation, nobody has any clue about several facts and all wrong means have become legitimate causes for all disorders inside India. The concept of currency itself is not properly understood, and proper knowledge transfer is being done by universities and so called "Experts" as well.

Here I have to give you one information, you may usually find people as Market Analysts, Share Market Analysts, Banking Specialists, Finance Experts and Economists. Every one of them except economists usually have only some part of understanding and they would be projecting that as good for economy because the underlying fact is that they get benefit for future developments due to their predictions or conclusions. Economists are supposed to have 3D 360 understanding but only those who have exposure to other economies could only be able to make out what is happening. However such fellows also usually only give preference to their personal achievements and recognitions and do not care anything about a benefit to nation at macro level. The systems are conceptualized and implemented in such a way that if you work to the bias of global forces, especially to the benefit of first world nations, you will be given access to global platforms and would be given all international prizes. Otherwise, your papers will be trashed and your books will be termed as nonsense and you will completely fail in your career. The same has been happening to me as well. Every leader of India knows me and my effort but none of them ever called me to support me.

Refer here my emails about RBI intentional devaluations and Manmohan Singh's acceptance of intentional devaluation. In order to cover up the crimes against the nation, all those involved have started promoting the concept of Full Currency convertibility and Free trade of Rupee against global currencies by allowing Rupee in the Currency future market.

What Indians don't know here is, "the process of continuous rise of Expenditure" was automated and left to the trade markets which is the core reason why prices always rise inside India unless that is removed. "Rising Expenditure was automated through Forex market trading" by Manmohan Singh, importing money as investment or loan, and converting them and using the converted money.

That did not happen easily. Several industrialists and several export oriented unit fellows are stuck in there in Delhi corridors. Because they did not bring back their forex income to India. Let me give you some details.

Hope recall the Trade deficit. It is the difference between Imports and Exports. If Imports are more means, expenditure is more, if exports are more means income is more. If imports are more than exports, means your account has more expenditure than income. Means you are running in losses.

You mean, Indian Economy here.

There are 16 different ways, some of those are not visible to common eye how expenditure can be injected into a nation.

In a nation, expenditure can be raised by all the following activities.

1. Weak Currency Value against other global Currencies.
2. Rising Taxes
3. Rising Waste Spending
4. Rising Government Employee Salaries
5. Rising Fuel Prices
6. Printing and injecting more Quantity of Money that is more than the ACTUAL ECONOMY
7. Disruption of Administration and Management Structure of the nation

8. Wrong projection of Development Figures
9. Rising Fixed asset values
10. Poor Quality Public Works
11. Irrational taxes
12. Large Money Transaction Charges in Banks
13. Slow movement of Rupee in Banks
14. Large Interest Rates in banks
15. Large CRR in banks
16. Large margins (Lending Rate – Interest on Deposits) to Banks

In all the above, points 1, 5, 6 and 11 will have 360 Degree NEGATIVE effect on the Economy and our lives and we start behaving ERRATICALLY.

Indian economy never had any Surplus Account, it has always been running under deficit account. However, RBI has forex reserve. When a nation has deficit, how could it have Reserve?

I wrote an article about the same which was published is available in the Appendix–II of this book.

Also one more thing, when Indian companies like software companies, send their manpower to abroad for onsite services, the income on them doesn't come to India. Also several regulations in those nations, demands the offices of service provider in those nations for which do not allow the forex income to India at all.

This is another major dent to the inflow of Indian economy.

Like this Indian Economy has been losing a minimum of US$500 billion worth of wealth and resources till date every year.

By now the reader may have reached a point to understand none of these are happening or occurring "out of blue" but a very carefully strategized plots are in the execution mode.

Such plots are supposed to be investigated and stopped at seeding level itself by Union Civil Service executives, since that is not happening, now question arises, if they are capable of administration. Administrators may cover their inefficiency with "India despite of all world conspirables on it but is still surviving because of them".

In fact they are also participants of such plots. Now one may say that these bureaucrats are not concerned for all developments but we are in democracy where everybody is responsible to perform their duties when getting benefited from Government as salary.

Let us look at the kind of inflow and rise in forex reserves with RBI has been very misleading. As FDI or FII, whatever the money came into nation has raised the liquidity that resulted into two things.

1. Large rise in Real estate prices
2. Rapid conversion of land to real estate from actual purpose.
3. Loss of food production due to rapid conversion of fertile land and agrarian land to real estate.
4. Huge money in the system.

Such money reached the people who may not have any skill but just some inherited land and/or brokers who live in real estate.

Large Fixed asset prices are symbols of poor economic system.

In real terms, let us say a person who has earned his skills, may be done M.Tech or something else and had started a company to give employment. Now this person would be struggling due to rising Prices and suffering from being creative, working on meeting his rising expenditure and making profit, even after he put 20 hours a day performance with utmost efficiency.

At the same time, no performance is required by those real estate owners where prices are growing without any effort and that real estate owners are becoming wealthier day by day where their contribution towards creating new economy is big ZERO.

The first skilled fellow would be committing all kinds of blunders under pressure and complications of Government and placing himself in a position of "CRIMINAL" by violation of Government norms.

The real estate fellow would be the useless fellow without skill from whom the Government officials can squeeze money as bribery in registration offices. Similarly all those fellows those are now visible as "Mines Mafia" would be born and become neo rich fellows of the nation influencing the government and economy wrongly.

The skilled fellow who wants to lead a life on skill cannot even start another business or industry of new economy.

We see further disorder in the society as rowdies in real estate sector in land grabbing. Police corruption, murders in real estate, common man suffering due to loss of assets to rowdies and many more.

This is the result of injection of large money into the system for the forex inflow and weak rupee value.

I wrote several emails to stop the creation of more and more liquidity to then Finance Minister of India, Pranab Mukherjee, but he was reluctant to change and control as similar as Chidambaram. You can see all my emails in my online forum.

Such large spurt in real estate prices and large money with people those are not having knowledge or skill started influencing the local politics and political parties.

People, for money started spoiling all natural resources. Fixed asset sector has been behaving like a regular commodity sector which is a reflection of poor economic planning. Such rapid conversion of large quantities of land have been resulting into the following negative impacts.

1. Food production is falling
2. Pollution started increasing further
3. Easy money making ill qualified into political circles
4. Easy money has been creating new income to Government through real estate which is not a good liquidity
5. Product prices rise started inflation of prices

6. Productivity is falling
7. The raise in real estate has been evaporating the options of self-employment because rentals and land for industries have become more expensive.

People have started constructing the buildings for no reason. Requirement is less and construction has become more. Wastage has risen inside the nation.

The entire Money quantity availability has been creation of more and more uselessness and useless fellows as well.

These all sounds very virtual and apprehensions but they are facts and real near future, India is going to have such horrible poverty and Indians become so much unskilful that recovering will take generations.

Such horrible conditions are today visible as we are "buying" water for drinking, there is no worst situation than this can be referred as example.

Who is responsible for such large liquidity?

I told you that I wrote several emails about stopping the devaluation of Rupee. Chidambaram from Finance Minister Position was moved out and Pranab Mukherjee, who later became President of India, was in the chair of Finance Minister, during when, I wrote several emails about consequences of such rise in liquidity inside the nation.

What was his crime, he did not allow the appreciation of Rupee along with the inflow of Forex into India, instead he made to devaluate Rupee and helped to lead to more and more liquidity injection into India.

He was adamant and I don't think he has the nature of paying attention towards learning any new things because he doesn't have that nature.

As and when he travelled to USA, Indian rupee used to fall.

Please read the article in Appendix–II of this article that I wrote about the same.

A wrong without knowledge could be mistake but a wrong with awareness is intentional crime beyond excusable limits.

# 33 VALIDITY OF CURRENCY TRADING

In the present currency value based virtual economies, "Currency Value" is the representation of Sovereign Power of the nation.

Any acts that hurts it, is nothing but playing with sovereign power of our nation which is in other words "Independence" of Nation.

A "virtual instrument" trading with another "Virtual Instrument" by a Gambler and generates "new Virtual Instrument (gain/loss)" that impacts the real economy. Does this make sense? Isn't this very foolish? But it is made as legitimate and scientifically proven theory and made us to accept and practice it in our daily life by so called "World renowned Economists."

In order to save themselves from the crimes of intentional devaluation, all those in the chairs of Government of India as economists/financial experts/bureaucrats/ministers have started the Rupee Trading as Commodity in the Currency Futures market. This way they put the entire nation's economy in the hands of a Gamblers on Currency trading.

Indian Nation sovereign is put in the hands of the Gamblers. How shameful it is!!

This is such a large crime, unfortunately, since India has jokers as "Experts" appearing in TV commenting on Economy, nothing has been happening.

Is it possible to audit the Quantity of Currency or any other CRIMES committed on them? Impossible.

Is it possible to find out if a nation did correct or wrong with respect to their nation's Currency? Is it possible to say that America or Britain committed such and other crimes in order to maintain their Currency values?

Impossible. But there are some relevant facts that clearly shows that there are unbelievable crimes being committed by USA and UK in the area of Currency and Quantity of Currency.

The objective of Global forces is to destabilize the nations through their financial systems.

Here one thing needs to understand is "Success" of Industry and Commerce is the success of the nation and wealth of the nation.

They don't want to keep the nations in stable condition which might lead to economic growth of that region which is not good for the economic growth of First world nations.

Their target always would be to destabilize the structure of the nations for that they use all different kind of techniques and tactics.

Please refer the Change Management "Participants". They use all kind of tricks where the participants themselves will not have a clue about their involvement and especially their work that they are involved in. They may not be even able to recognize that they are working or involved to work against their own welfare.

This doesn't mean that this cannot be noticeable. If intelligent enough, these can be noticed and stopped.

They provide indirect support to all such activities which create instability in the region. The global forces existence cannot be noticed.

Everybody talks about Poverty, Global warming, Pollution, Corruption. In fact all such are the result of this economic terrorism.

Due to killing of affordability with some nations in terms of Numbers, those nations are not able to adopt of all that knowledge and technology that can be nature friendly.

In fact there are many nature friendly technologies but all of them are being killed with one and only poison that is Money. Such activities have been creating Corruption. Such corruption have been creating pollution and such pollution is resulting into Global warming.

What else it is resulting into? Suicides of Farmers, Child labour creation, Atrocities on woman, poor sanitation facilities and many more.

Now is it money that is causing such disasters? No it is not money. It is the trading of money or currencies against each other.

Currency should not transact against each other but it is introduced in order to benefit illegally against all natural principles.

Such poisonous system were established across the world using some corrupted crooks. Now those crooks are not interested to take back their own blunders and not ready to agree their blunders hence it is becoming worst day by day.

Now there is no new activity required to do new corruption activities. Already the system is established as corrupted and everything that happens in this system would be wrong. How to stop this?

This cannot be stopped without spreading knowledge.

The economic terrorism crimes are very process and procedure oriented and finding wrong is tough, if found proving it is another major complex thing.

I have written so much till now, still I am sure you have not got information about some of the things. Especially about the following:

1. Why currencies should not be traded against each other?
2. Why one currency should not enter into another currency area?
3. What is wrong in that?
4. What is wrong in the currency trading each other?

5. The currency value represents the strength of the economy, then what is wrong in that?
6. Strength of the strong economy is being passed to other economies in order to strengthen the weak economies.

I will give the details in a crisp manner.

If an economy has excess liquidity, it raises prices in that economy, which reflects as Inflation in terms of money.

If an economy currency is sent to other economy, as we already discussed, it is not valid to use.

Currency trading against each other is not valid transaction and also Currency future trading system is also not a valid system.

Because as I said above, currency should be against a Product and Service and not against other currency. Hence trading against each other is not valid.

One Currency entering into Second economy is supposed to weaken the First currency as its availability has increased to the second economy. But around the world opposite has been happening.

However, there is another major crime committed by so called experts, it is not allowing Rupee to trade against first world nation's currency and not appreciating it as well.

Am I making you go in rounds around this?

360 degree in 3D will be like this only.

One more thing I would say here, I wrote earlier, USA looks at the currency as DEBT instrument, means, if a new activity is being created, they will calculate the future economy and print money for that economy now itself as Debt which will be credited and adjusted from future economic activities Income.

Whereas we are made to believe that Currency is a CREDIT instrument which a nation can only have only when there is INCOME.

Don't think that how did I figure this out or did anybody say this to me by any government officials of USA or those first world nations? Stop creating these questions and understand the concept and meaning. I figured the above said difference by continuous analysis as Systems Analysis. Because it is my skills to find the root cause of the systems. Nobody tells me each and every RECORDED reasons with numbers or proofs for finding problem. I have to find reasons and then the root causes by myself from several different data.

Do you as a reader be able to understand how big fools we are being made by this difference at the core?

The so called Economists, joker economists, were used on us and made us believe that we cannot plan our economy with our own currency as your currency don't have Margin in it and your economy don't have income to meet your expenses.

Since then we have been taking loans from them and have been printing money for that imported money and using it for our purposes.

Just imagine one simple way, what is the difference between Rupee and US$? Why not we use US$ instead of Indian Rupee, whatever currency, how and what does it matter, we need a transaction instrument as Currency, instead of Rupee let us use US$. Will US accepts it? No. never. This might have explained you how we are being fooled.

Also one more fact, I will give you, US$ is being used as world mostly accepted currency. Right?

A currency that is supposed to be used by 30 crore people is made to be used by 600 crore people around the world. All such currency is supposed to be made available to USA citizens only.

Less prices means, government is supposed to make less money availability to the nation. The "margins left over" cannot be pushed on to other economies. But they successfully sold their idea and transferred their margins as investments into other economies. One question that arises here—are they genuine margins?

Now you may argue that, where 600 crore people are using it? Only it is being used as acceptable currency in the export market.

Now recall the investments by World Bank in infrastructure projects around the world. They are in US$.

Means, US$ is there in other economies behind all transactions.

Now, how can 30 crore people currency be used by 600 crores? How that much money got created? It means "fake money was created as Debt money and injected into the world" by USA. When such large money is created, how could that have so much value against other currencies?

Second angle to it. We in India use Indian Rupees, Right?

Hope you remember the variable concept in Maths.

Let us now say, "Indian Rupee" is a variable name representing value of transaction.

Earlier days, we used to have "Varahas" as currency, hope you recall this in folk tales.

Now why we not rename our currency as "Varaha". One more thing is, today Indian rupee is ₹60 per US$, why not we use another currency within our economy as "Varaha" and start using it as Equal to US$ and use that Currency as Official Currency of Indian Economy? Do you recall any similar activities on this globe in the last 20 years. It is Euro creation.

What I am trying to say here is, we are talking about numbers and they can be called with any name and with any meaning and assigned value to it.

After all we and our understandings are being hijacked by global forces, first world nations or USA, UK, Australia, Canada and other nations which were occupied by good old European Immigrants.

So much I explained. Why Indians are not able to understand this?

The reason for this is the Immigration system that was established by those old European Globe trotters.

When Indians are not allowed to expose to other economies, everything on the other side is a black box. This is equal to black holes of the universe, however here the universe is in the form of numbers and concepts.

Since people in third world nations are completely made to be swamped up with lot of expenditure then to some of them when achieved to migrate as immigrants to first world nations, after lot of hard work, have been usually afraid of returning to their homeland and engage themselves in the efforts of settling themselves in the new land such as USA, UK, Australia or Canada, never take risk of even thinking of reasons for their mother land sufferings.

It is because of this such large conspiracies based on concepts which have been cherishing on this earth.

Why am I worried? How am I able to notice?

Probably, I am better than others and/or I may have faced incidents different from others.

Trust me I always faced completely opposite situations than any others experience with immigration also. My parents entered into USA without entry stamp at immigration desk, when approached the immigration office for stamp, they simply said, enjoy man with parents. Who cares about immigration stamp!!

Even after 9/11 incident, I used to hear such a large stories about immigration which was completely different from my experience. I had a friendly chat with not one but five different officers, who offered me coffee at immigration desk, of course, I was the last one left at the immigrant desk and there were no immigrant left to verify, this was in Dulles international airport, Washington DC.

One more example I will give. This will connect you better than any other said above.

Several Indians were migrated to outside India. They move out of India and live in foreign nations as Immigrants for minimum of 7 years and could only become citizens there after minimum of 12 years which is 20% of active life of human.

In this active life, they earn money. They are immigrants, means they are resources of India. The revenues on them are income to India. Their earnings never come to India. If the revenues on them come to India as forex inflow then Rupee never gets negative impact.

The revenues on them are due to their knowledge base that they gained in India. As long as they don't get the citizenship, their revenues should be routed to Indian economy and then again send back to the foreign nation.

This way Indian Economy can do two things. One Export duties can be levied on them after which they can pay tax in the foreign nation.

India has been losing forex income worth several billions of US$ every year as inflow to its economy.

"Vasudhaika Kutumbam", all Indians know this phrase. Some of such words make me feel that whatever I am trying to mention in this book or similar situations which I have been trying to find today in real world were once occurred in this world earlier. Whatever details mentioned in those old epics were being misinterpreted by us.

In my terms, "Vasudhaika Kutumbam" is representation of Uniform value currency system.

# 34 UNIQUE ID—CREDIT HISTORY

Aadhar card in India is similar to SSN but not 100% the same. In USA, everybody gets Social Security Number or Tax Identification Number.

Social Security Number is for those who is either citizen or authorized to work in USA. 7.5% of income will be deducted towards Social Security benefits. If a person pays US$3,900 per year, he gets four points and who gets 40 points is eligible to take retirement, he/she and his/her dependents get social security benefits which we in India refer as Pension.

The amount would be sufficient enough to live well as low middle class person in USA.

The same social security number will be used everywhere as identification of the person. Also one important associated link to this SSN is Credit history.

Credit History is the record of all the "Credit" one has at present and has not paid. Pay more attention here, a person's credit history doesn't have to be with bank or loans, but every payment.

Telephone bill, rental records, insurance, car loan, home loan, education loan, credit cards and traffic violations etc. many more.

There are three credit bureaus in USA. Similarly, there are credit bureaus in all first world nations. Those credit bureaus maintain the records and when a person approaches a bank for loan that person's credit history will be checked in order to provide him loan.

If a person by virtue of his fate could not maintain it well, his HELL life will start on earth itself.

Heaven and hell are on earth itself and nowhere else. There is no lateral world. As I said above, USA is a man-made heaven but hell is also there in the same nation when credit history is spoiled.

However, there is a provision in US Law. As the credit history is an ILLUSIONARY system or VIRTUAL system, the provision available for them is "File Bankruptcy" stating that my Fate is screwed up and I need relief.

However in India, the meaning and understanding of bankruptcy is different.

Bankruptcy doesn't mean that they will not get loans again.

Also one more thing, even a convicted by law and sentenced by law is supposed to get job under the provision of equal employment opportunity.

People will not mind to hire due to one reason, the "Credit History". Everybody knows the impact of it.

When I landed in USA, Citibank was facing heat from public for charging high interest rates for all those with poor "credit history".

I received a call stating that you open account for US$ 1000, deposit that money, we credit card for US$800 at interest rate of 18% + additional charges if not paid the loan within 50 days of transaction. The additional charges are calculated at DAILY Compounded interest rate which accumulates to 1.5 times of actual interest rate.

What happened to me is not useful to this book but this was the situation in USA.

The credit history was later attached to Criminal History, resident history etc.

This credit history is such a tool there that sucks up the individual's life, everybody has been experiencing for generations.

What I observed and understood was "Credit History" is the reason for the "no marriage", "no commitment" life in USA.

They are afraid of such commitments as the expenses could not make them live at all. This is also the reason why they behave differently as “No Sentiments”.

*In simple terms, USA is a large open air prison with borders are ring fenced and controlled by border security forces and satellites and everybody is numbered and monitored.* You might have watched the Matrix Movie, it is all about the same.

In the account of Government, the systems treats every individual as an “intelligent computing machines”. However, they are human and have feelings and natural urges.

Both male and female will have urges of nature, hence they behave such openly in USA when it comes to their Sexual Life. A male approaching a female as similar as any male animal to female animal and flirting or seducing is not an “unacceptable” behaviour, just expressing interest or not is the only response. As they consider communicating back is a very normal behaviour.

This is another reason why those nations have such large “Homosexuals”/”Gays”/“Lesbians”. Male and female approach to each other has been leading to a severe psychological issues and associated social issues.

It is a Psychological disorder developed due to psychological pressure on “Teenagers or youngsters” from too many rules, regulations, laws, violations, social understandings, traditions and many more around the Natural urges that is clubbed with the Credit history sort of financial pressures.

Sometimes I feel that these were the reasons that led to the creation of arranged marriage system in India by Indian ancestors to avoid all such Psychological disorders. Probably that is the reason why all epics explain more about value and respect around male and female relation through marriage.

In India, the situation is slowly deteriorating and we could see the development of same disorders in the society.

Let us come back to economy, economy is nothing but healthy society.

The individual person will have a life in digital world. That digital world is around this credit history and information on that person. *Every person living on this earth with a number as SSN or unique ID card will have a character and personality in that digital world.*

I pity for USA citizens those are looking for relief from their Digital world life that is created using Currency as base by CROOKS considered as Economists and Finance Specialists.

The impact due to this on the individual person's psychology is such huge one, this is another reason why they go mad and do all those killings. If you are in the same situation, you would also do the same because of psychological pressure.

I need to give information about two things. One is credit history with traffic violations and second is the psychological pressure.

If a person violates traffic rules, he/she gets penalized in terms of Money and later this violation will become base for insurance companies to raise car insurance premium. Means his/her expenditure goes up and he/she will incur more problems without income raise. Imagine the psychological pressure one would have due to that. The violation could be a mistake but it is the penalty for life time of two years in future of individual life.

Your violation is your sin for which you will be put through hell punishment here itself.

Regarding psychological pressure, I happened to watch a program in Discovery. This program was a Real Case Study in a prison in USA. A convict whose harsh behaviour led him to psychological treatment. He was locked in a room with hardly 5 ft × 10 ft size where the same room will have a Toilet as well with only one window for ventilation and door with a small slide of size 3 inches by 12 inches through which he will be medicated. He cannot even interact well with doctor. He has to communicate through the voice exchanger fitted to the door. Psychologist cannot see him and vice versa. He might be there in the room till he will be certified by Doctor as "Safe".

Pay attention here towards the Doctor and his/her career. If the patient is not there, Doctor will not have a career and income. It is the doctor who should certify and that all depends on the Doctor's revenue strength.

Similarly this world is in the hands of so called "World Renowned Economists" who live on virtual concepts weaved around numbers.

See how big fools are making us behave as they feel like.

Imagine yourself by being in such situation in that room. How do you feel? What would be your psychological state?

During the onset of winter, crime rate in USA rises. This is because most of the impoverished fellows do crimes to go to jail to get away from the homeless and winter chillness. In order to save themselves from the winter or cold temps. Those lie below zero for 10 months in a year with all drugs and liquor and there are news articles of consumption of petrol or breathing petroleum evaporation to get numbness to their body, this is even by kids there.

I am not trying to create situations here. I am giving information as I saw from the news articles showed by live TV channels.

Imagine here the hardships that our freedom fighters had been in Andaman jails. You don't get that feeling in reality and none can imagine the real pressure on those great leaders who really took the life risk while fighting against such an uncertain and cruel opponent during freedom fight.

I somehow feel that all the successors of those old Global Crooks of British rule are in the Global organizations and doing Economic Terrorism in all nations around the world being in USA, because such large similarities in the behaviour of systems can be found in the present situation since last one century.

However in India, there were no credit bureaus until CIBIL was started by Private organization. Later some more foreign credit bureaus started their operations when the foreign loans were started pouring into the nation.

They were in need of a unique number system hence the Aadhar Card. However my study says that this was not started as simple as that.

This was related to the Credit Card business in India. RBI changed laws in order to allow foreign credit card businesses in India. Foreign Credit business with scope up to 48% interest rates lured banks in India and their management, mostly PSU banks owned by Government.

The reasons given for such large interest rate were "loans without security" hence risk requires such large margin.

However in USA, the interest rates on credit cards, though base rates stay very low at around from 3% till 9% on credit cards, there will be revolving interest rate compounded daily on the amount which will make the total interest rate anywhere between 12% to 36%.

However, banks insure their risk on advances and also make the customer insure their loans so that on unforeseen events their credit history don't get hurt due to lack of ability of payments of credit cards.

The insurance will be available for any kind of RISKS.

When banks were caught in the credit card mess till neck deep, they were pressurizing the Government and RBI for Credit history.

You might have understood by now that a person's private life information is being collected by a private company for the purpose of making profit on the information and for controlling his life.

Parliament of India was not apprised or involved in such large issue introducing a record system on 100 crore Indians. Law was not made to legalize the Credit history documentation. Even without law this has become an unofficial law to follow by Citizens of India.

Credit Card network was established in order to make money from money transfers through electronic network where banks would pay, as I learnt last time, about 0.025% per transaction amount to Credit Card Electronic Networks. This is like a drop of water that makes ocean of water to Credit card companies.

They have been cashing this like hell and taking that money as profit to their nation and converting them from Rupee to their currency. Same as with Credit Bureaus.

What else worst could happen with Credit history in your life? Since Credit history is not legally position with proper framework, correct or wrong information could be registered there.

Unless a person knows about flaws, when would they know, when they apply for loan, when they are looking for desperately for a relief from life problem by taking loan, then he/she has to fight to correct the information, for this, he/she has to go in rounds in order to correct it and courts also takes days or months or years to resolve the issue.

The first thing required here is Credit History cannot be updated with information without first confirming the righteousness of information from that same person.

In USA, as per my information, courts have been discouraging the credit card recovery companies, usually legal agencies, from claiming the money unreasonably considering the life events of human in this complicated world that lead to, Credit Card companies to collaborate with the defaulters in order to adjust the EMIs in order to retain the business in order and recover later days. This happens by reducing interest rates as well. This explains how they do business and how much value they give to human life against the profits in terms of money. The situation related to same could be unimaginable in India.

I was having loan in USA on car. I missed one EMI, I received a red letter. I explained the situation as I was out of nation. They simply removed penalty and allowed me to pay the money and set right all the impacts to 0. All this with a phone call.

In India, I was on bed due to accident, every time, I used to withdraw money for car EMI on 6th of every month, I used to deposit money on 3rd and found that cheque was bounced.

There were penalties. I said that I was on bed in hospital to bank but bank was repeatedly asking me to pay the money. One more interesting point is it was 58th cheque out of 60 cheques of EMI.

See the difference between USA and India.

Let us recall here one more thing about Priming and Sub Priming Issue.

Recall here the Insurance system and Risk Management. In USA or around the world, there is a practice of selling loans of one company to another company.

Companies which do business in Finance adopt insurance system to cover their risk exposure.

Say Company A has sold its 100% Debt to Company B at 90% of price by taking 10% loss. Company B to Company C similarly at lower level. At the end, the loss is evenly distributed among all companies. Now the companies just claim their loss as Insurance Claim. That is all. The Insurance recovers all the "loses".

People in India used to talk a lot about Sub-Prime lending crisis. But the approach that USA Government takes would be different that Indian analysts don't understand well.

Recall here the Anderson Consulting, Price Waterhouse Coopers issue that I explained earlier to understand the behaviour of USA Government.

This is again the same Water bed formula. The Liquid is evenly distributed and evenly recovered. (Not sure you have understood but it is not that complicated)

Manmohan Singh who has been loyal servant of global forces wanted to serve for the agenda of Global Forces in India. The same was true with Pranab Mukherjee who was supported by Nandan Nilekani sort of business men for profit who always prefer to work with association of World Bank and IMF in order to have their reach on global platforms through different nation's bureaucrats and with those clones who are projected intellectuals by Global Forces.

There is a catch between SSN and Aadhar Card. Aadhar card was introduced for corrupted purposes and SSN was being used for welfare.

Aadhar was said a Unique ID for reimbursement of Subsidies. But was forced to share with Banks. PAN was introduced earlier but it was only available with those who pay taxes.

But the World Bank loans or credit cards or other foreign invested loans were given through micro finance to several Indians who don't have a PAN and never pay any tax in their life time.

How to bring them into Credit History net was a challenge to be answered, there was only one way it can be done that is by linking it with Subsidy on LPG at first level and making it mandatory by impacting the general life of public, though there was no subsidy and it was only a Financial adjustment by Government in its tax collection.

Here let us talk about subsidy again. Earlier days when Subsidies used to be directly given to Manufacturers by Government because it was easy to monitor. However, it was tough also as manufacturers may not provide actual production and actual sold but claims of false production capacities in order to get more reimbursement from Government. Even today such thefts are possible as Government has very minimum vigilance on it. Though subsidy was projected as basis for implementing aadhar card and system but hidden fact is credit history.

Aadhar only helped those foreign nations who export Digital cameras to India and also the systems used in them.

The simple one was made as complicated one.

The impact of Unique ID on individual young citizens would so horrible in India without proper framework. We are so much sentimental due to complicated systems around us that we follow all sort of astrology predictions. Even the vehicle numbers also we look at with sentiment, if a number that is lucky to a person.

Recall here the Nude dances that I mentioned above. People in USA do anything whatever they find it "returns" money in order to meet their credit commitments otherwise life would be hell.

The future of Indians with Aadhar card is visible today in the form of "Suicide Farmers".

# 35 TREACHERY

We all talk about Corruption in the systems of India. Usually Politicians would be targeted for this purpose in media. Everybody abuses a Politician like anything. Politicians would be projected as villains of the nation as well.

My study shows completely opposite. It is not politicians who are responsible for bad shape of India but Government employees. No Government employee is spared from this.

As we all know that our job and related power and privileges are like Sedatives. We live and die for them. We struggle for them. This is the Employee Culture and nature.

Employee is totally tightly bonded to his personal ambitions. I wrote above that Indian Systems are created by British and later new ones were created under the influence of Europeans and/or Americans directly or indirectly.

Employees are also very tightly networked. Their contribution and ambition would always be from the point of yielding a benefit to them. Usually we listen words like, in what way it helps your career?

This explains what the nature of employee is. At the same time employee wants to keep the control in his hands without responsibility. Why I am saying this? Since employee is getting paid for services but would not usually take the liabilities associated with that payment and responsibility.

Politician on other side does not get paid but spends his own wealth in order to be a politician or leader. What he/she expects for his spending is pure business proposition. When the system has flaw expecting a sincere politician is a wrong wish.

Leaders define what is required as Strategy. Administrators design what to implement suitable to that strategy. Managers implement what Administrators Designed. Supervisors supervise and accounts the implemented design and its performance. Monitors perform on and monitoring the implementations. Workers perform on the implementations.

In this entire six step, the major responsibility lies with Administrators who transform a concept from virtual to reality. It is the responsibility of administrator to implement flawless or fool proof systems. If required SME need to be involved appropriately for this.

The flaw in the systems is originating at Union Civil Service Executives who are committing irrecoverable blunders and getting away under the brand name of "intelligent". However from my findings, I found that the flaws are being introduced into the systems of India are not flaws by mistake but flaws by intention.

Every one of us faces several situation where we some or other way will become non-compliant to the law defined. We always immediately look for remedy to get over the situation. However we don't pay attention towards the reason why we have become non-compliance to the stipulated law.

The actual disorder here is "Creating a law or rule or regulation with conditions which cannot be met by Citizens". Defining the law without first considering existing conditions it is the starting point of the flaw.

Very simple example to prove the malicious intention of bureaucrats, I will tell you, none of the Government offices will have Application forms. They tell some format to be followed collecting from nearby Photo Copier Center.

Application will not have any information about required attachments.

Application will not have any guidelines about how to fill the data.

Application will have confusing fields to fill in.

Application when submitted, no acknowledgement will be given.

As an example, I will give one of my own experiences, my car registration was kept under suspension due to lack of documentary evidence of "Proof of *Permanent* Address". Following are flaws in this intentionally introduced condition in order to trap citizen and cash from his/her non-compliance to rule.

1. There is no process or procedure or entity of Government that provides a Permanent Address of a Citizen.
2. The citizen may not have a Permanent address at all.
3. The citizen may not own a house.

Indian economy is technically faulted. Such Technical faults by Government employees are forcing Citizens to become illegalized and getting incriminated. Probably the kind of "Crimes" being committed by Government Policy designers could not be compared with any other crime by any citizen, again the main culprits are Government employees in Administrative chairs and Subject matter experts.

My driving license was expired, second time. First time, all that I did was submit an application with a photo with address proof and got the Renewal Stamp in less than 15 days.

Second time, the procedures were changed, I was asked to get "No Objection Certificate (NOC)" for renewal from the office where it got renewed.

I was asked to carry a legal document that is supposed to be couriered between offices securely in order to avoid tampering of the documents.

I had to take a TV Media person's help to record live about the problems. Under such conditions, approaching the RTA in-charge of the office called the Additional Commissioner explaining about my situation of resisting to go and get the NOC personally, they were giving a "Special Case" Consideration.

Such several illegal processes and procedures are being introduced by bureaucrats.

Following would give some of those I can recollect now for this book purpose in order to give you a feel of where and how anarchy is being legitimized.

Corruption is being implemented through processes and procedures so that the disorder cannot Spotify and identify and proving corruption could become impossible.

Courts are not exempted from this. Everybody is taking advantage of their available means to create a localized trap for citizen and cash from his/her troubles.

Some of those disorders are

1. Farmer insurance—farmer is not supposed to pay in premium for this. Why? Please read my article in Appendix–II
2. Land Revenue Books
3. Poor Road Designs causing Road Accidents
4. VAT is good but there were huge confusion created around it in its Implementation
5. Vehicle Taxes for Road Construction but again Toll taxes
6. Tender System in Liquor retailing
7. Levy System for Rice Mills
8. Power purchase agreements
9. Pay Review Commissions
10. Land registrations
11. Law creation through Gazette Order
12. Land and building regularizations
13. Four Lane Roads with commercial building, direct approach without parking lots
14. In Commercial area, parking charges
15. Parking charges in Government office complexes
16. Poor Sanitation
17. Poor Quality Roads
18. Regulated drinking water
19. Selling Water

20. College Permissions
21. Passport clearance by police
22. Railway reservations
23. Bus reservations

And many more.

If we delve through, we can find so many "lethal disorders" that they are not unintentional or unexpected or a mistake. They are lethal disorders because they are leading to committing suicides by sufferers.

Every bureaucrat can be put to jail if these are properly analysed and finding the origin for such disorders.

Due to lack of skills with those writing analytical articles in media, such disorders are being properly attributed to Politicians failures.

Politicians are only a temporary entrants with only privilege but not power. Bureaucrats are the long term with power.

This "long term employment life with power in a close employee network and protection from application of law without prior permission from top chairs" has become an advantage and the procedurising the corruption is becoming a major advantage to them to get away from corruption activities.

The "long term" opportunity is also leading to killing scope for reforming the Government system with new skills.

Also one more major blunder with Bureaucracy is their incapability of understanding the problem. Such incapability is resulting into a situation where they are drafting something on paper and expecting people to follow.

# 36 FOOD SECTOR

Following was published as Editor Page column in Andhra Jyothy that tells what is the solution for India's fundamental sector problem.

Farmer and agriculture are in total Jeopardy. No, the fact is FOOD sector of India is in complete Jeopardy.

"Farmer completely lost confidence and sustainability". "Farmer must be saved". "Show Mercy at Farmer." "I will go to any extent until "farmer is saved" by Government of India".

Present days the above said are the frequently used phrases by all Political Parties and leaders.

Farmer—who usually being referred as "Food Donor" is today in trouble and is made as BEGGER for MONEY.

Farmer is trapped in the clutches of SYSTEMS OF MONEY—which need not be—a farmer IF decides not to depend on external world that runs on money then every one of us have to suffer for food.

There is no alternative for this.

First to be understood here is FARMER is not third party or second party but is our FOOD. We must recognize that we are talking about our FOOD and need to respect Farmer and stop the cheap tricks or activities of SAVING him/her. We are not doing any favor to him. We are saving ourselves. Every educated Indian is responsible for saving him and responsible for contributing to it.

As per MLAs statements in Andhra Pradesh State Assembly approximately two to three lakh farmers committed suicide in this nation and many more every day. What for? for virtual money. MONEY/numbers those are not real but imaginary.

Farmers are committing suicides because of FEAR of MONEY. They are completely terrified by MONEY.

The major fact is very clear from the economic policies of India is that between first world nations (who introduced the currency concept in this world) and India, "Currency Concept is not understood properly by Economists of India in India".

## Economy by Money Is Not Understood Properly

Every nation in the present world will have two economies. 1. Virtual Economy made and run by Money 2. Real Economy made by God.

Our Government and its CORRUPTED policies made Indians give more value to Virtual Issues, like Money, loans, agreements etc. but not for real LIVES of Farmers and Real losses of Agriculture.

One more very pity part is that the VIRTUAL systems in India are not COMPLETE but left over INCOMPLETE.

This is the reason why we are TIGHTLY bonded ourselves to VIRTUAL world made of MONEY and making suffer ourselves in our day to day life in our MONEY Matter issues.

Every Indian including Government of India has been losing a lot due to this INCOMPLETENESS in the VIRTUAL systems of India.

After looking at loss of so many lives and orphaning so many families for the sake of "virtual numbers" and looking at the present continuously spoiling sorrowful lives of farmers due to corrupted economic policies by SO CALLED economists of India, I am unable to resist myself from stating this here that they are clearly not ECONOMISTS but ACCOUNTANTS.

Agriculture/weaving/fishery/dairy and any other food related professions belong to Real world Economy.

These are our fundamental professions without which we cannot survive. Any Indian in those professions will not have enough expertise or skill of understanding and the intelligence of dealing with MONEY matters effectively in this CONTINUOUSLY changing GLOBALIZED FINANCIAL world.

Individuals those are considered experts or specialized in Financial Matters also sometimes fail to handle some of the MONEY matters effectively in this complex financial world. In such case, how a poorly educated farmer can handle money matters efficiently or sufficiently.

If we go to the roots of the problem, one issue that is not being noticed by every one of us including financial experts is that Government of India and its financial experts FORCEFULLY dragged and trapped Farmers from the Real World economy into the complex financial world without NOTICE to farmers. This is an UNWANTED and INJUSTICE act towards farmers. Today farmers are suffering a lot only due to this TRAP made around the neck of Farmer.

In order to untie the knots or unwind loops made around the farmers, today there is every need to work on evolving means and ways that can keep these FUNDAMENTAL professions away from the clutches of financial matters.

The loops made around farmers must be put back as responsibilities on the shoulders of all those FINANCIAL experts of Government of India and Banks in India.

Responsibilities and commitments which are supposed to be on the shoulders of the FINANCIAL experts of Government of India and Banks are today forcefully placed on the shoulders of farmers. These responsibilities are at the size larger than farmers can bear.

This clearly reflects INEFFICIENCY and INCAPABILITY of Economic and Financial Experts of Government of India which include from Manmohan Singh. Four hundred crores relief given by Manmohan Singh to farmers is also saying the same.

In order to save the farmer and our FOOD, we must do the following immediately.

Today the situation is as follows:

1. Banks are reluctant of giving loans to farmers because of insecurity of recovering of loans from debtor and his activities.
2. Farmers are not able to repay the loans because of loss of crop due to natural calamity, pest effects and price fall in the market.

The natural phenomenon that none of us can change even after so much of Scientific and Technical Advancement on the earth in human world, agriculture patterns will always be as per the Mother Nature. All Farmers get their yields all at one specified time defined by Mother Nature. The fact that we must keep in mind is every activity or matter that a Farmer handles or deals with never lies in his control any time. This includes Price of his product in the market.

So farmers should not be held responsible for any Financial Liabilities. Government and financial experts should take the responsibility of all liabilities of Farmers in the nation.

Today every real economy in every nation around the world is being driven by CURRENCY based virtual economy. Banks in currency based economies are FACILITATORS of Money flow. Unfortunately Due to lack of understanding of CURRENCY CONCEPT with SO CALLED Financial Experts of the nation of India, today banking is categorized and considered as BUSINESS in lieu of facilitator and banks behaving more as financial institutions instead of facilitators of currency transactions.

Consider these fundamental facts and blunders and misunderstandings with respect to the situation.

In order save the food sector of the nation Government cater fund of ₹ 2,00,000 crores as Insurance reserve fund right away to secure food sector of India. This fund can be categorized from money rests with RBI under the category of CRR.

This is to protect both banks and farmers, food sector of India.

This insurance works as Debt Protection for banks and Debt Relief for farmers simultaneously.

This strengthens the confidence of Banks and would give loans to farmers. Instead of farmers, Banks will pay premiums to secure their loans given to these professions. The premiums paid by banks will be added up to this 2,00,000 crores Insurance reserve fund.

Farmers should be kept away from Financial liabilities. His liability must be discounted and determined based on the statistical data yields.

For example:

If a farmer has procured ₹10,000 loan for an acre paddy field.

If we consider maximum paddy yield per acre would be 2,000 kgs and if the kg paddy is calculated at ₹10 per kg, means per acre farmer should get a gross return of ₹20,000.

After the crop, farmer liability should be "discounted" on average yields per acre in the area calculated against market price.

In case actual yield is only 1500 kgs per acre and now the market price is only ₹8 per kg, the total now comes to farmer as ₹12,000. The total loss to farmer from actual is 40%. So the farmer loan should be discounted by 40% by banks and banks should recover their losses from the insurance pool of Government. Also the Interest part of the farmer must be discounted accordingly.

Every loan of farmer must be TRUNCATED by the March 31st.

Government must work out on averaging the financial matters at the national level and should be kept away farmer from his financial liabilities.

Government must constitute a body that keeps on surveying the production yields of Agriculture around the nation after all natural calamities and pest effects. Government must declare YIELD ratio Max vs Actual after all calamities by

LOCALIZED VILLAGE wise and make the farmer relieve from all liabilities by the end of the CROP SEASON.

These must be done immediately to regain confidence in the nation's fundamental sectors.

Money is a USELESS concept when compared with food and life and all those are deal with them are USELESS fellows when compared with Farmer/weaver.

The above said may not completely solve the problems of farmers directly but rests responsibility of the financial matters more on the shoulders of the Financial Experts of Government of India and banks.

I am 200% sure this shift of responsibility will fix several other hidden blunders made by Indian Financial Experts due to which today INPUT cost of Farming is at unbearable levels to Farmers.

I urge everybody to send an appeal to Government of India for starting this insurance scheme.

# 37 EDUCATION

Our Education and its capability is good at building a Follower or Worker or Slave but not a Leader.

In order to talk about education, I should start from the point of my experience in USA.

I was working as computer software engineer in USA. One of my colleagues was an upper primary school pass out who was a truck driver and learnt vocational computer courses and has been working as Computer Software Systems Analyst along with me and drawing double the salary than what I was.

Here in India, Indian software companies used to recruit best scored fellows from top schools and used to project as a highly intelligent field where no ordinary fellow can enter and work. Here a person who was not even school pass out was working in Computer field.

Flights will be driving by uneducated farmers also. Here in India, flight driving would be for persons whose IQ is extraordinary and requires unimaginable natural intelligence.

In USA, anything can be done by anybody is the type of social psychology. Here in India we follow silly things as axioms of life and make things complicated.

If we look around, people with skills of nowhere related to their jobs that they have been performing are in the jobs. For example, Civil Engineer will be in Information Technology Field. Electrical Engineer in Finance Field. Finance Fellow in Engineering Field etc.

This is also the result of one of the negative impact due to large weak Rupee Value against Global Currencies. The excess realization of Money for small services is resulting into people develop the "awareness" level to get into jobs as soon as possible without fundamentals. If they have fundamentals or not but further involvement with "interest" to create new from the experience will not be there.

What is the end result due to this? Scope for new Creativity is being murdered which is one more reason for why there is no technology creation in India.

I wrote an email about this to Finance Minister of India once.

Once I tried to establish internet service provider business, during then internet was not there in India. During then I asked for permission to visit the STP data centre in Vijayawada. I did not get access to the server room and the projections they gave me was, accessing that room is only allowed for authorized personnel with permission from STP commissioner Hyderabad. I was surprised. Government units are supposed to expose the technology to everybody so that knowledge can be spread and new innovations can be developed.

As I said earlier, Innovation doesn't have to be the size of Einstein invention. I will give one simpler example. I am not sure if you have heard about Taste Engineering. Taste of food that we human eat and drink. Taste doesn't have to be Sweet always to be acceptable by everybody and be in demand. We also know that Taste could be sweet/sour/bitter/salty/spicy or could be combination of them.

However, Taste engineering is a technique of creating taste and flavour of food that attracts the human repeatedly.

This is how the world, not Indians, are living in this world in a tangible world which is what Indians need to focus on in future in order to survive.

But the present state of India might require another five generations to get there as, I already said this, Indians lost their fundamentals.

Hope you heard the word "Heaven of Thrishank" that is where India is in now with lot of "Liquidity" or "Money".

In USA, even a beggar house will have a telephone connection. In India, even after 40 years of independence, telephone was considered as Luxury instrument where MP recommendation was required for it. For this, not the politicians or political leaders were responsible but the bureaucrats and the employees of telephone industry who want to enjoy the monopoly system which is a new form of Feudal System where power will be used in order to enjoy the monopoly illegally.

The other name in the nation of India to this is "License Raj". This kind of monopoly system has different names at different levels, however the final result is "monopoly" and "anarchy" control in the hands of Government Employees, especially bureaucrats.

When I was doing my graduation, there used to be only around less than 25 engineering colleges in Andhra State. Education was also regulated. Not everybody was allowed to learn what ever course they feel like. This was one of the blunders at the core of Indian Education.

*One major problem in India, is lack of skill of identification of problem.* "Problem" always is identified wrongly and solutions would be created for wrong problems.

Let us look at the actual problem of Indian Education system. I already wrote about Indian Economy is not a Creative Economy but a trading economy.

In order to understand the problem with Indian Education system, let us consider learning driving a vehicle by reading a book. This is the fact of our education.

A person who by hearted content of the book will become a teacher and start teaching others as well. What is this saying to you, one idiot is creating another idiot.

We used to have a system where learning skills by practice used to be there but they were more tied to the caste system where caste segregation was considered as representation of Profession. Let us not get into "Correct" or "Wrong" or I am trying to talk about "Caste" system.

This was helpful in passing the secrets of trade by elders to their children without reservation. However, this was completely destroyed by British Employment and introduction of Money and Power in the society as Revenue officers and as lawyers.

People were forced towards reading and writing and several left their native skills and started running behind the virtual skills for money.

We have reached a point, a person who has mugged up the "book of driving" and can "rewrite it in new words in new conditions out of imagination" is Expert, further excellence in such reproduction as "Doctorate".

I said about my effort and changes in the real world due to them. I felt that I deserve some credits and tried to see if I am eligible to get Doctorate. What I found by a Doctorate person was, "Ph.D. is a Course of Learning better learning and not representation of Expert".

This sentence tells that they are covering their actual capability and second they are not interested to lose their credits.

In my opinion, unless a person's research yields a "real" time impact in the "real World", that person should not be awarded with "Doctorate". All the present doctorates also should be discontinued.

I would advise here to the reader to understand the sorry situation we are in so that we can correct it to make it better.

I wrote earlier about "Trading" economy.

Even education in our nation is in the same mode where teacher is just "trading" his "awareness" for "money".

There is nothing wrong in learning new improved skills in life but leaving the original skills was the wrong occurred in Indian Economy. This leads to the situation where Indians lost all their skills. This destruction was supported by Bureaucratic practices of restricting all native practices by meaningless policies as part of Government.

When I found several hurdles, I wrote about the need for opening up the education sector to all because nobody knows where the talent is available in India in what form. Some may be good at reading and reproducing. Some may be good at learning while watching. Some may be good at learning by listening. Somebody good at experiencing. However, at the end people should be able to innovate a new thing.

Since Innovation has come to discussion. The real reason for Indians are not able to be innovative is because of above said all problems and global forces were not allowing the consolidation of knowledge base of India.

I should mention here one important fact. Since I have been doing this kind of systems analysis and root cause analysis and several of my findings were not found by anybody earlier and all my emails were resulting into some actions by Government, I was believing that I am qualified for receiving a Doctorate as all the Ph.D. Students invent something in order to get their doctorates.

However, I was not post graduate so I started looking for options about gaining some credits for my efforts those may help to get enough support from Media. What I found was, the Ph.D. Program is a three year course of "Learning a Better Learning" and not an expert of the field or subject in which he/she has gained Doctorate.

I strongly believe that Doctorate program must be corrected in such a way that only if the Thesis of the Candidate has a real time effect on the society, then only doctorate should be given to that candidate.

Also some more blunders are, Indian Education Cycle does not match with the life cycle of the Human at all. Also, the content of the education.

What I mean by this is, if a human misses an exam, he misses some time of his life which cannot be recovered.

Also the structure of the program, unless a person completes three or four year of course, he/she will not get any credit for his effort.

I wrote above the cycle of a stages of a human from user to scientist, our education has this structure but not properly being maintained with enough hands on learning cycle. Our education system has been training persons to look at the world through books which is what I was talking about 2D to 3D.

The courses should be modularised and each and every subject should have its own credits and credits should have accreditations and at the end, the confluence of such should result into a large credit like graduation or post-graduation etc.

The long duration of study result into psychological disorders in young persons which at its first state is visible as "poor expressions". Indian education and evolution system instead of building positions strengths builds negative characterise and humiliates one person.

Coming back to Innovation, the percentage of inventions by highly scored individuals are very less than average achievers.

One more major deficiency in Indian education is, how to apply it?

Since education is more on stuffing the brain with awareness and information and not practice, the student does not have a clue how to use what he/she learnt.

Also what he learns would be more of imaginary and he/she will not have enough resources for learning in practice.

Sometimes what I feel is, since new born baby does not have the skill of interaction with Highly intellectual fellows of the earth like all those we consider as educationists in Government of India, new born are spared, otherwise, they will be asked to learn by reading a book about how to consume milk from mother, then only consume milk, until then don't do it.

How to be innovative?

Just look around for problem that you can solve with your skill, your skill may not be a kind of Einstein one but just a logical thinking within your reach. Then one can become innovative in no time.

One thing to be cognitive is that the Indian Economy is designed in such a way that "Creativity" has no scope to be successful.

Hope the reader is aware of Six Sigma Quality assurance technique. The evolution of it and popularization of it has close relation with Flight Maintenance by GE.

GE has Flight maintenance division. Once a flight cock pit window was fitted with a screw that is nearly of the same size but having smaller width head size less wide than required size.

This leads to a major flight mishap.

Why I am mentioning this here?

We are not even capable of making proper quality nails even after having engineering qualifications and lot of engineering graduates from premier institutes.

We do not have Material Engineering knowledge at all which is fundamental to any Technology. Material engineering is nothing but knowledge/knowledge base of Science.

In order to be a good technologist, one should have strong knowledge/knowledge base of Science.

This is not building up due to large resource costs due to falling rupee value.

This leads to kill all the technology capabilities in India. Not only that, if we look around whatever the technical skills learnt will be reset due to which education institutes or even teachers of India getting reset in their skills and becoming outdated.

Education institutions or teachers are supposed to be the Solution Providers but they are in the state of complaining on everything. They are supposed to offer guidance but they are at the state of insulting youngsters under different names. They are supposed the Anti-Virus of Nation and its society but they are in the state of catalysts of Virus. Here they means, I am not referring their physical presence or profession but their knowledge.

The best scorer in the present education system could be a "good worker" but not "good leader."

I would consider that the reader has understood the impact of information on us. There has been proposal about allowing foreign universities into India to direct the indirect influence on India and its knowledge.

I would rather say about the result in order to understand the large number of reactions due to wrong policies.

Our brain is emptied and filled with Junk. Our Physical performances and capacities are completely destroyed.

We are made as mentally retorted and physically handicapped despite of having all body parts perfectly functioning.

Reading and getting awareness requires exposure to the actual ambience of what is read and understood.

Indian's chance for getting exposed themselves to other parts of world is being killed by two means, raising 'unaffordability' and 'restricting accesses' through immigration systems.

The real fact is we are making ourselves as "dumb heads". You look at the books of our learning, none of them will have examples from Local place but will have from foreign location.

Here I would like to give one example. We have been using chemical pesticides, fertilizers on our food crops. Also we have been consuming lot of chemicals as medicines. Now we all know that chemicals are of two types, organic and inorganic. Every creature on this earth carries several chemical compositions and components. Extracting those natural chemical components as medicines is Ayurveda and using direct chemical is Allopathy. The natural chemical components will never have any side effects.

# 38 INVESTMENT OPPORTUNITIES

I wrote earlier about my ambition of buying a 50 acre land and return to India with ₹10 lakh. This kind of talk you would usually notice in Movies. Of course, common man life is no different from it.

However, I always have the ambition of starting my business, may it be industry or trading business, but something on my own.

I always used to come up with some or other kind of concept for it. I might have tried about 20 to 30 different businesses. Some of them were not there in India when I started working on them. One of them was retail chain. This was when I did case study on USA retail chains.

Initially, I started a trading company and within three months moved out of it to software job.

During then I also looked at starting a Cold Storage but was not possible to start because of two reasons. One lack of technical consultants in India and lack of government promotion programs.

Why Government Promotion program need to be understood here! Unless government gives a subsidy in investment and in electricity charges or kind of tax rebates, starting and running a business is not possible in India due to its cost structure as I gave you details above in Cost Account section.

I looked at old sick industries those can be revived and start doing business which also did not workout. Several multinationals bought Sick industries in India at throw away price and became profitable from first day itself.

I looked at Coconut fibre + cement sheet manufacturing unit. It was also not good. Investment was more and acceptability was less, returns were less.

When I gained some money while working in USA, I thought of starting a power generation unit of around 1 MW plant, especially in Windmill sector. What I figured out was, 1 MW wind mill was priced at around four to five crore and is feasible only when Government subsidy and/or European green credits is applied to investment. Government subsidy is applicable to people who might have an income level of ₹5 crores and above. Such large income earners can opt for it to avoid Income tax and depreciation of up to 40% in first year itself. Also the income from windmill power generation is also not taxable.

What many of Indians don't know is most of the Multinational companies or American companies operate in India have similar tax benefits. Hence their investments stay in positive profits at the start of the business itself and Indian investor will be in negative at the start of the investment in his/her new ventures.

Similarly several other policies were created only for the benefit of certain wealthy entities of nation. Small investor's options were completely destroyed.

There was time when I was trying to look at options those may help to generate employment opportunities in India. One of that I found was FM radio. In USA, anybody can start a FM radio from their garage. I did not get it by myself, an African American/Negro teenager started a FM radio station from his garage and became popular in USA. I immediately wrote an email about how Opening up of Media especially Radio stations could generate more employment. Then Policy on FM radio stations in Government of India was initiated later there was a big issue around, if it has to be given to everybody or to only some entities etc. At the end again bureaucratic tag resulted into such a way that only wealthy investors can take advantage of it.

Why and how did I focus on this? You all know Cell Phones. They operate on FM communication. Discussion about one of my friends who was working on Qualcom cell phone projects created interest in me about this. The information that I collected here gave me the clarity about how restriction of information about a specific technology would limit the growth of knowledge in the nation.

We are able to get aware of the subject but our brain is not digesting them and we are not able to be "maturing" in the subject we learnt.

Jaipal Reddy from Andhra Pradesh was Minister of IB then. He quit the ministry, not sure why.

In fact I tried to start a radio station but the options were not available.

Also I tried to start a wireless internet service provider business which also was a major expensive one.

Many may surprise to know that Dish Antenna was a garage business in USA.

Dell computers was the same. Microsoft was the same.

Amazon, enterprise car rentals, several businesses in USA were started small and became global conglomerates.

What I figured out is the continuous rise in investment requirements and expenditure and also several other restrictions led to the situation where one cannot establish any self-employment business on their own and succeed in that venture.

There was a proposal from OIL PSUs about establishing reticulated system for LPG. I tried for it. This was when I got into depth of OIL PSUs. When calculated and prepared a project report, the price of LPG per KG was feasible if OIL PSUs provide us at less than ₹5 per kg. However, what the company says that they give a margin of only ₹3 per KG.

The version of OIL PSUs management was, investment is a FIXED asset and one should calculate the ROI on investment.

Also one more thing was, OIL PSUs operate at huge margin but they expect people work at meagre margin. Gross

ROI per year at 60% of investment with 50% as expenditure and another 50% of 60% equal to 30% is a good ROI was their version.

I am not pessimistic but in India, unless there is business margin of 100% in each transaction, one cannot survive in small businesses.

India does not have any aspect where a business can be started and can be run successfully.

The main reasons for such policies are usually being referred as Politicians or political policies but it is only tip of the iceberg. The actual fact lies in the systems of Government that is in the control of Bureaucrats.

Several Government rules are prepared in such a way that an investor will be easily trapped and convicted by some or other means. In fact, those rules are not possible to maintain at all by individual citizens.

It is the responsibility of bureaucrats and experts of Government to see that such rules should not get created. It is the responsibility of bureaucrats and experts of Government to continuously analyse the situations and conditions of the nation and see that such rules and conditions are corrected appropriately. Both are not happening in India.

In fact such responsibility is being pushed on to the Political leaders in order to cover their inefficiency and incapability by those bureaucrats and experts of Government.

Investing in India by Indian has become a Sinful act of Indian in India.

Mostly we always find success business men from USA. The reason for their success is the policies of Government and supporting programs to them.

In India, Infosys or TCS or Wipro sort of companies are successful because of the US$ vs Rupee Valuation.

Wipro is successful in other hi-tech equipment sector because of having distributionships with those companies as trading partner.

I did start a Software Development company and produced 7 unique products those were not there when started. I was technically successful but commercially failed.

Do you remember that I said about the stages of Cognition process? I believe I attained the Moksha that is why I was able to create new products for existing problems.

I will give one of my experiences related to my products. This is related to a Banking Product. Hardware + Software. Developed it to simplify certain complications of banks. Banks productivity will improve by this product. Very simply and effective. I filed patent as well but I did not pursue the complete patent process.

We went to a public sector bank and demonstrated the product. Bank asked for integration with their existing computer system provided by Indian's one of the many largest IT companies where only more than 60% scored persons from higher school education are allowed to work.

The software is such a horrible quality one, it is negative quality product. I made my machine compatible to one of the bank process. Then they asked for another process while claiming that first synchronization "Demo" was not efficient enough. It was a Demo and they were expecting me to provide them all the world comfort during demo.

We as usual tried to convince by explaining how it can be improved. This effort resulted into the situation of a comment from bank that tomorrow investors of Bank may question their integrity and sincerity for introducing such products those are not good.

The strange thing in this incidence was "Bank spent Crores of Rupee and bought printers which were not compatible to their existing systems and were laying idle in bank". Bank officials were asking us if we can integrate them with their systems.

They were talking about Cloud and ATM and operating and controlling from a central station and many more without proper knowledge.

What at the end I found was, all those old fellows who don't have any technical skill are heading the IT departments of banks.

Later in my restarted job life when I came across systems those were done by me, I always used to feel bad luck.

What I understood was, my failure is due to lack of supporting environment in India. It is because of this talent of India is being murdered and it is becoming a "Trading" economy.

Let us call the vigilance cameras being promoted by Government through its policies. Such policies are helping foreign economies to make money and India is becoming weak and getting disabled.

I was the pioneer in online bus ticketing in India that failed to take off due to denial of payment gateway services from banks. I created one solution to simplify the processes of bank that was also failed due to insufficient support from banks. There is no policy that creates an ambience where large business houses engage new techniques from start up companies.

# 39 DISORDERS

So far I have been explaining all the activities which may create problems or have been creating problems in our life and our society. Let us see what those problems are. These are not complete list, preparing complete list takes longer time and needs larger effort. All these are because of corrupted financial policies.

1. Dowry
2. Girl Child Abortions
3. Corruption
4. Cheating
5. Blue Collar Crimes
6. Large Expenses
7. Poor Roads
8. Drinking water for sale
9. Lack of Food
10. Lack of fruit juices and protein foods
11. Accidents
12. Lack of creativity
13. Lack of Innovation
14. Share Market losses
15. Thefts
16. Poaching
17. Deforestation
18. Child labour
19. No doctors or medical services
20. Land grabbing
21. Murders for wealth

And many more.

The virtual world corruption taking its toll of Real world and transforming human to Monster.

# 40 SOLUTIONS

There are solutions in order to make India better. These are not complete. These are not complete list, preparing complete list takes longer time and needs larger effort.

1. Dissolve the Currency Trading System in Global Market and volunteer to make Rupee as is equal to all currencies.
2. Administrative chairs should not be made available to persons whose age is below 40 years.
3. Administrative chairs should not be available for more than 10 years job life.
4. Any Government employee total job life should not be more than 15 years.
5. No Indian with Government employment record is allowed to get into Rajya Sabha.
6. No Indian with Government employment record is allowed to sit in Ruling chair or constitutional chairs.
7. Employee unions or any form of association, either formal or informal, for Government employees should be banned.
8. Ruling chairs should be only for Lok Sabha members.
9. Government organizations should not be used for amendment/creation of law.
10. All Democratic bodies should be valid for fixed duration and elections should be at fixed intervals.
11. Elected members should not be allowed to resign unless on complete health failures during tenure.

12. One person should not get chance for more than two times for the same elected position.
13. Rajya Sabha members should not be allowed to any Central or state Government minister positions.
14. All citizens, starting from President of India should have the same Provident Fund.
15. All Citizens should get complete coverage of the Health Insurance at minimum comforts, additional facilities costs them more.
16. Banks loans to farmers should be protected by themselves through insurance system created among themselves.
17. No CRR for banks and No minimum cash amount in Bank Accounts.
18. Ban foreign currency loans to public infrastructure projects.
19. Bureaucrats should not be allowed into any constitutional nominated positions.
20. Bureaucrats should be deputed in different nations for at least 10 years before allowing them in Indian Services.
21. Magisterial powers from bureaucrats should be removed and give it to the Ruling body. Ruling body should have at least one legal expert consultant from public.

# 41 CLOSURE

Accepting facts requires guts.

The world is a going concern. This is the phrase of commerce. Nothing stops.

One major issue will be created to cover the earlier major issue but behind the screen both issues will continuously be progressive towards their destination.

Are you thinking of your welfare through your nation welfare? Please stop it, because, the economy of India is designed and implemented to make its citizens work for foreigners benefit as traders to be successful, else you would be loser and moron.

Because every act of all those, many Indians, have been working inside India to "solidify" the strengths of India internally have become acts of "Voluntary" and "non-profit" activity due to which many "strengths", individuals with capabilities, have been losing their financial strengths and are becoming "helpless". Refer here what I wrote about "voluntary" organizations funded by global "profit" organizations.

Indian economy is "Technically Correct" and "Functionally faulted". Here "Correct" is what is made us believe and understood as "Correct". We are taught by the global forces to consider that they showed it as "Correct" is "Correct" due to which we are being "Functionally faulted".

What I figured out is "Bad" always cherish and live for long time and Good in the human life and society is as similar as "Spike" once in a while. It is similar to Road with Speed Breaker. Where Speed Breaker representing the Good and

Road representing the Bad, not literally the same but I am saying to represent its physical form.

In the Management, everybody know about the word "Demography". It is one word that represents many things.

USA and UK has created organizations those are meant to manage Demography issues in individual nations in order to maintain positive environment for MNCs.

They work from micro level to macro level due to which several issues stay beyond the control of respective nation's government.

In this effort of mine.

I was in National Capital region for a year time during when I tried to contact, L.K. Advani, Chidabaram, Venkatiah Naidu.

I called L.K. Advani's office for appointment. I was in Delhi and called on Chidambaram on his home phone, whoever attended the phone, asked me to call office on next Monday. I did not go as you know the bureaucracy there in Delhi. I must say this here if it was not Chidambaram. India might be gone todays. He saved India.

I was in Bangalore and met Deve Gowda.

I met Chandrababu Naidu about four or five times.

I must say this here about Chandrababu Naidu. I said about acknowledgements from him to my emails when he was as CM of AP. It is his highness to do that which I have not seen with any leader that I met or wrote emails to. I might not be able to write this book if his acknowledgements were not there.

Listening a person is the first quality of Leadership for ruling.

I can say that or I admit that he is the right leader to India, it is ill fate of Indians that they are not letting him to win.

I am writing this in Closure document because India should understand what it is losing.

By just the above said four lines about Chandrababu Naidu, do not brand this as political (party) document.

I went to media offices to meet editors.

I called on some MPs, communist party presidents etc.

Most of the times, content that I have is not a regular public related one. Hence I used to find weak real time support or response.

However, I have seen change in several different places due to my effort.

You may consider this book as a fantasy document and all those names I mentioned resemble to real time but never mean to refer real persons.

But my aim is to stimulate thoughts. I am 100% sure I might have caused that in your mind.

In this book I have written several details, none of those were ever written by anybody. Several blunders those I exposed were never exposed by anybody. Why am I saying that I am first in this!! Because refer here that until 1999, until I started explaining this world about the Significance of Currency values and negative consequences of Currency values, there was a major campaign and belief in the nation that weak currency is good for the nation and its economy and economic growth.

I am the one who changed that understanding through different means.

May be around, 40 to 50 corrections were made in the economy of India, even those who did changes also might not know what the end result is. Whatever facts that I exposed were never said by anybody. I am supposed to receive doctorates or other Title for each such findings which may help me in earning my livelihood as an expert of economy. But that option in Indian Economy is not available.

At one time, Sir John Mayor, former PM of UK visited India for a media conducted leadership summit, he stated that we did not expect or we are surprised or it is commendable or it is astonishing to see such bounce back recovery or startling recovery or startling growth of Indian Economy!!

Somewhere I read that when Indian Freedom fighters were demanding for "freedom", British used to say that Indians are not ready to rule by themselves. Probably this book may have given you the information that why, what, where and how we as Indians are not yet ready to rule ourselves.

Everybody spoke about India becoming superpower then. What I understood from his statement was, John Mayor was referring the currency value concept. He/American/British did not expect Indians would understand this Currency value concept and the immigration systems.

It has been written in the news media that Raghuram Rajan, one of the RBI governors, predicted the economic crisis during 2007 or 2008 or 2009, the actual fact what none knowns was, it was intended result due to stopping of devaluation of rupee intentionally.

The economic crisis then was due to strong Indian Rupee. You may argue that, how Indian Rupee could do that result. As I said earlier, the world is closely knitted by Currencies and their values and associated top so called economists.

A difference in action from a nation's finance ministry from its earlier one or two decade behaviour is a major issue to be focused on and understand why there has been a change. Global forces are not fools. They are more intelligent than Indians.

The crisis in first world nation's economy was an intended result of strong rupee which occurred due to acts of Chidambaram, then Finance Minister of India on my repeated emails about the negative consequences of Rupee fall against global currencies.

Here you may get another doubt, is Chidambaram so dumb that he reacted on my emails. For this what I could say is, if it is one change then that might not be a believable matter but it is a continuous four years of behaviour.

At one point, I was frustrated of not having timely action at finance ministry and used to write emails with abusive words.

My concern was, the lack of action from finance ministry was resulting as loss of lives in the economy in the form of Suicides by Innocent farmers.

Though there were actions taken against others those used abusive language, I never used earlier as long as they were stern action, I only started using it when I did not find timely action, my concern was my nation's welfare, they did not take against me. I am not proud of it but I felt that there is sincerity with top leaders of the nation and bureaucrats as well who found that my findings are good for nation.

But I could not receive one acknowledgement email from Chidambaram. If I had, I could have been nation's top intellectual who saved this nation from collapse several times.

I firmly believe that I deserve "Bharat Ratna".

Laughing or finding me as "clone".

Yaar, you have read the book till this extent, lot of the information that I wrote here in this book, you might not have got it to your imagination at least, means I am the best, right, then what is wrong aspiring the nation's top most title.

So much I wrote, hope you might have understood now what Economy is.

Economy means health of our living standards. If we are able to get all that is required for our good living with in our income then that is considered as GOOD ECONOMY.

Hope now, let me genuinely ask one question.

Am I not qualified to be called as Economist? Am not qualified to receive doctorate? Am I not qualified to receive "Bharat Ratna"?

Economy is a System. An Economic Analyst should be a Systems Analyst first to be a Good Economist.

Look at the below picture. He received "Bharat Ratna" for the job duties he performed which was his duty for which he got paid.

Also he was President of India who is using a *COMMERCIAL DRINKING WATER* which is against respecting the NATURAL RIGHTS of Human. He, being Supreme of India, should have targeted to such situation where Business on Drinking water, drop of Life, is completely destroyed.

He did not. He failed in his duty of Ruling a nation as President of India. I don't have anything personal to him but the youngsters of the nation requires a clarity in the way how systems could impact us and our lives.

When I compare myself to him.

I did not get any benefit for all my effort.

I worked though I had lot of risk from several different power chairs.

I have put my own money and my career at risk for the betterment of this nation believing that it is my minimum duty to correct my nation where I was born and live and die. I am correcting my house.

However, there is one sector I did not cover which is "Defense" forces. I don't want to but I would put one single question to put out all my thoughts to the reader. After so much reading, what would be the real capability of defence forces? At what capability levels are we at in this regard?

India is in need of lot of systems analysts those can do continuous analysis of systems of real time and correct them.

As an average Indian who has put effort to dig out the conspiracies those could never get exposed easily by anybody, why I am not qualified for "Bharat Ratna"?

If I get "Bharat Ratna", I might use that popularity for the reform of this world.

The gigantic problems of Poverty, Global warming, pollution and corruption can be eradicated.

Today the science and technology is being used for selfish purpose which can be changed to the benefit of all the world population.

Science and technology can be put to action for right purpose.

Poverty can be eradicated from this earth.

An Indian, as citizen of the world, who got the life of human form and would use it for the betterment of this world.

Lastly I would give you one simple practical experience about our life in India.

Find out a "Drain Pit or Garbage Pit". Take a "Marble Stone" of sufficient size where it can surface out and you can stand on it. Drop this "Marble Stone" in that "Drain Pit". Then clean stone well and stand on it. This is how we have been living in India, including the "Billionaires".

Do we still continue living like this? It is our choice.

The final word to everybody is, I am a common man who is curious of world I did some service that I felt is good and I am satisfied with it.

I am a representative of my generation and my lateral generation Indians who are made to live with inhibitions developed due to continuous meaningless failures in life.

I did not have any power but able to achieve several. I saved India several times from several political plots and saved it from collapsing.

# APPENDIX–I

This is the link for groups that I used to send my analysis reports to Ministers of India, MPs of India and Editors of Indian News Media.

http://groups.yahoo.com/group/Indian_Economics

Details of Suggestions those I sent and corrections made in Indian Economy. Following are only limited, I wrote about several different issues in about 3000 emails.

1. Wrote several emails about avoiding the participation of OIL PSUs buying forex from open market to Finance Minister of India.
2. Check dams. During the regime of Chandrababu Naidu, there was huge drought. There was need for water. I found the need for Check dams.
3. Stopping of Intentional Devaluation of Rupee against global currencies and necessary steps to appreciate to Rupee till 38 against US$.
4. 0.25 paisa interest scheme to Farmers.
5. Identifying the Economic Terrorism plots of World Bank and IMF in India.
6. Resisted, looks like resulted as stopped by Government of India, the FDI and FII into Primary Rights sector of India through Public Private Participation in basic infrastructure of India scheme.
7. Stopping the effort of Globalization of OIL PSUs, on which 98% of Indian Fuel needs are depending on.

8. Exposed how the Subsidy on Domestic LPG was bogus and how OIL PSUs are making double profits on the same scheme.
9. ₹1 per head per day premium for complete Health Insurance which resulted into Arogyasree. I wrote above this during Chandrababu Naidu was in office as CM of AP, I was surprised when during election, YSR took this as his election item.
10. Three tier Quality audit system in Government Contracts.
11. Exposed how Tax Rebates on 100% EOU industries is a big Global Economic Terrorism plot of World Bank that was initiated by Manmohan Singh in India.
12. Exposed how all the policies initiated by Manmohan Singh are Economical Terrorism Plots on India.
13. How Expenditure was doped into Indian Economy that is leading to Farmers committing suicides.
14. How Manmohan Singh economic policies are leading India to a situation where farmers are committing suicides.
15. Exposed how Manmohan Singh Policies are sky rocketing basic Food prices in India.
16. FM radio stations need and necessity for generation of employment.
17. Need of fund by Government that helps individual technocrats carry on their R&D activities. Technical Incubation fund was initiated by Government of India.
18. Exposed how NREGS National Rural Employment scheme is Economic Terrorism Plot on India.
19. Exposed how Indian Stock markets were converted into Corporates with shareholding from Consortium centres and sold them to NASDAQ.
20. How Indian Companies are being sold to USA by means of FII, FDI and Participatory Notes sort of Foreign investments.

21. Exposed What are Financial Terrorism plots and how they are being executed on india.
22. AT PAR Cheque introduction in banks at 0 service charge.
23. Clearance of Cheques in maximum five days. http://groups.yahoo.com/group/Indian_Economics/message/108.
24. Energy Meter Installation at every distribution point of AP State Electricity to cut the pilferage of Electricity.
-. Introduction of PPF as retirement scheme for all citizens.
26. Removal of disparity in Small Savings schemes.
27. FDI into multi-brand retail was halted.
28. Sulabh Complexes for the comfort of Women of the nation.
29. Education Committees in schools with parents as members.
30. Farmers debt relief package.
31. Crude Index in Commodity Exchange.
32. De-aligned Indian Economy with USA in 2005 which was reinstated again by Pranab in 2008.
33. Fringe Benefit Tax was my result of suggestion given on tax reforms of removing the IT exemption to salaries under certain provisions that was being misused and reducing the tax rate to 10% uniformly to improve tax collection.
34. The proposed extension of Income Tax slab rebate from present levels of ₹1.5 to 2 lakhs was halted after my request with President of India by exposing about instead of controlling the rising cost of living inside the nation.

# APPENDIX–II

## ఆర్థికఉగ్రవాదం!

## -కొడాలిఏకాంబరరావు

ఎకానమీ(ఆర్థికవ్యవస్థ), ఫైనాన్స్(విత్తం- డబ్బునుసేకరించడం, దానినిఉపయోగించుకొనేశాస్త్రంలేదాకళ) అనేవిరెండుభిన్నపదాలు. ద్రవ్య(డబ్బు) సరఫరాసమృద్ధిగాఉన్నంతమాత్రానఒకఆర్థికవ్యవస్థపటిష్టంగాఉన్నదనితప్పనిసరిగాభావించనవసరంలేదు. అలాగేఒకఆర్థికవ్యవస్థశక్తిమంతంగాఉంటేదానివిత్తంపటిష్టంగాఉన్నదనిచెప్పలేము.

మనంస్వాతంత్ర్యవిజయోత్సవాలుజరుపుకొంటున్నతరుణంలోప్రపంచంలోపలుమార్పులుసంభవించాయి. వాటిలోఅధికభాగంభారతీయులదృష్టికిరాలేదు. భారతప్రభుత్వమూ, వివిధరంగాలనిపుణులుకూడాఇందుకుమినహాయింపుకాదు.

ఆమార్పుల్లోముఖ్యమైనవి-కరెన్సీలప్రమాణీకరణ,
వివిధదేశాలకుస్వతంత్రకరెన్సీలఏర్పాటు,
ఆర్థికవ్యవస్థలహద్దులనిర్దేశం,
క్రాస్కరెన్సీవిలువలనునిర్ణయించడం(రెండుకరెన్సీలమధ్యమారకపు
రేటునుమూడవకరెన్సీదృష్ట్యానిర్ణయించడం).

యూరోపియన్లు,
ముఖ్యంగాబ్రిటిష్వారుప్రపంచవ్యాప్తంగాగలతమవలసలనుంచిఉపసం
హరించుకొనివాటికిస్వాతంత్ర్యాన్ని ఇచ్చినసందర్భంలో ఈమార్పులు
చోటుచేసుకున్నాయి. ఈమార్పులనుగమనించినవారు,
వాటిభావిపర్యవసానాలనుపసిగట్టకలిగినవారుచాలాకొద్దిమందిమాత్ర
మే.
స్వాతంత్ర్యతొలినాళ్ళచరిత్రనునిశితంగాపరిశీలిస్తేభారతీయులుప్రపంచ

[illegible]

[illegible]రూపించినదాఖలాలుకానరావు.

1945లోరెండోప్రపంచయుద్ధంముగిసినతరువాతమానవాళిచరిత్రలో
ఒకకొత్తయుగంఆరంభమయింది.
[illegible]
మానవజీవితంద్రవ్యసమీకరణంఅయిపోయింది.
[illegible]
సమస్తయంత్రాలకుకొత్తఇంధనంగాక్రూడ్‌ఆయిల్‌నుగుర్తించారు.

రసాయనఎరువులనువాడిపండించడంతోవ్యవసాయంలోఆహారోత్పత్తి
ఇబ్బడికరంగాముందుకుపడింది. పారిశ్రామికరంగంకొత్తపుంతలుతొక్కింది.
స్వతంత్రరాజ్యాలఆవిర్భావం,
[illegible]
తప్పుడుదారిలో[illegible]
ఉన్నాయనుకున్నాయి.

అభివృద్ధిలోముందుగావెళ్ళినదేశాలప్రతిపోటీగా.
ప్రపంచవ్యాప్తంగాసంబంధాలు,
తమవిదేశీవాణిజ్యానికిఆమోదయోగ్యమైనకరెన్సీగాడాలర్‌నువాడు
[illegible]
1960దశకంలోడాలర్‌కుమార్కెట్‌ప్రారంభమయింది.
అదేకాలంలో[illegible].
ముఖ్యంగాఅమెరికాదేశాలతోపరోక్షయుద్ధాల్లోపాల్గొంది.

తత్ఫలితంగాతనఆర్థికవ్యవస్థనుస్వీయనియంత్రణలోఉంచుకోగలశక్తి నికోల్పోసాగింది.

ఆదేకాలంలోఇందిరాగాంధీబ్యాంకులనుజాతీయంచేశారు. దీంతోభారతఆర్థికవ్యవస్థ'నియమితఆర్థికవ్యవస్థ' (క్లోజ్డ్ఎకానమీ) అయిపోయింది.

ఈచర్యమనఆర్థికవ్యవస్థక్రమంగాపరాధీనంకావడానికిదారితీసింది. విదేశీమారకద్రవ్యానికినిత్యంకటకటపడాల్సివచ్చింది. దివంగతప్రధానిచంద్రశేఖర్విదేశీమారకద్రవ్యంకోసంజాతిసొత్తుఅయిన బంగారాన్నిలండన్‌లోతాకట్టుపెట్టడంభారతీయులుమరచిపోలేనివిష యం. ఇదిజరిగింది1990లో.

అప్పుడుప్రపంచబ్యాంక్మనఆర్థికవ్యవస్థలోకిప్రవేశించింది. తదాదిఅమెరికన్డాలర్నిధులనుఅందిస్తూమనఆర్థికానికి'రక్షకుడు'గా వ్యవహరిస్తోంది. భారత్తనక్రూడాయిల్, ఎరువులఅవసరాలలో70శాతాన్నిదిగుమతులద్వారాతీర్చుకొంటోం ది. అవిరెండూలేకపోతేపారిశ్రామికప్రగతి, ఆహారభద్రతమనదేశానికేకాదు, ఏదేశానికైనాపూజ్యమే.

మరిఆదిగుమతులకుమనకుడాలర్నిధులుఅవసరం. ఆనిధులకోసమే1990 నుంచిఇంతవరకుఅధికారంలోఉన్నప్రతిఒక్కరూ, ప్రతిరాజకీయపక్షమూప్రపంచబ్యాంకుతోఒప్పందాలుచేసుకోవటంజ రుగుతోంది.

ఇంతవరకుప్రపంచబ్యాంకునుంచివేలకోట్లడాలర్లను(రుణంగా)

తీసుకోవడంజరిగింది.
ఇప్పుడుమనదేశంలోనివివిధరంగాలలో7600
కోట్లడాలర్లమేరకుప్రపంచబ్యాంకుపెట్టుబడులుఉన్నాయి.
మనంఏటాఅమెరికానుంచి26,000
కోట్లడాలర్లవిలువైనసరుకులనుఅమెరికానుంచిదిగుమతిచేసుకొంటున్నాము. అమెరికాకుఏటా16,000
కోట్లడాలర్లవిలువైనసరుకులనుఎగుమతిచేస్తున్నాము.
అంటేఅమెరికాతోమనవాణిజ్యలోటు10,000 కోట్లడాలర్లు.

డాలర్విలువపెరిగినప్పుడల్లామనచమురు,
ఎరువులకంపెనీలుఫారెక్స్మార్కెట్(విదేశీమారకంవిపణి)
నుంచిడాలర్నిధులనుకొనుగోలుచేస్తాయి. క్రూడాయిల్,
ఎరువులదిగుమతులకుడాలర్నిధులనుకొనుగోలుచేసినప్పుడల్లా
మనరూపాయివిలువతగ్గిపోతుంది.
తత్ఫలితంగాదేశంలోఅన్నిసరుకులధరలుపెరుగుతుంటాయి.

అమెరికాతోపదివేలకోట్లడాలర్లవాణిజ్యలోటుతోపాటుమనదేశంఏటాప్రపంచబ్యాంకురుణాలపైవడ్డీలనుడాలర్లరూపంలోచెల్లించవలసివుంది.
ఒకవేళరూపాయలలోచెల్లించినాప్రపంచబ్యాంకుఆసొమ్మునుడాలర్లలోకిమార్పిడిచేస్తుంది.
భారతీయఆర్థికవ్యవస్థప్రపంచీకరణపేరిటమనప్రభుత్వంఅనుసరిస్తోన్నవిధానాలన్నిటినీవాణిజ్యలోటు,
ప్రపంచబ్యాంకురుణాలునిర్ణయాత్మకంగాప్రభావితంచేస్తున్నాయి.
వివిధరంగాలకువిదేశీపెట్టుబడులనుఆకర్షించడానికేఈవిధానాలు.

సదరుపెట్టుబడులతోవచ్చినలాభాలనుతిరిగిడాలర్లేదామరేదైనారూ
పాయేతరకరెన్సీలోకిమార్పిడిచేస్తారు.
దీంతోరూపాయివిలువతగ్గిపోతుంది.

ప్రపంచదేశాలజాతీయప్రభుత్వాలకుద్రవ్యపరమైనవనరులుసమకూ
ర్చేబ్యాంకుప్రపంచబ్యాంకు.
ద్వితీయప్రపంచసంగ్రామంలోఅతలాకుతలమైపోయినవివిధదేశాలఆ
ర్థికవ్యవస్థలనుసంస్కరించి,
పునరుద్ధరించేందుకుగానుఈబ్యాంకునునెలకొల్పారు.
తనఅరవైఐదేళ్ళప్రస్తానంలోప్రపంచబ్యాంకుచాలాదూరంపయనించిం
ది.

ఇప్పుడుఆబ్యాంకునుఅమెరికానెలకొల్పిన,
అమెరికానుంచిఅమెరికాతరఫునతనకార్యకలాపాలనునిర్వహిస్తున్న
బ్యాంకుగాఎవరూనేరుగాచెప్పకపోవచ్చు.
ప్రపంచబ్యాంకువెబ్సైట్ప్రకారంఅదొకసహకారబ్యాంకు. 184
దేశాలకన్సోర్టియం(సహాయతాసంఘం-
భిన్నసంస్థలు/దేశాలుఒకానొకపనికోసంకలసిఒకసంస్థగాఏర్పడటం).
దానిలావాదేవీలన్నీఅమెరికాడాలర్లలోనేనడుస్తాయి.
ప్రపంచవ్యాప్తంగాఉన్నదానికార్యాలయాలలోవివిధదేశాలకుచెందిన
వారుఉద్యోగులుగాఉంటారు.
ప్రధానిమన్మోహన్సింగ్ప్రపంచబ్యాంకుమాజీఉద్యోగి.

ప్రపంచబ్యాంకుమౌలికఎజెండాగురించిసాధారణంగాఎవరికీసందేహా
లురావు.
లోకానికిఎలాకన్పిస్తున్నప్పటికీప్రపంచబ్యాంకునిజానికిఒకబ్యాంకుకా
దు; అదిఒకరాజకీయసంస్థ.
బ్యాంకురూపంలోపనిచేస్తున్నరాజకీయసంస్థ;
అమెరికారాజకీయకుతంత్రాలనుఇతరదేశాలఆర్థికవ్యవస్థలలోద్రవ్యవి
ధానాలరూపేణాఅదిఅమలుపరుస్తోంది.

ఇతరదేశాలఆర్థికవ్యవస్థలపైఅమెరికాడాలర్నియంత్రణనుస్థాపించడ
మేప్రపంచబ్యాంకునుఏర్పాటుచేయడంలోనిఅసలులక్ష్యం.
అమెరికాయేతరకరెన్సీలనుబలహీనపరచి,
తద్వారాప్రపంచసహజవనరులనుచౌకగాకైవసంచేసుకోవడానికిఅమె
రికాకుతోడ్పడడమేప్రపంచబ్యాంకుప్రధానలక్ష్యం.

ఇప్పుడుప్రపంచబ్యాంకుప్రభుత్వాలనేనియంత్రించగలిగేదశకుచేరుకోం
ది. ఇందుకుమనదేశమూమినహాయింపుకాదు.
దీనికిరెండుకారణాలున్నాయి.
ఒకటిప్రపంచబ్యాంకుమాజీఉద్యోగిఒకరుఇప్పుడుమనప్రధానమంత్రి;
రెండోదిప్రపంచద్రవ్యరాజకీయాలగురించిమనరాజకీయవేత్తలకుసరైన
అవగాహనలేకపోవడం.

కరెన్సీమారకపురేట్లు,
వాటిప్రభావాలతోవ్యవహరించేవిషయంలోమనఆర్థిక,
విత్తవ్యవస్థలనిపుణులకుసైతంసరైనఅనుభవంలేకపోవడంకూడామ

రోకారణంగాచెప్పవచ్చు.

రూపాయివిలువఅంతకంతకూపతనంకావడానికిప్రపంచబ్యాంకుసృష్టించినపరిస్థితులుమూలంగానేడుసంఖ్యానేకభారతీయులుఅమెరికాజీవనశైలిఆకర్షణలోపడిపోయారు; అలాంటివారుభారతరాజ్యాంగాన్నివంచించిఅమెరికారాజ్యాంగాన్నిపాటించడానికిసంసిద్ధంగాఉన్నారు.

రూపాయివిలువపతనంప్రతిభారతీయుడినీనిత్యజీవితంలోముప్పతిప్పలుపెడుతోంది. ధరలపెరుగుదలతోఎక్కడిడబ్బూదేనికీసరిపోవడంలేదు. దీంతోమరింతధనార్జనకుప్రతిఒక్కరూఆరాటపడుతున్నారు. ఈఆరాటంలోఅవినీతికిపాల్పడుతూదేశాన్నిమోసగిస్తున్నారు. ప్రపంచబ్యాంకుసహాయంఆర్థికసహాయంకానేకాదు, అదిఆర్థికఉగ్రవాదం.

యూరోపియన్యూనియన్దేశాలఆర్థికవ్యవస్థలపైఅమెరికాడాలర్ప్రభావాన్నినిరోధించడానికిగతశతాబ్దితుదిసంవత్సరాలలోయూరోనుసృష్టించారు.

ప్రపంచసహజవనరులపైఇంకాగణనీయమైననియంత్రణనుకలిగివున్నబ్రిటన్సహజంగానేయూరోలోభాగస్వామికాలేదు. ఆదేశంతనవిదేశీవాణిజ్యానికితనకరెన్సీనిడాలర్లలోకిమార్పిడిచేసుకోవల్సినఅవసరంలేదు.

బహుళకరెన్సీలుఉన్ననేటిప్రపంచంలోమనరూపీఆర్థికవ్యవస్థలోడాల
ర్నిర్వహిస్తోన్నపాత్రచాలాప్రమాదకరమైనది.
ప్రపంచవ్యాప్తంగారూపాయివిలువకోల్పోవడంఅంటేఅణ్వస్త్రదాడికిగురి
కావడంతోసమానమే. అమెరికన్డాలర్నురూపాయిల్లోకిమార్పిడిచేసి,
ఆనిధులనుమనదేశంలోవివిధరంగాలలోపెట్టుబడులుగాఅనుమతిం
చడంసునామీకిలోనవడమేసుమా.

సరే, భారతీయులు,
భారతప్రభుత్వమూడాలర్కరెన్సీప్రపంచవ్యాప్తంగావివిధఆర్థికవ్యవస్థ
లలోసృష్టిస్తోన్నఅల్లకల్లోలాన్నిఅర్థంచేసుకొంటున్నారు.
డాలర్ఆధిపత్యంతోమనఆర్థికవ్యవస్థఎదుర్కొంటోన్నసమస్యలుఏఒ
క్కభారతీయుడూపరిష్కరించలేడు.
మనలోప్రతిఒక్కరూఆసమస్యలకుబాధ్యులే.

నిజానికిరూపాయిబలహీనపడడానికికారణమైనవిధానాలన్నీద్రవ్య
సంబంధమైన, ఆర్థికపరమైనభారీనేరాలే.
గతనలభైసంవత్సరాలుగాభారతప్రభుత్వంలోఉద్యోగిగా,
పార్లమెంటుసభ్యుడుగాకీలకబాధ్యతలునిర్వహిస్తోన్నమన్మోహన్సింగ్
నుఈనేరాలలోప్రధాననిందితుడుగాపరిగణించాలి.
పూనుకుంటేమనంఆనేరాలనునిరోధించగలం.

-కొడాలిఏకాంబరరావు

(వ్యాసకర్తఆర్థికశాస్త్రవేత్త)

# కంచేచేనుమేస్తోంది!

# -కొడాలిఏకాంబరరావు

తేనెపూసినకత్తులు-ఆర్థికకుట్రాజకీయాలు!

మనకువ్యతిరేకంగామనదేశంలోనేఈఆర్థికకుతంత్రాలుజరిగిపోతు న్నాయి. శీఘ్రఆర్థికాభివృద్ధికిదోహదంచేసేఅవశ్య, అత్యుత్తమసంస్కరణలుగాకన్పించేఆకార్యక్రమాలవెనకఉన్నకుట్రల నుఆర్థికనిపుణులేపసిగట్టలేరుమరి. అవేమిటోకొన్నిపేర్కొంటాను. ఉద్దేశపూర్వకంగారూపాయివిలువతగ్గింపు; భారతీయకార్పొరేట్కంపెనీలలో75 శాతంవిదేశీపెట్టుబడులకుఅనుమతి; ప్రభుత్వరంగంలోనిచమురుకంపెనీలప్రైవేటీకరణ; జాతీయగ్రామీణఉపాధిహామీపథకం; ప్రభుత్వోద్యోగులకుభారీగావేతనాలపెంపు; మౌలికసదుపాయాలప్రాజెక్ట్‌లప్రైవేటీకరణ; ప్రభుత్వరంగసంస్థలనుంచిపెట్టుబడులఉపసంహరణ; రైతులకుసబ్సిడీలసదుపాయంరద్దుమొదలైనవి.

ప్రస్తుతంకేంద్రంలోఅధికారంలోఉన్నలేదాభవిష్యత్తులోఅధికారంలోకివచ్చేవారినియంత్రణలోలేని, ఉండబోనివ్యవస్థఒకటిఉంది. అదేఆర్థిక, ద్రవ్యవ్యవస్థ.

ఐదుదశాబ్దాలక్రితంవలసదేశాలనుంచిఉపసంహరించుకున్ననాటి

నుంచిఅభివృద్ధిచెందినదేశాలుప్రపంచంపైతమఆర్థిక, రాజకీయపెత్తనాన్నిమరింతగాపెంచుకోవడానికిప్రయత్నిస్తున్నాయి.

ఈప్రయత్నాలలోభాగంగానేవివిధదేశాలఆర్థికనిపుణులనుఅంతర్జాతీయఆర్థికసంస్థలైనప్రపంచబ్యాంకు, ఐఎమ్ఎఫ్‌లలోనియమితులవుతున్నారు. క్రమంగావారికికీలకబాధ్యతలుఅప్పగిస్తారు. వాటినిసమర్థంగానిర్వహించినవారిలోఎంపికచేసుకొన్నకొంతమందికి మరింతప్రాధాన్యమిస్తారు. ఇలాప్రాధాన్యంపొందినవారిలోమనప్రధానిడాక్టర్మన్మోహన్సింగ్ఒకరు.

మనదేశంలోగాని, ఇతరవర్ధమానదేశాలలోగానిఆర్థిక, ద్రవ్యవ్యవస్థకుసారథ్యంవహిస్తున్నవారుఎవరోనిశితంగాగమనించండి. వారుఎవరైనా, గతంలోఏదోఒకసందర్భంలోప్రపంచబ్యాంకు, ఐఎమ్ఎఫ్కార్యకలాపాలలోతప్పకభాగస్వాములైనవారైవుంటారు. అంతేకాదువారికివాషింగ్టన్ప్రభువులమద్దతుకూడాఉంటుందిసుమా! ప్రపంచబ్యాంకు, ఐఎమ్ఎఫ్‌లలోపనిచేయడంతప్పా? తప్పుకాదు.

అయితేస్వదేశానికితిరిగివచ్చి, తమజాతీయప్రభుత్వంలోపనిచేస్తూ, ఆసంస్థలవిధానాలకనుగుణంగాదేశీయఆర్థికవిధానాలనునిర్ణయించడంలేదాప్రభావితంచేయడంముమ్మాటికీతప్పు. ఎందుకని? ప్రపంచబ్యాంకు, ఐఎంఎఫ్విధానాలుఅమెరికాకుఅనుకూలం; భారత్సహావర్ధమానదేశాలకువ్యతిరేకం. అంతర్జాతీయరాజకీయవ్యవహారాలనుప్రభావితంచేసేశక్తిసామర్థ్యాలు

భారతీయరాజకీయనాయకత్వానికికొరవడడానికికారణాలేమిటో ఇప్పుడుఅవగతమవుతున్నాయా?

ఈఆర్థికనిపుణులఒత్తిడిలేదాప్రభావంతో మనఆర్థికవిధానాలుఎలారూపొందుతున్నాయోచూద్దాం.
ఉదాహరణకువిదేశీపెట్టుబడులనేతీసుకోండి.
విదేశీప్రత్యక్షపెట్టుబడులు(ఎఫ్‌డిఐ),
విదేశీసంస్థాగతపెట్టుబడుల(ఎఫ్ఐఐ)నుఅనుమతించకపోవడంపైతొలుతమీడియాలో గగ్గోలుపుడుతుంది.
వాటినిఅనుమతించాల్సినఅవసరంఉందనిప్రతిఒక్కరూఘోషిస్తారు.

లేనిపక్షంలో మనఆర్థికవ్యవస్థకుప్పకూలిపోతుందనిభయాందోళనలనురేకెత్తిస్తారు. అధ్యయనాలునిర్వహించి,
విశ్లేషణలుజరిపివాస్తవాలుఏమిటోతెలుసుకొనేవ్యవధికూడాలేకుండాభారతప్రభుత్వంపైఒత్తిడితీసుకొస్తారు. తక్షణమేఎఫ్‌డిఐ,
ఎఫ్ఐఐలకుఅనుగుణంగావిధాననిర్ణయంతీసుకునేలాచేస్తారు.

విదేశీపెట్టుబడులవిషయంలోనేకాదు,
పలుఇతరవిధానాలవిషయంలో కూడాఈఘటనలక్రమంమనదేశంలోకనీసంరెండుదశాబ్దాలుగాచోటుచేసుకొంటోంది.
అన్నిటికీఆరంభంమన్మోహన్సింగ్ఆర్థికసంస్కరణలు.
వీటికితోడుఒక'సంప్రదాయక' కార్యకలాపంఒకటిఉంది.
దానికొకలాంఛనప్రాయమైనప్రక్రియకానీ, కార్యవిధానంకానీఉండదు.

అదేరిజర్వ్బ్యాంకుఉద్దేశపూర్వకంగాచేపట్టేరూపాయివిలువతగ్గింపుచ
ర్య.

[illegible]

[illegible]

మరివిదేశీమారకద్రవ్యముంటేఅమెరికాడాలరేసుమా!

[illegible]

లకనుకలుసదుపాయాలుకల్పించడమేకాకపాటికినూయుశాలింపను

రాయితీకూడాఇస్తోంది.

కనుకఅన్నాపారసంస్థలనుంచిపైనాఅదాయంరాకపోగాఆసంస్థలకు

[illegible]

మవుతుంది.

[illegible]

డి. మనకున్నఅప్పుల్లోస్వల్పకాలరుణాలేఎక్కువకావడం.

మనదగ్గరున్నదంతాకేవలంఊహాజనితమైనదనిపిస్తోంది.

ఇదెలాజరుగుతోంది?

ప్రతిసందర్భంలోమనదగ్గరున్నవిదేశీమారకద్రవ్యనిల్వల

గురించిమనంకూడాఆలోచించాల్సివుంటుంది.

ఉత్పత్తులకుఎగుమతికేంద్రీకరించినసంస్థలకుప్రోత్సాహంగా

ఋణసౌకర్యాన్నిఅందించడమేకాకపెద్దఎత్తునరాయితీలనిచ్చి

ఆకర్షిస్తున్నారు. అయితేవారుదేశీయమార్కెట్లోనూ

వ్యాపారంచేస్తున్నారు. అంటేలాభాలుదండుకుంటున్నారు.

చౌకధరలకుఎగుమతిచేయడంద్వారాసంపాదించినఆదాయాన్ని
భరించేందుకుప్రపంచబ్యాంకు,
[illegible]
ఇదిరాజకీయకుట్ర.

ఇక్కడొకమెలికఉంది. దీన్నిఅర్థంచేసుకోవడంచాలాముఖ్యం.
[illegible]
శపూర్వకంగారూపాయివిలువనుతగ్గించడంజరిగింది.
[illegible]
[illegible]
కరెన్సీవిలువతగ్గింపుఅంటేవ్యయంపెరుగుదలేకానిఆదాయంపెరుగు
దలకాదు. వ్యయంపెరుగుదలఅంటేసరుకుధరపెరగడం.

[illegible]
అంటేతక్కువడబ్బుకుఎక్కువసరుకులువెళ్తాయి.
రూపాయివిలువతగ్గినప్పుడుఅమెరికాలోభారతీయసరుకులుచౌకగాల
భిస్తాయి. 1 డాలర్విలువ20 రూపాయిలయితే1 కిలోబియ్యంధర1
డాలర్. అయితే1 డాలర్30 రూపాయలయితే1
డాలర్కుఒకటిన్నరబియ్యంకిలోవస్తుంది.
[illegible]
[illegible]

ఇదిఎగుమతులకుసంబంధించినవాస్తవం
ఇకదిగుమతులసంగతి[illegible]

మనకుక్రూడాయిల్, ఎరువులుఅవసరం. 1 బ్యారెల్క్రూడాయిల్1 డాలర్అంటే20 రూపాయలు. రూపాయివిలువతగ్గింపుతో1 డాలర్30 రూపాయిలుఅయితే1 బ్యారెల్క్రూడాయిల్30 రూపాయలు. అంటేక్రూడాయిల్ధరపెరిగింది. అంటేదిగుమతిచేసుకొనేఇంధనంధరేకాదుదేశంలోసమస్తసరుకులధరలూపెరుగుతాయి. ఇప్పుడు1 డాలర్విలువ47 రూపాయలు. అంటేభారతీయవనరులు, సరుకులుఅంతర్జాతీయమార్కెట్‌లో47 రెట్లుచౌకగాలభిస్తాయి.

విదేశీసరుకులు, వనరులు(భారతీయసరుకులు, వనరులుకూడా) 47 రెట్లుప్రియమవుతాయి. తక్కువడాలర్లకుఎక్కువభారతీయసరుకులులభించడమంటేదిగుమతులుచేసుకోగలసామర్థ్యంమనకుసన్నగిల్లినట్లే. మరింతస్పష్టంగాచెప్పాలంటేభారత్తనవనరులన్నిటినీఎగుమతిచేసినతరువాతకూడాతనకుఅవసరమైనక్రూడాయిల్, ఎరువులనుదిగుమతిచేసుకోవడానికిఅవసరమైనవిదేశీమారకద్రవ్యాన్నిసమకూర్చుకోలేదు.

ఉద్దేశపూర్వకంగాకరెన్సీవిలువనుతగ్గించుకోవడంఏదేశానికైనాఆత్మహత్యాసదృశమే.మనక్రూడాయిల్, ఎరువులఅవసరాలలో70 శాతందిగుమతులపైనేఆధారపడుతున్నందునదేనికీమినహాయింపులేకుండాప్రతిసరుకుధరపెరిగిపోతుంది. ఉద్దేశపూర్వకంగారూపాయివిలువతగ్గింపుపర్యవసానమేరైతులఆత్మ

హాత్యలు.
ఉత్పత్తివ్యయంపెరిగిపోవడంవల్లేరైతులకుఆదుస్థితిఏర్పడింది.

రిజర్వ్బ్యాంకు, భారతప్రభుత్వవిభిన్న విభాగాలలో వివి« దస్థానాలలో ఉన్న ఆర్థికనిపుణులప్రాథమికబాధ్యతరూపాయివిలువ నుపరిరక్షిస్తూఅంతర్జాతీయంగాదానివిలువనుమరింతగాపెంపొందించ డమే.
మనఆర్థికవ్యవస్థసౌష్ఠవాన్ని దెబ్బతీయడానికిఅంతర్జాతీయంగాజరు గుతోన్న కుతంత్రాలగురించిమనరాజకీయనాయకత్వాన్ని ఎప్పటిక ప్పుడూఅప్రమత్తంచేయడంకూడావారిబాధ్యతే.
కానిజరుగుతున్న దేమిటి?
వారుతమఇష్టానుసారంరూపాయివిలువనుతగ్గిస్తున్నారు.
తానురూపాయివిలువను16
శాతంమేరకుతగ్గించినట్టుప్రధానిమన్మోహన్స్వయంగాఅంగీకరించారు.

దేశఆర్థికవ్యవస్థలోఅమెరికాపెట్టుబడులనుమరింతగాపెంచడానికిఈ ఆర్థికనిపుణులంతాతోడ్పడుతున్నారు.
ఇదిమనదేశంలో జరుగుతోన్న నేరాలన్నిటికంటేఘోరమైననేరం.
వారికితమనిర్ణయాల, చర్యలపర్యవసానాలుఏమిటోబాగాతెలుసు.
తమవిధానాలవాస్తవలక్ష్యాలనుసామాన్యులుగాని, రాజకీయపక్షాలుగానీఅర్థంచేసుకోలేవనేవిశ్వాసంవారిలో నిండుగాఉం ది.

ఉద్దేశపూర్వకంగారూపాయివిలువనుతగ్గించడంఎటువంటినేరాలతోస మానమోచెప్పమంటారా? జాతికివ్యతిరేకంగాతిరుగుబాటుచేయడం, జాతికివ్యతిరేకంగావిదేశీశక్తులరాజకీయకుతంత్రాలకుసహకరించడం, భారతరాజ్యాంగానికివ్యతిరేకంగాపనిచేయడం, జాతిద్రోహానికిపాల్పడడం, జాతినితప్పుదోవపట్టించడం, జాతినిదగాచేయడం.

విచారకరమైనవిషయమేమిటంటేఈనేరాలకుపాల్పడుతున్నవారంద రూభారతప్రభుత్వఉప్పుఅంటేభారతప్రజలసొమ్మునుతింటున్నారు; ఎవరిసొమ్మునుతింటున్నారోవారికిద్రోహంచేస్తున్నారు. ద్రోహంచేయడానికేప్రభుత్వమూవారికిభారీవేతనభత్యాలనిస్తోంది! భారతీయఆర్థికవ్యవస్థనుఇప్పటికేఒకవ్యూహంప్రకారం, చాలాపకడ్బందీగాతప్పుదోవపట్టించారు. భారతీయులారాఇప్పటికైనామేల్కొంటారా?

-కొడాలిఏకాంబరరావు
(వ్యాసకర్తఆర్థికశాస్త్రవేత్త)

# ఆహారభద్రతకురెండులక్షలకోట్లనిధి

# -కొడాలిఏకాంబరరావు

రైతురైతుగాబతకలేకపోతున్నాడు. వ్యవసాయానికిపూర్తిగాచెడ్డరోజులుదాపురించాయి. నిజంచెప్పాలంటేభారతదేశఆహారరంగమేపూర్తిగాప్రమాదంలోపడింది.

'రైతునుఆదుకోవాలి';

'ప్రభుత్వంరైతునుఆదుకొనేలాచేసేందుకుఎటువంటిత్యాగానికైనావెనుదీయం'-ఇవీనేడువివిధరాజకీయపక్షాలనుంచి, వాటినాయకులనుంచివినబడుతున్ననినాదాలు.

అన్నదాతగాలోకప్రసిద్ధుడైనరైతుడబ్బునుఅడుక్కునేవాడుగాదిగజారిపోయాడు. డబ్బుపైఆధారపడినవ్యవస్థకోరల్లోరైతుచిక్కుకున్నాడు. డబ్బుపైఆ«ధారపడ్డబాహ్యప్రపంచంపైఆధారపడకూడదనిరైతునిర్ణయించుకంటేమనలోప్రతిఒక్కరమూఆహారభద్రతనుకోల్పోవాల్సివస్తుంది.

ఈపరిస్థితికిప్రత్యామ్నాయంలేదు. ఇక్కడమనంమనఆహారంగురించిమాట్లాడుకొంటున్నాం. కనుకరైతునుమనంగౌరవించితీరాలి. రైతునుఆదుకోవాలి, రక్షించాలిఇత్యాదిచౌకబారునినాదాలకుస్వస్తిచెప్పాలి. అన్నదాతకుమనమేమీఉపకారంచేయడంలేదు. మనల్నిమనమేరక్షించుకొంటున్నాం. రైతునుఆదుకోవడమనేదితననైతికబాధ్యతగావిద్యావంతుడైనప్రతిభారతీయుడూగుర్తించాలి. చట్టసభల్లోప్రజాప్రతినిధులువెల్లడిస్తున్నవివరాలప్రకారంఆత్మహత్యలుచేసుకున్నరైతులసంఖ్యవేలు, లక్షల్లోఉంది.

ఆఆత్మహత్యలుఇంకాకొనసాగుతూనేఉన్నాయి. రైతులఆత్మహత్యలుఎందుకుచేసుకొంటున్నారు? డబ్బుకోసం. తమశ్రమకుతగినరొక్కంఅందలేదనేబాధతో; అందదేమోననేభయంతో. భారతప్రభుత్వంఅనుసరిస్తున్నఆర్థికవిధానాలుఒకవాస్తవాన్నిస్పష్టంచేస్తున్నాయి.

కరెన్సీఅనేఆర్థికభావననుప్రపంచంలోప్రవేశపెట్టినమొదటిప్రపంచదేశాలు(అమెరికామొదలైనసంపన్నదేశాలు), భారత్‌కుమధ్యఒకవ్యత్యాసంఉందనేదేఆవాస్తవం. భారత్‌లోనిభారతీయఆర్థికవేత్తలుకరెన్సీభావననుసరిగ్గాఅర్థంచేసుకోకపోవడమేఆవ్యత్యాసం.

ప్రపంచంలోనిప్రతిదేశానికీరెండుఆర్థికవ్యవస్థలుఉంటాయి. ఒకటి-డబ్బురూపొందించి, నిర్వహించేకాల్పనికఆర్థికవ్యవస్థ; రెండోదిదైవప్రసాదితమైనలేదాప్రకృతిసిద్ధమైననిజఆర్థికవ్యవస్థ. నగదు, రుణాలు, ఒప్పందాలుమొదలైనకాల్పనికఅంశాలకేమనప్రభుత్వఆర్థికవిధానాలుప్రాధాన్యమిస్తున్నాయి. రైతులజీవితాలు, వ్యవసాయరంగపువాస్తవాలుమొదలైనఅంశాలకుఅవిప్రాధాన్యమివ్వడంలేదు. మరోశోచనీయమనవిషయమేమిటంటేభారత్‌లోనికాల్పనికఆర్థికవ్యవస్థలుసంపూర్ణమైనవికావు; వాటినిఅసంపూర్ణంగావదిలివేస్తున్నారు. ప్రతిఅంశాన్నిడబ్బుతోముడిపెట్టుకోవడంవల్లనేమనంఅనేకవిధాలనష్టపోతున్నాం.

రైతులదుస్థితికిమూలకారణాలనుఅన్వేషిస్తేభారతప్రభుత్వమూదానిఆర్థికనిపుణులూరైతులనునిజఆర్థికవ్యవస్థనుంచిడబ్బుపైఆధారపడ్డసంక్లిష్టఆర్థికవ్యవస్థలోకిబలవంతంగాలాగడంవల్లేఆదయనీయస్థితిఅనివిశదమవుతుంది. ఇదిఅవాంఛనీయం. అంతేకాదురైతులకుజరుగుతున్నఅన్యాయంకూడా. రైతునుఈఉచ్చునుంచిబయటకులాగినప్పుడేఅతనికిపూర్తిసంక్షేమంసమకూరుతుంది. ఇందుకుమనంచేయవల్సిందివ్యవసాయం, నేత,

పాడిఉత్పత్తులు, చేపలవేట,
వడ్రంగంమొదలైనమౌలికలేదాప్రాథమికఆర్థికకార్యకలాపాలనుసంక్లిష్టఆర్థిక
వ్యవహారాలబంధనాలనుంచిబయటపడవేయాలి.

ఏఅంశాలైతేరైతులకుసంకటంగాపరిణమించాయోఆఅంశాలనునైతికనిష్ఠతో
నిర్వర్తించాల్సినబాధ్యతలుగాభారతప్రభుత్వఆర్థికనిపుణులు,
ప్రభుత్వరంగబ్యాంకులభుజస్కంధాలపైమోపాలి.
రైతునుఆదుకొనిమనంఆహారభద్రతనుసమకూర్చుకోవాలనుకుంటేమనం
తక్షణమేకొన్నిచర్యలుచేపట్టాలి. ప్రస్తుతపరిస్థితిఇలాఉంది:

(అ)
రైతులకుఇచ్చినరుణాలుతిరిగివసూలుకావేమోననేభయంతోవ్యవసాయరం
గానికిరుణాలుమంజూరుచేయడానికిబ్యాంకులువెనుకాడుతున్నాయి; (ఆ)
ప్రకృతివిపత్తులుచీడపీడలు,
మార్కెట్టమదిగుబడులకుకనీసధరలభించకపోవడంమొదలైనకారణాలవల్ల
రైతులుబ్యాంకులనుంచితీసుకున్నరుణాలనుతిరిగిసకాలంలోచెల్లించలేకపో
తున్నారు. కాగా, వాతావరణపరిస్థితులుగాని,
మార్కెట్‌లోధరలుగానీరైతులచేతుల్లోఉండవనేవాస్తవాన్నివిస్మరించకూడ
దు.

ప్రపంచవ్యాప్తంగాప్రతినిజమైనఆర్థికవ్యవస్థాకాల్పనికఆర్థికవ్యవస్థఅంటేడ
బ్బుఆధారితఆర్థికవ్యవస్థప్రభావంలోనడుస్తున్నాయనేవాస్తవాన్నికూడామ
రచిపోకూడదు.
డబ్బుఆధారితఆర్థికవ్యవస్థలోబ్యాంకులుఅనేవిధనప్రవాహానికిసదుపాయ
సంధాత(ఫెసిలిటేటర్)గావ్యవహరిస్తాయి.
దురదృష్టవశాత్తుకరెన్సీభావననుమనంసరిగ్గాఅర్థంచేసుకోకవపోవడంవల్ల

బ్యాంకులనుఫెసిలిటేటర్స్‌గాకాకవాణిజ్యసంస్థలుగామననిపుణులుపరిగణి స్తున్నారు.

ఆహారరంగాన్ని సంరక్షించుకోవడానికిప్రభుత్వంతక్షణమేరెండులక్షలకోట్లరూ పాయలతోఒకబీమానిల్వనిధి(ఇన్సూరెన్సిజర్వ్‌ఫండ్)నినెలకొల్పాలి. ఈనిధిని, రిజర్వ్‌బ్యాంక్‌ఆధ్వర్యంలోసిఆర్‌ఆర్గాపరిగణింపబడేనిధిగాపరిగణించాలి. బ్యాంకులు, రైతులు, ఆహారరంగాన్ని కాపాడడానికిఈనిధిఎంతైనాఅవసరం. ఈనిధిఏకసమయంలోబ్యాంకులకురుణరక్షణగాను, రైతులకురుణసహాయంగానుపనిచేస్తుంది. రైతులుబ్యాంకులనుంచితీసుకునేరుణాలకురైతులకుబదులుబ్యాంకులేప్రీ మియంచెల్లిస్తాయి.

ఇలాచెల్లించినసొమ్ము ఆబీమానిధికిఅదనంగాజతఅవుతుంది. రైతులకుసంభవించేనష్టాలనుదిగుబడులవివరాలప్రాతిపదికనగణించాలి. ఉదాహరణకుఎకరంవరికమతానికిపదివేలరూపాయలరుణాన్ని తీసుకు న్నాడనుకుందాం. ఎకరానికి2000కిలోలవరిధాన్యందిగుబడిఅయితే, కిలోపదిరూపాయలచొప్పునధరలభిస్తేఅప్పుడుఆరైతుకురూ.20 వేలులభిస్తాయి.

ఒకప్రాంతంలోమార్కెట్టరఆధారంగాసగటుదిగుబడినిఅంచనావేయాలి. వాస్తవానికిరైతు1500 కిలోలధాన్యాన్నే పండించాడనుకుందాం. మార్కెట్టరకిలోఎనిమిదిరూపాయలుఉంటేఅప్పుడుఆరైతుకులభించేదిరూ. 12 వేలుమాత్రమే. ఈదృష్ట్యారైతుకు40 శాతంనష్టంవచ్చిందనుకోవాలి. ఈ40 శాతాన్ని బ్యాంకులుప్రభుత్వంనెలకొల్పినబీమానిధినుంచితీసుకోవాలి.

తదనుగుణంగారైతులుచెల్లించాల్సినవడ్డీనికూడామినహాయించాలి.
మార్చి31నాటికిప్రతిరైతురుణభారాన్నితగ్గించాలి.

దేశవ్యాప్తంగాప్రకృతివిపత్తులు,
చీడలుపీడలకువీగామిగిలినపంటదిగుబడులనుకచ్చితంగాగణించడనాకిప్ర
భుత్వంఒకసంస్థనునియమించాలి. మొత్తందిగుబడులు,
గ్రామంప్రాతిపదికనగణించినదిగుబడులదామాషాఆధారంగాసగటుదిగుబడి
నినిర్ణయించాలి.
పంటసీజన్ముగిసేనాటికిఅన్నినష్టాలనుంచిబయటపడేలారైతుకుసహాయప
డాలి.

వ్యవసాయం,
చేతివృత్తులుమొదలైనప్రాథమికరంగాలుఆర్థికసౌష్ఠవాన్నిసమృద్ధిగాపొంద
డానికిపైనసూచించినబీమాపథకాన్నితక్షణమేఅమలుపరచాలి.
ఈపథకంవల్లసమస్యపూర్తిగాపరిష్కారంకాకపోయినప్పటికీఆర్థికవ్యవహారా
లబాధ్యతలుభారతప్రభుత్వఆర్థికనిపుణులు,
బ్యాంకులకుఅప్పగించడంసాధ్యమవుతుంది.
ఈవాస్తవాలనుదృష్టిలోఉంచుకొనిబీమానిల్వనిధినితక్షణమేప్రారంభించాలి.

-కొడాలిఏకాంబరరావు

మన ఆర్థిక విధాన కర్తలు రూపాయి విలువను ఉద్దేశపూర్వకంగా తగ్గించి వేశారు. ఇది మహాదోషం. మరి మన ఆర్థిక వ్యవస్థ స్థితిగతులను మెరుగుపరిచేందుకై రూపాయి విలువను ఉద్దేశపూర్వకంగా పెంచే ప్రయత్నాలేవీ చేయడం లేదు. ఇదొక మహాపరాధం... రూపాయి విలువను నిర్ణయించడమనే ప్రక్రియను మార్కెట్ శక్తులకు వదిలివేశారు. ఏ దేశమైనా తన కరెన్సీ విలువను నిర్ణయించే ప్రక్రియను అంతర్జాతీయ విదేశీ శక్తుల ప్రభావానికి వదిలి వేయడమంటే జాతి సంపదను పూర్తిగా ఇతరుల చేతుల్లో ఉంచి, వారి దయను పొందడమే అవుతుంది.

# తాకట్టులో రూపాయి

- కొడాలి ఏకాంబర్‌రావు

# విలోమ వృద్ధి

**భారతదేశపు వనరులు భారతీయులకు అందుబాటులో ఉండడం లేదు. దేశవ్యాప్తంగా ప్రజలు తాగునీటిని కొనుగోలు చేసుకోవడమే ఈ వాస్తవానికి నిదర్శనం. నీరు భారత ప్రజల ప్రాథమిక హక్కు. నీటిని కొనుగోలు చేసుకోవడమంటే తమ ప్రాథమిక హక్కును కొనుగోలు చేసుకోవడమే. మరింత స్పష్టంగా చెప్పాలంటే మీకు ధనం లేకపోతే మీరు ప్రాథమిక హక్కులు పొందడానికి అర్హులు కారు. ఇదీ భారతదేశ పౌరుల జీవిత వాస్తవం.**

ఒక వస్తువు 'విక్రయ ధర'ను నిర్ణయించే అంశాలు లేదా ఉత్పాదకాలు ఏమిటి? ఒకటి- ఆ వస్తువు తయారీకి ఉపయోగించిన ముడి పదార్థాల ఖర్చు. రెండు- ప్రాసెసింగ్ (తయారీ) ఖర్చు. మానవ వనరులు, రవాణా, విద్యుత్తు, అద్దెలు, లాభాలు, పన్నులు, నగదు లావాదేవీల చార్జీలు - ఈ ఏడు అంశాలు తయారీ ఖర్చు పరిధిలోకి వస్తాయి. లాభాల్లో హెచ్చుతగ్గులు అనేది ఇతర ఉత్పాదకాల మూల్యాలపై ఆధారపడి ఉంటుంది. ముడి పదార్థాలు, విద్యుత్తు, అద్దెలు, రవాణా వ్యయం, పన్నులు అధికంగా ఉన్నప్పుడు లాభాలు అనివార్యంగా తగ్గిపోతాయి. అన్ని ఉత్పాదకాల ఖర్చుల పెరుగుదలలో ఒక ఉమ్మడి అంశం ఉంది. అదే, అంతర్జాతీయ విపణిలో విదేశీ మారక ద్రవ్యాలు, ముఖ్యంగా అమెరికా డాలర్‌తో రూపాయి మారకం రేటు. రూపాయి విలువ తక్కువగా ఉంటే అన్ని ఉత్పాదకాల ఖర్చు పెరుగుతుంది. తత్ఫలితంగా సరుకుల ధరలు హెచ్చుగా ఉంటాయి. 'ఆర్థిక సంస్కరణల' పేరుతో అమలుచేస్తున్న విధానాల ఫలితంగా జరుగుతున్నదేమిటంటే అన్ని సహజవనరుల ధరలను వాటి ప్రపంచ ధరలతో సమకాలీకరణం (sychronisation) చేయడం. ఇది, ఉత్పత్తి సామగ్రి (అవి పూర్తిగా దేశంలోనే లభ్యమవుతున్నప్పటికీ) ధరల పెరుగుదలకు దారితీస్తోంది.

రూపాయి విలువ తక్కువగా ఎందుకు ఉంది? ప్రణబ్ ముఖర్జీ ఆర్థిక మంత్రిగా ఉన్నప్పుడు ఐ.ఎమ్.ఎఫ్ నుంచి 700 కోట్ల డాలర్ల విలువైన బంగారాన్ని కొన్నారు. ఆర్థిక సంక్షోభంలో కొట్టుమిట్టాడుతున్న యూరోపును ఆదుకోవడానికై ఐ.ఎమ్.ఎఫ్‌కు ప్రధాని మన్మోహన్‌సింగ్ 1200 కోట్ల డాలర్ల ఆర్థిక సహాయాన్ని అందజేశారు. ఇటువంటి చర్యలు రెండు ఉమ్మడి ఫలితాలను సాధించాయి. అవి: అంతర్జాతీయ విపణిలో భారత్‌తో జరిపే విదేశీ వాణిజ్యంలో అమెరికా డాలర్ల లభ్యతను నిరాకరించడమూ, ఇతర దేశాల ఆర్థిక వ్యవస్థల్లో డాలర్ పాత్రను మరింతగా పటిష్ఠం చేయడమూ. పార్లమెంటు ఆమోదం పొందకుండానే ప్రణబ్, మన్మోహన్‌లు ఆ చర్యలు చేపట్టడం విస్మరించరాని విషయం. మరింత స్పష్టంగా చెప్పాలంటే పార్లమెంటు ఆమోదం లేకుండానే భారీ ఎత్తున బంగారాన్ని కొనుగోలు చేయడం, ఇతర దేశాలను ఆదుకోవడానికి భారీ ఆర్థిక సహాయాన్ని అందించడం ఒక ప్రధాన నేరం కిందకే వస్తాయి. ఇవి ఆర్థిక చర్యలే గానీ, విత్త చర్యలు కానే కావు. ఇవి మన ఆర్థిక వ్యవస్థను బలహీనపరిచాయి. ఉత్పత్తి వ్యయాలు పెరిగిపోవడానికి మరో ముఖ్యమైన కారణం పన్నులు. పంచాయతీ నుంచి కేంద్ర ప్రభుత్వ స్థాయి వరకూ మనం అనేక పన్నులు చెల్లిస్తున్నాము. ప్రత్యక్ష పన్ను పేరుతో కొత్త పన్నులు విధించడం సరిపోదు. ఎన్నో కొత్త పన్నులను చెల్లిస్తున్నప్పుడు ఇంకా ఆదాయపు పన్ను ఎందుకు? దాన్ని రద్దు చేయాలి. ప్రస్తుతం అమల్లో ఉన్న పన్నుల వ్యవస్థ మన ఆర్థిక వ్యవస్థ పటిష్ఠం కావడానికి తోడ్పడేది కాదు. ఉదాహరణకు వాహనాలపై రోడ్డు పన్నును తీసుకోండి. ఈ పన్నును అందరూ చెల్లిస్తున్నారు. వాహనాల రాకపోకలకు అవసరమైన మౌలిక సదుపాయాల కోసం ఈ పన్నును చెల్లిస్తున్నాము. మరి టోల్ గేట్ చార్జీలను కూడా వసూలు చేస్తున్నారు! ఒకే ప్రయాణంలో కనీసం రెండు మూడు రెట్లు ఈ చార్జీలను చెల్లించవలసి వస్తోంది. ప్రైవేట్, ప్రభుత్వ భాగస్వామ్యం (పిపిపి), నిర్మాణం, నిర్వహణ, బదిలీ (బిఓటి) పేరుతో జాతీయ హైవేలను ప్రైవేట్ యాజమాన్యాలకు అప్పగిస్తున్నారు. నిజానికి ఇది దేశాన్ని కొంచెం కొంచెంగా ప్రైవేట్ యాజమాన్యాలకు విక్రయించడమే సుమా! పిపిపి, బిఓటి విధానాల మూలంగా ప్రభుత్వం దేశ ఆర్థిక వ్యవస్థపై తన రాజ్యాంగబద్ధమైన యాజమాన్యాన్ని క్రమంగా కోల్పోతోంది.

విదేశీ ప్రత్యక్ష పెట్టుబడుల ద్వారా ఏ విదేశీ కంపెనీ కూడా మన దేశంలో భూమిపై యాజమాన్య హక్కులు కలిగి ఉండడానికి వీలు లేదు; అయితే విదేశీ కంపెనీలకు వాటాలు ఉన్న కంపెనీ సహజ వనరులపై యాజమాన్యం పొందడానికి అర్హమవుతుంది. ఇది మన ప్రభుత్వ విధానం. నీటి పారుదల, విద్యుత్తు, రోడ్డు ఇత్యాది రంగాలలో పలు ప్రాజెక్టులకు ప్రపంచ బ్యాంకు పెద్దఎత్తున నిధులు సమకూరుస్తోంది. వీటితో పాటు బ్యాంకింగ్ రంగంలో కూడా పిపిపి, బిఓటి ప్రాజెక్టులు అమలవుతున్న వాస్తవాన్ని మనం విస్మరించకూడదు. విదేశీ ప్రత్యక్ష పెట్టుబడులుగానీ, విదేశీ సంస్థాగత పెట్టుబడులుగానీ మన దేశంలోని నగదు లావాదేవీల ఆర్థికవ్యవస్థను సొంత ప్రయోజనాలకు ఉపయోగించుకోవడానికే వస్తున్నాయి; అంతేగానీ మన భారత్‌ను మరింతగా బలోపేతం చేయడానికై విదేశీ వనరులను తీసుకురావడం లేదు. ఈ వాస్తవాన్ని మనలో ప్రతి ఒక్కరూ అర్థం చేసుకోవల్సిన అవసరముంది.

ఉత్పాదకాల ఖర్చులు పెరిగిపోతున్నాయి. తరిగిపోతున్న లాభాలను నిలబెట్టుకోవడానికి యాజమాన్యాలు పలు ప్రయత్నాలు చేస్తున్నాయి. మానవ వనరుల విభాగంలో బాల కార్మికులను ఉపయోగించుకోవడం వీటిలో ఒకటి. అయితే లాభాలు లేని పక్షంలో దేశ ఆర్థిక వ్యవస్థ ఇంత అభివృద్ధి ఎలా సాధించిందని కొంతమంది ప్రశ్నిస్తున్నారు. వాస్తవమేమిటంటే విదేశీ ప్రయత్నాలకు భారత ఆర్థిక వ్యవస్థను తాకట్టు పెట్టడం ద్వారా విదేశీ ఆర్థిక సంస్థల నుంచి తెచ్చుకున్న రుణాలతో సాధించిన అభివృద్ధి అది. మరో వాస్తవం ఏమిటంటే రూపాయి విలువ ఉండవల్సిన విధంగా లేదన్న సత్యాన్ని దేశ ఆర్థిక వ్యవస్థ బాగోగులకు బాధ్యులైన వారందరూ గుర్తించారు. నోట్ల చెలామణీ అధికం

లేని దాన్ని అవసరమైన వ్యయంగా మార్చి వేస్తున్నారు. ఎవరైతే అధికంగా ద్రవ్యాన్ని పొందుతున్నారో వారు అంతగా తమ వ్యక్తిగత సంపదను పెంచుకుంటున్నారు. ఆ సొమ్ము ఆర్థిక వ్యవస్థలో భాగమయ్యేంతవరకూ దాని ద్వారా ప్రయోజనం పొందేవారు ఉంటారు. తయారీ ఖర్చులలోని ఏడు అంశాలలో ఒక్క రవాణా ఇంధనం మినహా మిగతావన్నీ మన దేశ వనరులే. అయితే మనం ఉపయోగించుకుంటున్న డబ్బు విదేశీ ధనం. మన ఆర్థిక వేత్తలు కావాలని ఈ పరిస్థితికి తీసుకువచ్చారు.

ఈ పరిణామం ఎటువంటి ఫలితాలకు దారి తీస్తోంది? భారతదేశపు వనరులు భారతీయులకు అందుబాటులో ఉండడం లేదు. దేశవ్యాప్తంగా ప్రజలు తాగునీటిని కొనుగోలు చేసుకోవడమే ఈ వాస్తవానికి నిదర్శనం. నీరు భారత ప్రజల ప్రాథమిక హక్కు. నీటిని కొనుగోలు చేసుకోవడమంటే తమ ప్రాథమిక హక్కును కొనుగోలు చేసుకోవడమే. మరింత స్పష్టంగా చెప్పాలంటే మీకు ధనం లేకపోతే మీరు ప్రాథమిక హక్కులు పొందడానికి కూడా అర్హులు కారు. ఇదీ భారతదేశ పౌరుల జీవిత వాస్తవం. మరి భారతదేశంలో నీటి కొరత ఉందా? లేదు. అయితే నీటి పునశ్శుద్ధీకరణ (ఉపయోగించుకున్న నీటిని మళ్ళీ ఉపయోగించుకోనే విధంగా చేసుకోవడం) ప్రక్రియ అవసరాలకు తగిన రీతిలో వేగంగా జరగడం లేదు. జల వనరులు సదా సమృద్ధిగా ఉండుకోనే విషయమై మనం శ్రద్ధ చూపడం లేదు. కలుషితమైన నదులు, కాలువలు, జలాశయాలే ఇందుకు ఉదాహరణ. అయితే నీటిని తిరిగి ఉపయోగించుకొనే ప్రక్రియను వేగవంతం చేసేదెలా? అందుకు డబ్బు అవసరం. ప్రభుత్వానికి ఆదాయం ఉంది. అయితే రూపాయి విలువ తక్కువగా ఉండడంతో వివిధ ముడి పదార్థాలు, ఇతర సామగ్రి ధరలు పెరిగిపోతున్నాయి. సహజవనరులను తీర్చగలిగే విధంగా మౌలికసదుపాయాలను సృష్టించే ఆర్థిక శక్తి ప్రభుత్వానికి లేదు. ఏ రంగమూ దీనికి మినహాయింపు కాదు. అధిక ధరల కారణంగా అవసరమైన ఉత్పత్తి సామగ్రి అందుబాటులో ఉండడం లేదు. తత్ఫలితంగా పారిశ్రామిక రంగానికి గానీ, వ్యవసాయ రంగానికి గానీ కొత్త పెట్టుబడులు రావడం లేదు. దీని వల్ల నిరుద్యోగం పెరిగిపోతోంది.

ఇక రవాణా అంశాన్ని పరిశీలిద్దాం. పెట్రోలియం ఉత్పత్తులు, వాటి ధరలు ఈ రంగంలో కీలకపాత్ర పోషిస్తాయి. చమురు రంగానికి ఇస్తున్న సబ్సిడీల వల్ల దేశప్రయోజనాలకు చాలా నష్టం కలుగుతుందని అధికారంలో ఉన్నవారు పదే పదే అంటుంటారు. మరి మన దేశంలో సబ్సిడీ అనేది నిజంగా ఉందా అనే విషయాన్ని చూద్దాం. ఒక బ్యారెల్ అంటే 160 లీటర్లు. ప్రతి 100 లీటర్ల క్రూడాయిల్‌లోను 44 శాతం పెట్రోల్, 26 శాతం డీజిల్, 1 శాతం ఎల్‌పిజి, 6 శాతం కిరోసిన్ ఉంటుంది. ఇప్పుడు ఒక బ్యారెల్ క్రూడాయిల్ ధర 100డాలర్లు (రూ.5700). 100 లీటర్ల క్రూడాయిల్ ధర రూ.3500. 44 లీటర్ల పెట్రోల్‌ను రూ.3300కి విక్రయిస్తున్నారు. 6 లీటర్ల కిరోసిన్‌ను రూ.90కి, 1 లీటర్ ఎల్‌పిజిని రూ.35కి విక్రయిస్తున్నారు. ఈ మొత్తం రూ.3450. ఇక 26 లీటర్ల డీజిల్‌ని రూ.1170కి విక్రయిస్తున్నారు. పై మొత్తంతో దీనిని కలిపితే రూ.4600 అవుతుంది. మిగతా పెట్రోలియం ఉత్పత్తులు 24 లీటర్లుగా ఉంటాయి. వీటిలో లూబ్రికెంట్ ఆయిల్ మొదలైన వాటిని లీటర్ ఒక్కింటికి రూ.300కి విక్రయిస్తున్నారు. డాలర్ మారకంలో రూపాయి విలువ 35 రూపాయలున్నప్పుడు 100 లీటర్ల చమురు ధర కేవలం 2000 రూపాయలు మాత్రమే. రూపాయి విలువ పతనం కారణంగా 100 లీటర్లకు రూ.3500 చెల్లించాల్సి వస్తోంది. రూపాయి పతనానికి ప్రభుత్వ విధానాలే కారణం.

కొవ్వు ఏ మాత్రం లేని పాలలో 88 శాతం ద్రవం, మిగతా 12 శాతం వెన్న, నెయ్యి భాగంగా ఉంటాయి. లీటరు పాల ధర రూ.30. పాలలోని వెన్న, నెయ్యిని అధిక ధరలకు విక్రయిస్తారు. పాల ధర ఒక సహజ సూత్రం ఆధారంగా నిర్ణయమవుతుంది. అధిక శాతం ఉన్న సరుకు ధర తక్కువగానూ, తక్కువ ఉత్పత్తి ఉన్న సరుకు ధర అధికంగాను ఉండడం సహజం కదా. మరి పెట్రోలియం ఉత్పత్తుల ధరలూ సహజ సూత్రం ప్రకారమే నిర్ణయమవుతున్నాయా? మన ఆర్థిక, పెట్రోలియం మంత్రిత్వ శాఖల అధికారులు పెట్రోలియం ఉత్పత్తులకు నిర్ణయిస్తున్న ధరల విధానం సహజ సూత్రానికి భిన్నంగా ఉంది. 44 శాతం ఉన్న పెట్రోలును అధిక ధరకు, తక్కువగా ఉన్న ఇతర ఉత్పత్తులను తక్కువ ధరకు విక్రయిస్తున్నారు. ఇది సహజ సూత్రానికి విరుద్ధం. పెట్రోలు ధర రూపాయి విలువపై నిర్ణయాత్మక ప్రభావాన్ని చూపుతుందని మనం మరచిపోకూడదు. ఇది విజ్ఞానాధార ఆర్థికవ్యవస్థల యుగం. ఈ సత్యాన్ని ప్రతి ఒక్కరూ గుర్తించాలి. ముడిపదార్థాలు అందుబాటులో లేకపోవడం విజ్ఞానం కొరవడడానికి దారితీస్తోంది. ముడిపదార్థాలు అందుబాటులో లేకపోవడం వల్ల శాస్త్రీయ పరిశోధనలు నిర్వహించడం, సాంకేతికతలను అభివృద్ధిపరచడం సాధ్యం కావడం లేదు. ఈ పరిస్థితి మెరుగుపడనంతవరకు దేశ ఆర్థిక వ్యవస్థ మెరుగుపడదు. పైగా గతకాలపు స్థాయికి దిగజారిపోతోంది. అదే జరిగితే మహాత్ముడు మళ్లీ పుట్టినా మన ఆర్థికవ్యవస్థను ఉద్ధరించడం అసాధ్యమవుతుంది.

- కె.ఇ.రావు